POST-POLITICS AND CIVIL SOCIETY IN ASIAN CITIES

Bringing together an interdisciplinary group of scholars, *Post-Politics and Civil Society in Asian Cities* examines how the concept of 'post-politics' has manifested across a range of Asian cities, and the impact this has had on state-society relationships in processes of urban governance.

This volume examines how the post-political framework—derived from the study of Western liberal democracies—applies to Asian cities. Appreciating that the region has undergone a distinctive trajectory of political development, and is currently governed under democratic or authoritarian regimes, the book articulates how post-political conditions have created obstacles or opportunities for civil society to assert its voice in urban governance. Chapters address the different ways in which Asian civil society groups strive to gain a stake in the development and management of cities, specifically by looking at their involvement in heritage and environmental governance, two inter-related components in discourses about establishing liveable cities for the future.

By providing in-depth case studies examining the varying degrees to which post-political ideologies have been enacted in urban governance across Central, South, Southeast, and East Asia, this book offers a useful and timely resource for students and scholars interested in urban studies, political science, Asian studies, geography, and sociology.

Sonia Lam-Knott was a postdoctoral fellow in the Asian Urbanisms Cluster at the Asia Research Institute, National University of Singapore. She received her DPhil in anthropology from the University of Oxford in 2015, for her research on youth activism in Hong Kong. Her research explores the socio-political ambiguities in post-1997 Hong Kong, viewed through the lens of heritage politics, nostalgia, and vernacular experiences of the city. She has published in journals such as *Asian Anthropology*, *Anthropology Matters*, and *Urban Studies*, as well as in edited volumes.

Creighton Connolly is a lecturer in the School of Geography, University of Lincoln (UK), focussing on development studies and the Global South. He is an urban political ecologist by training, having received his PhD in geography from the University of Manchester, where he was a member of the European Network of Political Ecology (ENTITLE). His research focuses primarily on contestations over urban (re)development and environmental governance in peninsular Malaysia. He has published this work in numerous journals, including the *International Journal of Urban and Regional Research (IJURR)*, *Cultural Geographies*, and *Geoforum*.

Kong Chong Ho was trained as an urban sociologist at the University of Chicago, and his research interests lie in neighbourhood and community development, heritage and place-making, the political economy of cities, and a more recent interest in higher education. He has produced edited volumes such as *Service Industries and Asia Pacific Cities* (2012, with Peter Daniels and Tom Hutton), and *Advancing the Regional Commons in the New East Asia* (2016, with Siriporn Wajjwalku and Osamu Yoshida). Forthcoming publications include *Neighbourhoods for the City in Pacific Asia* (2019).

Politics in Asia series

The Ever-Changing Sino-Japanese Rivalry
Philip Streich

Risk Management Strategies of Japanese Companies in China
Political Crisis and Multinational Firms
Kristin Vekasi

The Political Economy of Press Freedom
The Paradox of Taiwan versus China
Jaw-Nian Huang

Inequality and Democratic Politics in East Asia
Edited by Chong-Min Park and Eric M. Uslaner

India's Maritime Strategy
Balancing Regional Ambitions and China
Shishir Upadhyaya

Post-Politics and Civil Society in Asian Cities
Spaces of Depoliticisation
Edited by Sonia Lam-Knott, Creighton Connolly, and Kong Chong Ho

Chinese Constructions of Sovereignty and the East China Sea Conflict
Czeslaw Tubilewicz

For the full list of titles in the series, visit: www.routledge.com/Politics-in-Asia/book-series/PIA

POST-POLITICS AND CIVIL SOCIETY IN ASIAN CITIES

Spaces of Depoliticisation

Edited by Sonia Lam-Knott, Creighton Connolly, and Kong Chong Ho

LONDON AND NEW YORK

First published 2020
by Routledge
2 Park Square, Milton Park, Abingdon, Oxon OX14 4RN

and by Routledge
52 Vanderbilt Avenue, New York, NY 10017

Routledge is an imprint of the Taylor & Francis Group, an informa business

© 2020 selection and editorial matter, Sonia Lam-Knott, Creighton Connolly, and Kong Chong Ho; individual chapters, the contributors

The right of Sonia Lam-Knott, Creighton Connolly, and Kong Chong Ho to be identified as the authors of the editorial material, and of the authors for their individual chapters, has been asserted in accordance with sections 77 and 78 of the Copyright, Designs and Patents Act 1988.

All rights reserved. No part of this book may be reprinted or reproduced or utilised in any form or by any electronic, mechanical, or other means, now known or hereafter invented, including photocopying and recording, or in any information storage or retrieval system, without permission in writing from the publishers.

Trademark notice: Product or corporate names may be trademarks or registered trademarks, and are used only for identification and explanation without intent to infringe.

British Library Cataloguing-in-Publication Data
A catalogue record for this book is available from the British Library

Library of Congress Cataloging-in-Publication Data
Names: Lam-Knott, Sonia Yue Chuen, 1986– editor. | Connolly, Creighton, 1988– editor. | Ho, Kong-Chong, 1955– editor.
Title: Post-politics and civil society in Asian cities : spaces of depoliticization / edited by Sonia Lam-Knott, Creighton Connolly, and Kong Chong Ho.
Description: Abingdon, Oxon ; New York, NY : Routledge, 2019. | Includes bibliographical references and index.
Identifiers: LCCN 2019032280 | ISBN 9780367278823 (hardback) | ISBN 9780367278830 (paperback) | ISBN 9780429298530 (ebook)
Subjects: LCSH: Federal-city relations—Asia. | Civil society—Asia. | Asia—Politics and government.
Classification: LCC JS6950 .P67 2019 | DDC 300.95/091732—dc23
LC record available at https://lccn.loc.gov/2019032280

ISBN: 978-0-367-27882-3 (hbk)
ISBN: 978-0-367-27883-0 (pbk)
ISBN: 978-0-429-29853-0 (ebk)

Typeset in Bembo
by Apex CoVantage, LLC

CONTENTS

List of illustrations vii
Acknowledgements viii
Notes on contributors ix

    Introduction: theorising the post-political in Asian cities 1
    Sonia Lam-Knott, Creighton Connolly, and Kong Chong Ho

PART I
Post-political governance in Asia   19

1   A return to the political? civil society and post-politics in authoritarian regimes   21
    David Matijasevich

2   Managing grievances in the age of post-politics: the relocation of communities for the Thilawa Special Economic Zone in Myanmar   37
    Tamas Wells

3   Emerging post-political city in Seoul   54
    U-Seok Seo

4   Back to the land: post-political utopias of organic living   72
    Karl Beelen

PART II
Post-politics in heritage governance — 91

5 Between state and society: heritage politics in urban China — 93
   Yujie Zhu

6 'Connecting Emotions through Wells': heritage instrumentalisation, civic activism, and urban sustainability in Quanzhou, China — 106
   Yunci Cai

PART III
Post-politics in environmental governance — 121

7 Constructing space for participatory governance in Vietnam: reflections from the Hanoi tree movement — 123
   Seohee Kwak

8 Environmental civil activism in Central Asia: emerging civil society governance and fragile relations with the state — 140
   Reina Artur Kyzy

9 Post-political planning and insurgent mobilisation in the post-disaster city: the experience of Tacloban City, Philippines, after Typhoon Haiyan — 152
   Dakila Kim P. Yee

Index — *173*

ILLUSTRATIONS

Figures

3.1	Changes in the number of citizen committees	66
6.1	The Calming Pagoda after refurbishment	111
7.1	Thematic network of public participation contexts in Vietnam	132

Tables

3.1	The elected mayors of Seoul	60
3.2	Timetable of the 'Air Pollution Roundtable'	68
7.1	Timeline summary of the Hanoi tree movement	126

ACKNOWLEDGEMENTS

This edited volume was developed out of a 2018 conference, titled '(Re)conceptualising Asian Civil Society in the Age of Post-Politics', that took place at the Asia Research Institute (ARI) of the National University of Singapore. From the discussions and conversations at this event, we realised there was a need for scholarly work to further examine the relationship between the notions of post-politics, urban governance, and civil society, especially within the context of urban Asia. We thus decided to embark on this book project, inviting a number of individuals who presented at the conference to contribute.

We would thus like to express our appreciation to ARI for their generous financial support, and Sharon Ong of the ARI events team for providing us with much-needed administrative support, without which the conference would not have been possible. We would also like to thank Simon Bates at Routledge, who was receptive towards this edited volume since its inception, and has offered insightful feedback throughout the entire publication process. Our gratitude also extends to all the authors for their commitment and enthusiasm towards this edited volume, for their patience in responding to our editorial commentary, and for delivering their work in a timely manner. Thanks must be given to Nika Tay of ARI, who has offered indispensable editorial assistance. Finally, we would like to thank our family, friends, and colleagues whom supported us throughout the highlights and difficulties we encountered in convening this volume.

CONTRIBUTORS

Editors

Sonia Lam-Knott was a postdoctoral fellow in the Asian Urbanisms Cluster at the Asia Research Institute, National University of Singapore. She received her DPhil in anthropology from the University of Oxford in 2015, for her research on youth activism in Hong Kong, which looks at the emergent political subjectivities and the changes in state–civil society relations in the contemporary city. Her research explores the socio-political ambiguities in post-1997 Hong Kong, viewed through the lens of heritage politics, nostalgia, and vernacular experiences of the city. Of particular interest are the divergent history narratives that have emerged in the heritage spaces of the contemporary city, and how they are being received and experienced by ordinary citizens. She has published in journals such as *Asian Anthropology*, *Anthropology Matters*, and *Urban Studies*, as well as in edited volumes.

Creighton Connolly is a lecturer in the School of Geography, University of Lincoln (UK), focussing on development studies and the Global South. Prior to this, he was a postdoctoral fellow in the Asian Urbanisms Cluster of the Asia Research Institute, National University of Singapore. He is an urban political ecologist by training, having received his PhD in geography from the University of Manchester in June 2016, where he was a member of the European Network of Political Ecology (ENTITLE). His research focuses primarily on contestations over urban (re)development, and environmental governance in peninsular Malaysia. He has published this work in numerous journals, including the *International Journal of Urban and Regional Research* (*IJURR*), *Environment and Planning A*, *Cultural Geographies*, and *Geoforum*. Creighton's teaching expertise is largely focussed on heritage, development studies, and political ecology.

Kong Chong Ho was trained as an urban sociologist at the University of Chicago, and his research interests lies in neighbourhood and community development, heritage and place-making, the political economy of cities, and a more recent interest in higher education. Much of his published work is on East (Hong Kong, Seoul, and Taipei) and Southeast (Bangkok and Singapore) Asian cities. He has produced edited volumes such as *Service Industries and Asia Pacific Cities* (2012, with Peter Daniels and Tom Hutton) and *Advancing the Regional Commons in the New East Asia* (2016, with Siriporn Wajjwalku and Osamu Yoshida). Recent publications include "The Neighbourhood Roots of Social Cohesion: Notes on an Exceptional Case of Singapore" in *Environment and Planning C* (2018, with Vincent Chua), "The Cultivation of Research Labour in Pacific Asia" in *Asia Pacific Education Review* (2018, with Ge Yun), and "Discrepant Knowledge and InterAsian Mobilities: Unlikely Movements, Uncertain Futures" in *Discourse: Studies in the Cultural Politics of Education* (2018, with Francis Collins). Forthcoming publications include *Neighbourhoods for the City in Pacific Asia* (2019).

Contributing Authors (arranged in accordance to chapter order)

David Matijasevich is affiliated with the Department of Political Science at Simon Fraser University and is an independent researcher. He received his PhD in political science from Carleton University in Ottawa, Canada, in 2015. His interests lie at the crossroads of comparative politics and political theory, particularly contemporary democratic theory and practice and state–civil society relations.

Tamas Wells is a research fellow in the School of Social and Political Sciences at the University of Melbourne. His research focuses on meanings of democracy, governance, and accountability in Southeast Asia and the role of international aid agencies and 'civil society', and he has published widely on these topics in academic and practitioner literature, exemplified by his contributions to edited volumes such as *Conflict in Myanmar: War, Politics, and Religion* (2016) and to the *Asian Journal of Political Science*. His doctoral dissertation examined the Burmese opposition movement in the lead-up to the historic 2015 elections in Myanmar and diverging narratives of democracy within the movement, and amongst its international supporters. Before his doctoral studies, he has worked as an aid and development adviser and consultant with various NGOs, including Save the Children and Oxfam, and spent seven years living and working in Myanmar.

U-Seok Seo is a professor in the Department of Urban Sociology at the University of Seoul, where he also served as a chair of the Department of Culture, Arts and Tourism at the Graduate School of Urban Sciences from 2008 until 2016. He received his BA and MA degrees in sociology from Seoul National University, and his PhD in sociology from the University of Cologne, Germany. His research areas include cultural sociology, urban sociology, cultural policy, and research methodology. He published several book chapters and numerous articles in peer-reviewed academic journals. In the past year, he has edited two monographs focussed on Seoul. He currently serves as editor-in-chief for *Review of Culture and Economy* published by the Korean Association of Cultural Economics and as an editorial member of the *Journal of Arts, Management and Policy* published by the Korean Association of Arts Management.

Karl Beelen is an architect and urban designer by training, and currently a lecturer and researcher at the Karlsruhe Institute of Technology. He received his PhD in urbanism from Eindhoven University of Technology for examining the implicit, erasive urbanisms emerging in the margin of infrastructural logistics and urban planning. He was a postdoctoral research fellow at IIT-Madras (Chennai, India), during which he founded the Bypasslab in 2016, a research and design workshop based in Chennai focussing on the peri-urban frontiers of urbanisation in India. His current research engages with the cities of Chennai and Amsterdam, carrying a particular interest in grassroots urbanisms and 'everyday' notions of design.

Yujie Zhu is a lecturer at the Center for Heritage and Museum Studies of the Australian National University. Yujie is interested in the politics of cultural heritage, and its relation to issues like tourism, material culture, urban history, and religious practices in China. He is the author of *Heritage and Romantic Consumption in China* (2018) and the co-editor of *Politics of Scale* (2018) and *Sustainable Tourism Management at World Heritage Sites* (UNWTO 2009). He has also published more than 30 articles that appeared in leading anthropology, tourism, and heritage journals, including *American Anthropologist*, *Annals of Tourism Research*, and *International Journal of Heritage Studies*. In addition, Yujie is an executive committee member of the Association of Critical Heritage Studies (ACHS).

Yunci Cai is a lecturer in museum studies at the School of Museum Studies at the University of Leicester. She completed her PhD in museum and heritage studies at University College London (UCL) in 2017. Her PhD research explores the politics of heritage instrumentalisation at four indigenous cultural villages in Malaysia. Her research interests pertain to the cultural politics and museologies in and of Asia, and her recent project explores the politics of heritage instrumentalisation along the maritime Silk Road under China's Belt and Road Initiative. She has published in the *International Journal of Politics, Culture and Society*, the *Journal of the Malaysian Branch of the Royal Asiatic Society*, and the *International Journal of the Inclusive Museum*, as well as book chapters in the *Routledge Handbook of Urbanisation in Southeast Asia* (2018), *Citizens, Civil Society and Heritage-Making in Asia* (2017), and *Essays in Singapore's Legal History: In Memory of Professor Geoffrey Wilson Bartholomew* (2009, *Singapore Journal of Legal Studies*).

Seohee Kwak is a PhD candidate at the International Institute of Social Studies (ISS), Erasmus University Rotterdam, The Netherlands. Her current research focuses on citizen participation and government responsiveness in Vietnam. She worked as a researcher in the Korean Women's Development Institute and co-authored several publications in Korean on gender and development agendas. With a geographical interest in Vietnam and other Southeast Asian countries, her academic interests include democratic/good governance, accountability, civil society, human rights, and state-society relations in the field of international development.

Reina Artur Kyzy is a PhD candidate at the Otto von Guericke Universität in Magdeburg, Germany, and a visiting assistant professor and researcher at the American University of Central Asia, Kyrgyzstan. Her research interest areas cover, but are not limited, to civil society conceptualisation in post-conflict and authoritarian states in Central Asia, democratisation, human rights, gender issues, and environmental protection. She is a civil activist and one of the founding members of Feminists' Initiatives in Kyrgyzstan. She has been a co-editor for the book *Reimagining Civil Society in a Time of Uncivil Societies* (2017).

Dakila Kim P. Yee is an assistant professor of sociology at the Division of Social Sciences, University of the Philippines Visayas Tacloban College. He graduated with a master of arts in sociology from the University of the Philippines Diliman. His research interest covers disaster politics, disaster justice, and the production of neoliberal spaces and subjectivities in post-disaster cities. His recent publications appeared in the journals *Critical Asian Studies* and *Peace Review: A Journal of Social Justice*.

INTRODUCTION

Theorising the post-political in Asian cities

*Sonia Lam-Knott, Creighton Connolly,
and Kong Chong Ho*

The rise of the post-political city

Observing changes to contemporary state-society relations, scholars claim that we now live in a post-political era (Swyngedouw 2007; Wilson and Swyngedouw 2016). Whereas politics broadly refers to the production and circulation of antagonistic dynamics between different individuals and organisations (Mouffe 2005, 9), the concept of post-politics describes the absence and negation of such contentious relations in society. One aspect of this is the prevalence of political apathy and cynicism amongst citizens in democratic societies, given the perceived control of political and economic elites operating behind the façade of formal democratic political systems. Another is the commensurate rise in populism and right-wing politics around the world, which are seen as disproportionately influencing politics in democratic societies. As Ruming (2018) has observed, populism has emerged as a core element of post-political efforts to appeal to the ambitions and desires of a population.

More importantly, scholars identify tendencies towards depoliticisation in democratic societies as the product of 'post-political governance' where the state is perceived as embodying a technocratic and managerial role in decision-making processes (Raco and Lin 2012; Swyngedouw 2009; Žižek 2008). This mode of governance also strives to establish widespread societal consensus through producing "an external threat such as climate change and terrorism against which ideas of a united society are mobilised" (Cook 2018, 372; see Swyngedouw 2009), and by advocating for seemingly vague, 'inclusive', and 'progressive' objectives (Allmendinger and Haughton 2012). These objectives include economic growth, framed as the harbinger of cosmopolitanism and developmental modernity; environmental sustainability, presented as a moral issue and obligation; or cultural regeneration, portrayed as a humanistic endeavour which also contributes towards economic growth (Legacy et al. 2018; Ruming 2018). These objectives differ in theme and scope, but all appear as non-political issues geared towards realising the 'common good', becoming attached to notions of social responsibility in actualising good citizenship, thereby making them difficult to question or oppose. To rephrase, these objectives are not subject to critical reflexive thought and valuations by the population, processes that are central to political conduct.

Whilst the term 'post' in 'post-politics' infers that societies now exist under conditions that transcend 'the political', post-political governance is in itself a political act, involving the management of different opinions to establish consensus and minimise contestation. Existing literature on post-politics makes two inter-related observations about the ramifications post-political governance has on state-society interactions within the urban context. Firstly, in building societal consensus towards these normative objectives, governing bodies seek to control and mediate political discourse within societies. Decision-making has become centralised amongst politicians comprising of the governing institution and advisors, whilst the need for non-expert citizen involvement and input in such processes have been downplayed. Nonetheless, politicians strive to appear 'reasonable' by enabling civil society groups to partake in formal decision-making consultations (Haughton, Gilchrist, and Swyngedouw 2016). But to engage in such dialogue, civil society groups must adhere to the rules of engagement stipulated by governing bodies or risk expulsion and exclusion (Swyngedouw 1997, 2005, 1995). Furthermore, the topics of discussion have already been pre-determined, ultimately generating policies and outcomes deemed acceptable by the political elite. Secondly, political and economic elites enforce consensus not only by encouraging civil society to internalise and embrace these objectives through educational and propagandist campaigns, but by replacing decision-making processes using public debates and bargaining with referendum voting, which renders the voices of the dissenting minority obscure against the backdrop of majority consensus (Allmendinger and Haughton 2012; Deas 2014). The result is that "political decision making is virtually pre-ordained . . . where the outcomes of policy-making . . . are virtually known in advance" (Beveridge and Koch 2017, 33).

As a result, under post-political governance, the possibility of genuine political choice exerted by civil society is reduced, and explorations of potential alternative values and imaginings of the city have been denied (Beveridge 2017). Whilst initially developed by political thinkers like Jacques Rancière (2003), Chantal Mouffe (2005), and Slavoj Žižek (2008), these ideas have been translated by Erik Swyngedouw (2007, 2009) to theorise urban politics and governance. Indeed, cities have become the site where post-political tensions are played out, due to the gradual decentralisation of state power across different societies throughout the 20th century, whereby political power has been dispersed to local-level urban and regional governments. Post-political trends prevail in the cities of Western liberal democracies, where urban planning is reduced to consensus regarding depoliticised imaginings of the 'global city', 'creative city', 'smart city', or 'green city', which remain largely as empty signifiers (Beveridge and Koch 2017). For instance, new urban development and revitalisation schemes are presented as being structured around establishing the competitive city that can lead to future economic growth, which holds the promise of improving the quality of life not just for urban inhabitants, but also for regional and national populations (see Legacy et al. 2018; Swyngedouw 2007, 2009). For Swyngedouw, such discourses are associated with the rise of neoliberal governmentality and "the dominance of capitalism as an economic system" (Ruming 2018, 183).

The material form and characteristics of cities are also thus subject to controversies between the municipal government, its inhabitants, and various special interest groups. As Beveridge and Koch (2017) have noted, the urban form is the very thing at stake in the (de)politicisation of urban governance, given the centrality of cities for public contestation. Rather than merely structuring urban space in such a way as to cater to ideals of the 'creative city' or 'green cities', they must also include spaces for the representation of competing or marginalised interests (see Kohn 2004; Newman 2015). It is for this reason that contributors to this volume pay particular attention to the construction of heritage landscapes, in that such spaces of historicity can embody and reconfigure the political or cultural ideologies and power relations in any contemporary society (see Geismar 2015). Many ideological differences surrounding heritage often run along divisions between the agendas of civil society, local government, national government, and even transnational agencies (see Berliner 2012; Chu 2015; Peleggi 2005). Whilst such heritage dilemmas have prompted grassroots actors in some cities to act independently from state agencies, in other locations they have provided opportunities for new cooperative relationships to emerge between governmental and non-governmental actors (see King 2017; Sand 2013).

A further manifestation of post-political urban governance that this book examines is that of the urban environment and sustainability. Swyngedouw's (2009) initial work on the post-political city was also primarily concerned with issues surrounding environmental justice and sustainable environmental futures, which are increasingly urban questions. This has been documented through considerable urban research which has sought to interrogate the relationship between urban (political) processes and environmental transformations (e.g., Heynen, Kaika, and Swyngedouw 2006; Loftus 2012; Swyngedouw 2004). For instance, Swyngedouw (2009, 602) notes that cities produce 80 percent of the world's greenhouse gases, express the most acute forms of socio-environmental injustice, and are central to the production of more sustainable environmental futures. As Raco and Lin (2012, 193) observed, there was also a global convergence in urban development planning around the world in the 2000s, emphasising sustainability planning in urban and regional governance agendas, albeit in a depoliticised form. Moreover, cities are often the venue for social mobilisations and political struggles which have sought to shape alternative trajectories of urban development that are grounded in principles of environmental justice and sustainability (see Houston et al. 2018; Connolly 2019a). This is also one of the primary motivations for this volume, which seeks to interrogate how post-political tendencies have emerged in the sphere of environmental governance, and how they are being resisted by local actors.

Although the concept of post-politics was borne of observations made in the liberal democracies of Europe, North America, and Australia, it has also been applied to the Asian context, where scholars observe that governing bodies in the region impose consensus upon different stakeholders by championing ideals of economic growth and sustainability to facilitate urban development (see L.H.D. Hui and Au 2016; Kim and Cho 2017; Raco and Lin 2012). But at the same time, the ubiquity and pervasiveness of the post-political condition has been increasingly challenged (see Beveridge and Koch 2017; Larner 2014). Indeed, recent work has sought to question the extent and pervasiveness of post-politics across different cities, with some studies taking a reflexive step by noting that the seeming prevalence of post-politics is borne from our limited definitions and conceptualisations of what politics entails in the first place (Beveridge 2017; Davidson and Iverson 2015). In this regard, Raco and Lin (2012, 192) associate the Western bias in the literature on post-politics to a wider "Eurocentrism that seeks to generate universal theories from the post-war experiences of a relatively small, albeit powerful, group of countries". Therefore, there is a need for the development of more 'cosmopolitan' forms of theorising which are attentive to how social, political, and cultural differences can affect, for instance, the relationships between state and civil society in different places (see Robinson 2002, 546).

Responding to the bleak and confining nature of the post-political city, scholars argue for the dispelling of the post-political by rethinking the political as actually involving "an assemblage of distributed authority in which power is continually negotiated and renegotiated" not only within governing institutions, but within the realm of everyday life (Allen and Cochrane 2010, 1076; Sassen 2006). Building upon such ideas, other studies note that theorisations and descriptions of the post-political city do not reflect the on-the-ground reality of urban relations, with the recent eruption of protests challenging claims that post-political governance negates and "diminish the possibilities of the urban as a political space of resistance and emancipation" (Beveridge and Koch 2017, 32; see also Raco and Lin 2012; Ruming 2018). Contributors to this volume join other scholars in highlighting 'alternative' political strategies used by urban citizens to challenge the neoliberal inspired models of redevelopment pursued by political and economic elites (see Raco and Lin 2012; Ruming 2018). As such, examining the (re)negotiation of power relations in cities necessitates developing a nuanced understanding of state-society relations within processes of urban governance, which in turn are contingent on the socio-political and historical specificities of a geographic context, which is what this volume intends to do for the Asian case.

State-society relations in the Asian urban context

The notion of the post-political urban governance, and how this impacts upon the dynamics between the state and civil society, requires greater contextual specificity and differentiation. Although scholars claim that post-political trends have been observed in Asia, as noted previously, applying this concept to post-colonial and non-Western contexts poses conceptual challenges, due to the ambiguous manifestations of 'politics' and the relatively young state of democracy in such societies. Whilst contemporary Western nations are decentralising their state apparatuses to establish a form of post-political governance to enhance the effectiveness of their participative qualities and output delivery (see Crouch 2004; Kübler and Heinelt 2005; Sellers and Walks 2013), the political situation in Asia is more complex, due to the region's distinctive socio-political development throughout history. Unlike cities in Western liberal democracies that give the illusion of civic participation in driving urban development, urban changes in Asia have been blatantly dictated by the colonial and post-colonial regimes throughout the 16th until the mid-20th centuries, with little citizen input. This state-society imbalance was exacerbated towards the end of the colonial rule, when newly independent Asian states were driven by a politics of survival premised on attaining economic stability, and therefore established strong state bureaucracies. Many governments thus adopted non-democratic styles of governance, characterised by a dearth of consultative platforms for the public, and the suppression of dissent (Boudreau 2004; Spencer 1997). Whilst not all Asian countries were formally colonialised by the West or by other nations, most are still young democracies that arose from post-war restructuring.

Today, many cities in the region implement economically liberal policies enabling their markets and trade networks to expand and engage with the global domain. This is in part due to the "rescaling of state power from the nation-state to urban region, and the resultant entrepreneurial strategies adopted by city governments" (Connolly 2019b, 621; see also Allen and Cochrane 2010; Bunnell 2004; Davidson and Iverson 2015). Consequently, rationalities of planning and democratic governance are compromised as city governments bow to various developmental and political pressures. In some cases, such governance patterns can be characterised by their neglect and restriction of socio-political rights for the population, whilst in others, governments seek to adopt forms of 'good governance' which are focussed on participation and partnership (see Kim and Cho 2017; Raco and Lin 2012). However, in both cases, as Ruming (2018, 182) has argued, the implementation of such neoliberal planning strategies is post-political in that it seeks to "constrain participation, streamline decision making, create investment certainty, and deliver urban projects that benefit powerful state and market elites". This is certainly the case in many Asian states which have adopted a strong-state approach to achieving development, but may not be post-political in the true sense of the term that revolves around the notion of consensus.

Such modes of governance have attracted a plethora of scholarship analysing the socio-political and cultural particularities of Asian urbanism (see Jayne 2018; Ren and Luger 2014; Roy 2009). For instance, the chapters by Kwak and Kyzy (this volume) draw attention to the tensions within the central governments of many Asian states regarding the extent to which social unrest is seen as a marker of democratic maturity, on the one hand, and a threat to social and governmental order, on the other (see also Raco and Lin 2012, 192). The chapters by Wells and Yee highlight the emergent contradictions between Asian states attempting to adhere to 'international standards' of governance which embrace participatory practices, but at the same time, continue to marginalise their populations from decision-making processes. As various scholars have noted, we still need a better understanding of how particular actors in Asian and other post-colonial contexts understand issues like 'consensus politics' and who the agents of post-politics really are (Beveridge and Koch 2017; Raco and Lin 2012).

The political landscape of Asia underwent transition towards the end of the 20th century. In the wake of democratic movements in the region, a number of strong post-independent nations embraced a form of decentralised governance (see Presidential Committee on Government Innovation and Decentralization 2006; Painter 2004). Political power is transferred from the national government to local governing bodies such as city administrations, bringing the government 'closer' to the people, allowing for greater direct democratic involvement in political decision-making (see Crook and Manor 1998; Fritzen 2006). But how such democratic civic participation is construed and manifest in urban governance remains open to scrutiny (see Asian Barometer 2016; Thompson 2015). For example, policy-making power is retained by the national government in nations such as China, whereas nations such as Japan and South Korea conflate democratic practices with simply holding formal votes. At the same time, many contemporary Asian cities and nations remain quasi-authoritarian despite decentralisation, and have even seen the rise and growth of anti-democratic tendencies, with the state incurring upon the rights of the public sphere (Abramowitz 2019; Cheng and Chu 2018). In most Asian settings, municipal governments tend to lack formal mechanisms that can broaden citizen engagement with urban governance on an everyday basis, reducing civil society engagements to occasional social movements (see Ng 2013).

Although scholars observe the expansion of civil society across Asian cities, many of these organisations operate under strict regulations imposed by the state, struggle to receive recognition from their respective governments, and find it difficult to pose as a genuine opposition force to state power (see Alagappa 2004; Ogawa 2018). Instances of mass protests in public spaces, such as the anti-World Trade Organisation and Occupy Movements, would either not emerge in the first place (e.g., in China, where state control is strong) or would be quickly suppressed by the state through the use of force (e.g., as with the Sunflower Movement in Taiwan and the Umbrella Movement in Hong Kong). In light of the region having undergone a different historical and political trajectory than Western liberal democracies, and in light of the region's complex and variegated political conditions, the applicability of the post-political framework to the contemporary Asian urban context requires further critical inquiry.

We focus in particular on issues of heritage and environmental governance, as these topics have provided opportunities for new cooperative and contentious relationships to emerge between governmental and non-governmental actors (see Sand 2013). Heritage governance broadly refers to the conservation of material and immaterial aspects from the past in the present, whereas environmental governance involves the utilisation and rationing of natural resources and landscapes. Both are recognised by scholars as being inter-related components in the (re)constitution of urban space and urban social relations (see Connolly 2019a; Geismar 2015; Kooy and Bakker 2008), thereby rendering them into sites of ideological contentions between governments and civil society (see Bakker 2007; Bolaños 2011; Chu 2015; Y-F. Hui, Hsiao, and Peycam 2017). Whilst these issues are often distinct, and treated as such in this volume, they are also inter-related because they are construed by city governments and civil society actors as essential components in building more sustainable and 'liveable' cities for the future. Both heritage and environmental governance are aspects of the aforementioned convergence in urban development planning in the 21st century, which have brought the preservation of heritage and environmental sustainability to the fore, as represented through the Sustainable Development Goals of the United Nations (UN), for example. They are also commonly promoted by the UN, World Bank and other multi-national institutions as part of consensual approaches to developing 'good governance' and 'sustainability' in the Global South (Raco and Lin 2012, 193).

In this context, what are the alternatives and forms of resistance being developed to challenge such consensual politics in non-Western contexts such as Asia? In this volume, we seek to explore the strategies used by Asian civil society organisations in attempting to transform—even in minor ways—how cities are planned and developed, particularly through their involvement in heritage and environmental governance initiatives. By bringing together an interdisciplinary group of scholars, this volume provides a collection of empirical and ethnographic studies reviewing the extent to which the concept of post-politics applies in Asian cities. The chapters in this collection problematise how civil society has developed and is currently positioned in relation to local and national governing institutions. More significantly, they rectify an existing knowledge gap in urban governance literature by examining the capacities of civil society in effecting changes to urban governance dynamics and to the physical form and experience of the city itself. By broadening our scope of inquiry to both the cultural and natural dimension of cities, the contributions to this volume reveal how post-political conditions have hindered or opened up opportunities for civil society in shaping the politics and socio-environmental futures Asian cities. This is important to further understanding the geography of socio-political systems, and the growing multiplicity of political agency, in cities.

Structure of this book

This book is divided into three parts. The first section, 'Post-Political Governance in Asia', provides a theoretical examination of if and how notions of post-political tendencies are evident in Asian cities, whilst taking into account the diverse socio-economic and political histories within the region. Together, these chapters illustrate how the post-political condition is not exclusive to Western nations that have political systems characterised by more poly-centric forms of (democratic) governance but is also a useful political device to reinforce an anti-democratic governmentality in mono-centrically governed nations.

Subsequent sections of this volume address the 'on-the-ground' manifestations of post-politics across different Asian cities, by exploring state-society collaborations and contestations pertaining to the inter-related categories of heritage and environmental governance in the city. Despite the inherent political ramifications of heritage governance and environmental governance can have on society (e.g., relating to nation building or resource allocation), chapters in these sections show that heritage governance and environmental governance have instead been associated with values of sustainability and economic growth to attain support, consensus, and cooperation from the wider public domain across Asian cities. Yet these chapters also observe that such attempts at post-politicisation can be an incomplete process, or have in turn been used by civil society organisations as a strategy for them to engage with the political. This enables civil society across Asia to attain a stake in the governing of their cities, but with varying degrees of success, as noted by the contributors to this volume.

Puzzles and pathways in Asian post-politics

Our review of the literature in this introductory chapter suggests that the post-political condition occurs when political participation from the grassroots is curtailed by state-initiated structures which value expert opinion over debate and discussion involving a diverse range of citizens and stakeholders. Governments, in their attempts to be responsive to the needs and concerns of the citizenry, promote technocratic discourses accompanied by supportive narratives which speak to notions of openness, fair play, and the best interests of affected localities, as well as appeal to the wider interests of the entire city. But what should be questioned are how these 'interests of the city' are defined (see Baker and Ruming 2015; Colven 2017; Fainstein 2010; Harvey 2008). In actuality, those in power deem such urban interests as being aligned to the growth of the capitalist market, with municipal city governments supporting such capitalistic developments by justifying their contributions towards quality-of-life improvements. By being able to dictate what urban interests comprises of, national and local governments are able to exert control over the topics posited for public deliberation; more specifically, deliberations between citizens and the state become focussed on specific issues pre-determined by the latter. In sum, the widespread role of expertise, and the ritualised nature of deliberations, work to constrain and limit wider forms of public participation in the political sphere and in the decision-making processes of the city.

To conclude this introductory chapter to the volume, we take another look at the conditions and assumptions which underpin post-political theorising, noting the key points made by the chapters in this collection, and see if there are indeed post-political elements in the political development of Asian countries. By doing so, we then open up the discussion towards examining four potential developmental paths in Asian politics for the near future. The volume opens with a chapter by

David Matijasevich, who through a study of Thailand and Singapore, notes that post-political conditions in Asia are enforced by quasi-democratic and authoritarian rule, departing from existing literature linking post-politics with liberal democracies. He thus questions the extent to which Asian cities can truly be 'post' political, and in doing so, also discusses what the 'political' means in Asia. Matijasevich's work is then followed by contributions by other scholars that also question the extent and manifestation of the post-political in Asia, approaching this inquiry by examining the perspectives and experiences of civil society across a range of locales.

Many of the subsequent chapters in this book begin by looking at the relationship between the state and civil society in three ways. Firstly, the chapters demonstrate the vitality of civil society movements, noting a difference in the intensity and the degree of state antagonism these mobilisations incur, depending on whether they are addressing environmental or heritage concerns. For example, civil society movements pertaining to environmental issues are often met with strong state resistance. This is seen from Seohee Kwak's chapter examining the 2014 citizen movement against a state-led tree-felling project in Hanoi, Vietnam, illustrating how these grassroots oppositional voices with a political tone are suppressed by the state, prompting civil society actors to instead direct their energies towards engaging in social movements though online platforms such as Facebook (Chapter 7). Similarly, Reina Artur Kyzy's chapter explores civic mobilisations against the environmental ramifications of state-led urban development in Central Asian cities such as Bishkek, outlining the stymied development of civil society in the region due to suppression by authoritarian and quasi-democratic governing regimes. Referencing the works of Manuel Castells, Tim Bunnell, and other scholars on grassroots urban governance strategies, Kyzy reveals that civil society organisations in Central Asia are attempting to overcome state restrictions through the formation of on-the-ground and digital networks (Chapter 8).

Unlike environmental activism where relations between state and civil society are often antagonistic and conflictual, in turn, heritage activism appears to take on a different tone. As pointed out by Yujie Zhu examining urban development in Xi'an (Chapter 5), the local government associates heritage with tourism, evoking ideas of 'fun' and 'beauty' and even of national pride, which encourage widespread public participation and support of these initiatives. Despite occasions where state-society interests towards historical sites do not align, resulting in citizen mobilisations that have managed to vie for concessions from local officials, these concessions ultimately adhere to the interests of the state in facilitating tourism, so that state dominance over heritage governance remains unchallenged. This is echoed in Yunci Cai's observations in Quanzhou (Chapter 6), where state-endorsed civil society organisations promulgate the connection between heritage with positive ideals of sustainability and community building, which Cai interprets to be a form of governance to lessen public dissent towards state-led redevelopment and gentrification of the wider urban landscape. Thus, in heritage activism, there is arguably a depoliticisation process at work, as many state-led heritage schemes seemingly promise potential benefits to all the stakeholders concerned. Analysing the nature of state response towards civil society movements with regards to heritage activism, the chapters by Zhu and Cai suggest that states assume a milder and more accommodating response to heritage activism compared with environmental activism, where there is a clash of interests between state and society.

Secondly, the chapters in this volume explore state responses towards civil society mobilisations, which are dependent on a number of variables. State response is contingent on the issue addressed by civil society movements, as illustrated by the difference in state response towards heritage and environmental activism mentioned previously, but also on the eruption of unforeseen events or the presence of international agencies within Asian states. For example, during moments of socio-political and physical disruptions, such as natural disasters, states are given the opportunity to assume absolute control from the citizenry over the shaping of the city. Dakila Kim P. Yee's examination of Tacloban City shows that after Typhoon Haiyan took a severe infrastructural and human toll on the region, the Tacloban City government used reconstruction efforts as an opportunity to facilitate their neoliberal agendas of fostering urban development at the expense of the urban poor (Chapter 9). State responses to civil society can also be moderated by the presence of third parties who advocate for fair compensation for communities affected by urban development, as seen in the Thilawa Special Economic Zone of Myanmar, as discussed by Tamas Wells (Chapter 2). Wells explores how the Thilawa government strategically employs ideals of liberal democracy through its collaborations with third-party international corporations. Whilst these third-party international organisations are supposed to espouse practices of good governance and mediate state-society relations in Thilawa, in reality, Wells finds that these international entities are reluctant to assume responsibility over resolving local state-society contestations, ultimately enabling the state to enforce post-political conditions by stifling and curtailing dissent from civil society.

Thirdly, the chapters in this volume appreciate that the relative strength of the regulative and coercive powers of the state provides the context for understanding the nature of the relationship between state, the environment, and society in the contemporary era. This is best expressed by Kyzy's writing about the growth and advances made by civil society movements in Central Asia over the past decades, where it is clear that the state has and continues to assume an authoritarian stance in the area of urban governance. State control over urban development can similarly be seen in the Myanmar context, whilst the chapters by Zhu and Cai also infer the presence of a strong state apparatus in China whereby civil society organisations and the citizenry are subject to strong state control and restrictions. Civil society organisations are gradually challenging such authoritarianism, yet the state retains the ability to exert coercive and regulatory powers to stifle emergent grassroots movements. This tension represents *one pathway* for future political development in Asia.

But even in Asian nations that have undergone democratisation since the mid-20th century such that civil society actors and organisations are no longer met with state suppression, what is observed is that citizens' voices continue to be subject to state control, albeit in less visible ways. This is illustrated by Seo's assessment of the South Korean context (Chapter 3), a nation that has been a liberal democracy since the 1980s and is arguably the current forerunner for democratic practices in Asia. The South Korean state appears to cede some of its power to the public sphere in matters of political decision-making and urban governance, as evidenced by the growth of popular participation in Seoul in terms of the rapid expansion of citizenship committees. Yet these forms of citizen participation and engagement are also constraining, as they remain heavily influenced by the interests of the state. The question Seo thus raises is whether such citizen committees are constrained by the regulatory power of the state to become nothing more than window dressing, thereby adhering to post-political framings. An affirmative answer to this question folds nicely into the post-political argument where broader issues, pertaining to structural state-society power inequalities along with citizen rights and freedom of speech, are increasingly being herded by the state towards a limited range of issues.

Whilst the topics featured within state-society deliberations may be increasingly determined by the state, at the same time, we have witnessed South Koreans frequently taking to the streets to address instances of injustice and to protest against the dominance of corporate and government interests on the urban landscape. Thus the rise of liberal democracy in the nation has also had an ongoing effect in Korean society, continuing to shape citizen consciousness towards embracing their right to govern, as seen from citizen efforts in establishing and participating in citizenship committees, and from citizens taking to the streets to protest when necessary. What is seen in South Korea is that in the midst of post-political tendencies invoked by the neoliberalising state that advocates for an expanded role for citizens to become involved in issues of governance, albeit under the rules and conditions stipulated by the state, there are also vibrant attempts at the grassroots level to engage in urban politics on their own terms through street protests and social media campaigns. This tension within the political landscape in contemporary South Korea represents the *second pathway* to political development in Asia: where states that have undergone democratisation and neoliberalism have been pushed to create more spaces for public participation, opening up opportunities for citizens to enact their political rights and become more involved in the making of their urban realities in a manner deemed acceptable by the state, whilst at the same time, grassroots-led mobilisation and mass action that do not fall under state-approved channels of public political participation continues to persist.

Asides from exploring avenues of public political participation that is created by citizens and not the state, the chapters in this collection also open other ways to consider governance, in terms of the tendency for utopian spaces to be crafted. Beelen's observations of the back-to-the-land organic farming movement near Chennai, India, present the possibility of a retreat from the influence of the state (Chapter 4). Back-to-the-land farmers in India (and in other parts of Asia) are united by a shared ideology and practice towards what they believe to be 'simpler', non-urban forms of life (see Leng 2016; Shapiro 2015). In the case of India, these individuals are able to embrace a non-urban lifestyle by setting up farming communities outside of Chennai, thanks to the financial accumulation made possible by their middle-class professions. These back-to-the-land farmers thereby represent a new way in which the middle-class is successfully creating new political spaces that lie beyond the boundaries of the city. Their distancing from the city is also a way of escaping from the influence of the state, though Beelen acknowledges that adjusting to such new ways of living poses difficulties for its practitioners, and can be characterised by an element of exclusivity that is based on socio-economic class. Nonetheless, conceptually, such movements produce the potential of new utopias which are separate from, or at least minimally linked to, the infrastructures of state control that are denser in the city. As Beelen observes amongst the back-to-the-land farmers, a shared ideology and practice enables a sense of solidarity and community amongst this select portion of the citizenry to be formed, ensuring some level of mutual assistance and collective welfare to be realised amongst them. This inclination towards cooperation and self-sufficiency, combined with the financial stability of these back-to-the-land farmers who hail from the middle-classes, grants them a degree of independence from the welfare safety nets of the state. Also, the positioning of these back-to-the-land farmers outside of the city does create a buffer between these individuals from the policies and infrastructures developed by the state, along with other state-led influences and encroachments introduced in the interests of urban (re)development. These pockets of middle-class utopian spaces may represent the *third avenue* of political development in Asia, though they also present a conundrum in that these efforts contain divisive elements by excluding the working-class.

Finally, in our attempts to chart the possibilities of political development in Asia, we should also consider the applicability of the assumptions made by the post-political literature. Certainly, a number of inter-related key assumptions do apply. The first assumption is the state's dependence on the neoliberal market economy, which is perceived as being fundamental to the management and development of the city. The effects capitalist markets have on the city are clear. For example, a vibrant urban economy creates jobs in the city and raises tax revenues that will be of benefit for the municipal government, which can be used towards the provision and upgrading of infrastructure, thereby increasing the quality of life for urban dwellers. Furthermore, the incorporation of private business interests in urban governance partnerships are also increasingly vital for the redevelopment of the city, as seen from philanthropic initiatives from businesses and wealthy individuals whom finance social services or public infrastructural works (see Allmendinger and Haughton 2012; Deas 2014; Wade 2018), and as seen from privatisation schemes where public services are transferred to private ownership and management (see de Jong et al. 2010; Parker 1999; Pongsiri 2012). This is, however, an unhealthy dependence that keep states aligned with capitalist interests.

In contrast, cities with robust, diverse, and healthy economies may be less dependent on financial contributions from corporations, and can have a more powerful bargaining position with business on specific projects (Savitch and Kantor 2002).

For example, despite the Japanese economy being primarily oriented towards the services sector, it remains diverse, encompassing agricultural and industrial endeavours, which means that no one sector of private corporations can dominate the financial landscape. And for a number of other countries in Asia, their governments possess large revenue sources derived from state-owned enterprises (e.g., China), sovereign wealth funds (e.g., China and Singapore), oil (e.g., Brunei), the leasing of land (e.g., Hong Kong), and gambling revenues (e.g., Macau). The ability of these governments to retain ownership over major industry sectors, and generate income that significantly contributes towards their gross domestic product, places these governing bodies in a stronger position to withstand corporate influence. But it is not our intention to paint a utopian scenario in this last part of this introductory chapter. Redistributive expenditures by the state can only be sustainable to the extent that government revenues are sufficient over the long term. The fact remains that in many cities across Asia, with the rise of neoliberal practices, states are increasingly looking to the corporate sector to finance public services and structures, as exemplified by the rise of 'privately-owned public spaces', whereby corporations are tasked by the state to provide and maintain public spaces, as seen in Asian cities such as Hong Kong, Singapore, and Seoul (see Cuthbert and McKinnell 1997; Koo and Lee 2015).

This dependence of the state on businesses to finance and fund urban development constrains the type of democratic politics and public scrutiny that should be central to the planning process, and can result in the neglect of public interest. The role and positioning of public participation in matters of urban governance is of increasing interest amongst the populations of urban Asia who, perhaps inspired by international discourse and other civil society movements across the Euro-American context, now claim their 'right to the city' and celebrate notions of the 'urban commons', and are contesting state and corporate control over the urban landscape. Such trends can be observed from citizen-led anti-gentrification movements in democratic cities like Taipei and Seoul, but also in quasi-democratic cities such as Hong Kong, and even in non-democratic cities across the wider Chinese nation (see Lee and Hsing 2010; Lee 2018; Shin 2018). This represents the *fourth avenue* of political development in Asia, whereby it is the metropolitan scale of politics where issues of citizen rights and urban governance are most often contested, where the impetus for grassroots mobilisation is felt most keenly, and where the engagement between state and society is strongest.

References

Abramowitz, M. J. 2019. *Freedom in the World 2018: Democracy in Crisis.* Freedom House. https://freedomhouse.org/report/freedom-world/freedom-world-2018

Alagappa, M., ed. 2004. *Civil Society and Political Change in Asia: Expanding and Contracting Democratic Space.* Stanford, CA: Stanford University Press.

Allen, J., and A. Cochrane. 2010. "Assemblages of State Power: Topological Shifts in the Organization of Government and Politics." *Antipode* 42 (5): 1071–1089.

Allmendinger, P., and G. Haughton. 2012. "Post-Political Spatial Planning in England: A Crisis of Consensus?" *Transactions of the Institute of British Geographers* 37 (1): 89–103.
Asian Barometer. 2016. "Meaning of Democracy." www.asianbarometer.org/survey/meaning-of-democracy
Baker, T., and K. Ruming. 2015. "Making 'Global Sydney': Spatial Imaginaries, Worlding and Strategic Plans." *International Journal of Urban and Regional Research* 39 (1): 62–78. doi:10.1111/1468-2427.12183.
Bakker, K. 2007. "The 'Commons' Versus the 'Commodity': Alter-Globalization, Anti-Privatization and the Human Right to Water in the Global South." *Antipode* 39 (3): 430–455.
Berliner, D. 2012. "Multiple Nostalgias: The Fabric of Heritage in Luang Prabang (Lao PDR)." *Journal of the Royal Anthropological Institute* 18 (4): 769–786.
Beveridge, R. 2017. "The (Ontological) Politics in Depoliticisaton Debates: Three Lens on the Decline of the Political." *Political Studies Review* 15 (4): 589–600.
Beveridge, R., and P. Koch. 2017. "The Post-Political Trap? Reflections on Politics, Agency and the City." *Urban Studies* 54 (1): 31–43.
Bolaños, O. 2011. "Redefining Identities, Redefining Landscapes: Indigenous Identity and Land Rights Struggles in the Brazilian Amazon." *Journal of Cultural Geography* 28 (1): 45–72.
Boudreau, V. 2004. *Resisting Dictatorship: Repression and Protest in Southeast Asia*. New York: Cambridge University Press.
Bunnell, T. 2004. *Malaysia, Modernity and the Multimedia Super Corridor: A Critical Geography of Intelligent Landscapes*. London: Routledge.
Cheng, T-J., and Y-H. Chu. 2018. "Introduction: An Overview of East Asian Democratization." In *Routledge Handbook of Democratization in East Asia*, edited by T-J. Cheng and Y-H. Chu, 1–16. Oxon: Routledge.
Chu, C. L. 2015. "Spectacular Macau: Visioning Futures for a World Heritage City." *Geoforum* 65: 440–450.
Colven, E. 2017. "Understanding the Allure of Big Infrastructure: Jakarta's Great Garuda Sea Wall Project." *Water Alternatives* 10 (2): 250–264.
Connolly, C. 2019a. "From Resilience to Multi-Species Flourishing: (Re)imagining Urban-Environmental Governance in Penang, Malaysia." *Urban Studies*. doi:10.1177/0042098018807573.
———. 2019b. "Worlding Cities through Transportation Infrastructure." *Environment and Planning A: Economy and Space* 51 (3): 617–635.
Cook, N. 2018. "More-Than-Human Planning: The Agency of Buildings and Bodies in the Post-Political City." *Geographical Research* 56 (4): 368–381.
Crook, R. C., and J. Manor. 1998. *Democracy and Decentralisation in South Asia and West Africa: Participation, Accountability, and Performance*. Cambridge: Cambridge University Press.
Crouch, C. 2004. *Post Democracy*. Cambridge: Polity Press.
Cuthbert, A. R., and K. G. McKinnell. 1997. "Ambiguous Space, Ambiguous Rights—Corporate Power and Social Control in Hong Kong." *Cities* 14 (5): 295–311.
Davidson, M., and K. Iverson. 2015. "Recovering the Politics of the City: From the 'Post-political City' to a 'Method of Equality' for Critical Urban Geography." *Progress in Human Geography* 39 (5): 543–559.
de Jong, M., M. Rui, D. Stead, Y. Ma, and B. Xi. 2010. "Introducing Public—Private Partnerships for Metropolitan Subways in China: What is the Evidence?" *Journal of Transport Geography* 18 (2): 301–313.
Deas, I. 2014. "The Search for Territorial Fixes in Subnational Governance: City-Regions and the Disputed Emergence of Post-Political Consensus in Manchester, England." *Urban Studies* 51 (11): 2285–2314.

Fainstein, S. S. 2010. *The Just City*. Ithaca: Cornell University Press.
Fritzen, S. A. 2006. "Probing System Limits: Decentralisation and Local Political Accountability in Vietnam." *Asia Pacific Journal of Public Administration* 28 (1): 1–23.
Geismar, H. 2015. "Anthropology and Heritage Regimes." *Annual Review of Anthropology* 44: 71–85. doi:10.1146/annurev-anthro-102214-014217.
Harvey, D. 2008. "The Right to the City." *New Left Review* 53: 23–40.
Haughton, G., A. Gilchrist, and E. Swynegdouw. 2016. "'Rise like Lions after Slumber': Dissent, Protest and (Post-)Politics in Manchester." *Territory, Politics, Governance* 4 (4): 472–491.
Heynen, N., M. Kaika and E. Swyngedouw., ed. 2006. *In the Nature of Cities: Urban Political Ecology and the Politics of Urban Metabolism (Questioning Cities)*. London: Routledge.
Houston, D., J. Hillier, D. MacCallum, W. Steele, and J. Byrne. 2018. "Make Kin, Not Cities! Multispecies entanglements and 'Becoming-World' in Planning Theory." *Planning Theory* 17 (2): 190–212.
Hui, L. H. D., and C. Y. R. Au. 2016. "Spatial Governance and the Rise of Post-Politics in Hong Kong." *Journal of Asian Public Policy* 9 (3): 227–242.
Hui, Y-F., H-H. M. Hsiao, and P. Peycam. 2017. "Introduction: Finding the Grain of Heritage Politics." In *Citizens, Civil Society, and Heritage-Making in Asia*, edited by H-H. M. Hsiao, Y-F. Hui, and P. Peycam, 1–14. Singapore: ISEAS—Yusof Ishak Institute.
Jayne, M. 2018. "An Introduction to Critical Perspectives on Chinese Urbanism." In *Chinese Urbanism: Critical Perspectives*, edited by M. Jayne, 1–14. Oxon: Routledge.
Kim, J., and M. Cho. 2017. "Creating a Sewing Village in Seoul: Towards Participatory Village-Making or Post-Political Urban Regeneration?" *Community Development Journal*, 1–21. doi:10.1093/cdj/bsx051.
King, R. 2017. *Heritage and Identity in Contemporary Thailand: Memory, Place and Power*. Singapore: National University of Singapore Press.
Kohn, M. 2004. *Brave New Neighbourhoods: The Privatization of Public Space*. London and New York: Routledge.
Koo, B., and Y. Lee. 2015. The Influence of Surrounding Ground Floor Facilities on the Use of Privately Owned Public Spaces in Seoul. *Journal of Building Construction and Planning Research* 3 (2): 95–106.
Kooy, M., and K. Bakker. 2008. Technologies of Government: Constituting Subjectivities, Spaces, and Infrastructures in Colonial and Contemporary Jakarta. *International Journal of Urban and Regional Research* 32 (2): 375–391. doi:10.1111/j.1468-2427.2008.00791.x.
Kübler, D., and H. Heinelt. 2005. "Metropolitan Governance, Democracy and the Dynamics of Place." In *Metropolitan Governance in the 21st Century: Capacity, Democracy and the Dynamics of Place*, edited by H. Heinelt and D. Kübler, 8–28. Oxon: Routledge.
Larner, W. 2014. "The Limits of Post-Politics: Rethinking Radical Social Enterprise." In *The Post-Political and Its Discontents: Spaces of Depoliticisation, Spectres of Radical Politics*, edited by E. Swyngedouw and J. Wilson, 189–207. Edinburgh: University of Edinburgh Press.
Lee, C. K., and Y-T. Hsing. 2010. "Social Activism in China: Agency and Possibility." In *Reclaiming Chinese Society: The New Social Activism*, edited by Y-T. Hsing and C. K. Lee, 1–14. Oxon: Routledge.
Lee, S. Y. 2018. "The Evolution of Housing Rights Activism in South Korea." In *Contested Cities and Urban Activism*, edited by N. M. Yip, M. A. M. López, and X. Sun, 253–273. Singapore: Palgrave Macmillan.
Legacy, C., N. Cook, D. Rogers, and K. Ruming. 2018. "Planning the Post-Political City: Exploring Public Participation in the Contemporary Australian City." *Geographic Research* 56 (2): 176–180.

Leng, S. 2016. "Hong Kong's Agricultural Revolution: The Rise in Farming for Fun." *South China Morning Post*, July 30. www.scmp.com/news/hong-kong/health-environment/article/1996597/hong-kongs-agricultural-revolution-rise-farming

Loftus, A. 2012. *Everyday Environmentalism: Creating an Urban Political Ecology*. Minneapolis: University of Minnesota Press.

Mouffe, C. 2005. *On the Political*. Abingdon: Routledge.

Newman, A. 2015. *Landscape of Discontent*. Minneapolis: University of Minnesota Press.

Ng, M. K. 2013. "Got the Controversial Urban Planning Job Done? An Institutional Perspective." In *Evaluating the Tsang Years 2005–2012*, edited by J. Cheng, 347–373. Hong Kong: City University Press.

Ogawa, A. 2018. "Introduction." In *The Routledge Handbook of Civil Society in Asia*, edited by A. Ogawa, 1–14. Oxon: Routledge.

Painter, M. 2004. "The Politics of Administrative Reform in East and Southeast Asia: From Gridlock to Continuous Self-Improvement?" *Governance* 17 (3): 361–386.

Parker, D. 1999. "Policy Transfer and Policy Inertia: Privatization in Taiwan." *Asia Pacific Business Review* 6 (2): 1–20.

Peleggi, M. 2005. "Consuming Colonial Nostalgia: The Monumentalisation of Historical Hotels in Urban South-East Asia." *Asia Pacific Viewpoint* 46 (3): 255–265. doi:10.1111/j.1467-8373.2005.00289.x.

Pongsiri, N. 2012. "Public-Private Partnerships and Urban Infrastructure Development in Southeast Asia." In *Urbanisation in Southeast Asia: Issues & Impacts*, edited by Y. K. Sheng and M. Thuzar, 139–153. Singapore: Institute of Southeast Asian Studies.

Presidential Committee on Government Innovation and Decentralization. 2006. "Reenergizing Local Governance in Korea." http://innovation.pa.go.kr/eng/images/01.PDF

Raco, M., and W-I. Lin. 2012. Urban Sustainability, Conflict Management, and the Geographies of Postpoliticism: A Case Study of Taipei. *Environment and Planning C: Government and Policy* 30 (2): 191–208.

Rancière, J. 2003 "Comment and Responses." *Theory & Event* 6 (4). doi:10.1353/tae.2003.0017.

Ren, J., and J. Luger. 2014. "Comparative Urbanism and the 'Asian City': Implications for Research and Theory." *International Journal of Urban and Regional Research* 39 (1): 145–156.

Robinson, J. 2002. "Global and World Cities: A View from Off the Map." *International Journal of Urban and Regional Research* 26 (3): 531–554.

Roy, A. 2009. "Why India Cannot Plan Its Cities: Informality, Insurgence, and the Idiom of Urbanisation." *Planning Theory* 8 (1): 76–87.

Ruming, K. 2018. "Post-Political Planning and Community Opposition: Asserting and Challenging Conesus in Planning Urban Regeneration in Newcastle, New South Wales." *Geographic Research* 56 (2): 181–195.

Sand, J. 2013. *Tokyo Vernacular: Common Spaces, Local Histories, Found Objects*. Berkeley: University of California Press.

Sassen, S. 2006. *Territory, Authority, Rights: From Medieval to Global Assemblages*. Princeton, NJ: Princeton University Press.

Savitch, H. V., and P. Kantor. 2002. *Cities in the International Marketplace: The Political Economy of Urban Development in North America and Western Europe*. Princeton, NJ: Princeton University Press.

Sellers, J. M., and R. A. Walks. 2013. "Introduction—The Metropolitanisation of Politics." In *The Political Ecology of the Metropolis: Metropolitan Sources of Electoral Behaviour in Eleven Countries*, edited by J. M. Sellers, D. Kübler, M. Walter-Rogg, and R. A. Walks, 3–36. Essex: ECPR Press.

Shapiro, A. 2015. "For One Couple, Grub Farm Cures Stress of Modern Korean Life." *NPR (National Public Radio)*, August 9. www.npr.org/2015/08/09/431025516/for-one-couple-grub-farm-cures-stress-of-modern-korean-life?t=1556383895203

Shin, H. B. 2018. "Urban Movements and the Genealogy of Urban Rights Discourses: The Case of Urban Protesters against Redevelopment and Displacement in Seoul, South Korea." *Annals of the American Association of Geographers* 108 (2): 356–369.

Spencer, J. 1997. "Post-Colonialism and the Political Imagination." *Journal of the Royal Anthropological Institute* 3 (1): 1–19.

Swyngedouw, E. 1997. "Neither Global nor Local: 'Glocalization' and the Politics of Scale." In *Spaces of Globalization: Reasserting the Power of the Local*, edited by K. R. Cox, 137–166. New York: Guilford Press.

———. 2004. *Social Power and the Urbanization of Water: Flows of Power*. Oxford and New York: Oxford University Press.

———. 2005. "Governance Innovation and the Citizen: The Janus Face of Governance-Beyond-the-State." *Urban Studies* 42 (11): 1991–2006.

———. 2007. "Impossible/Undesirable Sustainability and the Post-Political Condition." In *The Sustainable Development Paradox*, edited by R. Krueger and D. Gibbs, 13–40. New York: Guilford Press.

———. 2009. "The Antinomies of the Postpolitical City: In Search of a Democratic Politics of Environmental Production." *International Journal of Urban and Regional Research* 33 (3): 601–620.

Thompson, M. R. 2015. "Democracy with Asian Characteristics." *The Journal of Asian Studies* 74 (4): 875–887.

Wade, M. 2018. "Hyper-Planning Jakarta: The Great Garuda and Planning the Global Spectacle: Hyper-Planning Jakarta." *Singapore Journal of Tropical Geography* 40 (1): 158–172. doi:10.1111/sjtg.12262.

Wilson, J., and E. Swyngedouw. 2016. "Seeds of Dystopia: Post-Politics and the Return of the Political." In *The Post-Political and its Discontents: Spaces of Depoliticisation, Spectres of Radical Politics*, edited by J. Wilson and E. Swyngeodouw, 1–22. Edinburgh: Edinburgh University Press.

Žižek, S. 2008. *Revolution at the Gate: Žižek on Lenin: The 1917 Writings*. London: Verso.

PART I
Post-political governance in Asia

1
A RETURN TO THE POLITICAL?

Civil society and post-politics in authoritarian regimes

David Matijasevich

Introduction

The purpose of this chapter is to present a critique of the 'radical democratic' proposals put forward by Erik Swyngedouw and others in relation to what has come to be known as the post-political condition. According to Wilson and Swyngedouw, the post-political condition can be defined as the

> untroubled, undivided, cohesive and common-sense society in which everyone knows his or her place and performs his or duties in their own (and hence in everyone else's) interest . . . organised through a diversity of institutional forms of organised representative government, aided and supported by participatory governance arrangements for all sorts of recognised problems, issues and matters or public concern.
> *(Wilson and Swyngedouw 2015, 3)*

Across the globe, consensus-orientated approaches to political decision-making and policy formulation have found their way into areas as diverse as economic and urban planning, environmental sustainability, and development (Raco 2015; Kamat 2015). In such arrangements, government technocrats, corporations, and semi-institutionalised members of civil society collaborate to manage problems and administer solutions across a wide range or socio-economic and socio-environmental matters, including some of the aforementioned. Mainstream politicians speak a language of 'beyond conflict' and 'beyond left/right' and emphasise the importance of non-ideological, non-conflictual, and pragmatic approaches to issues facing the polity (Mouffe 2013, 119). For those who have bought into such a manner of doing politics, these approaches are 'win-win' for the reason that, firstly, they allow multiple stakeholders in society to have their input into policy-making and implementation and, secondly, their non-conflictual stance provides assurances to investors, both domestic and foreign, whose economic health the polity relies on (Brown 2015, 25, 128).

It must be said, however, that not everyone shares such an optimistic appraisal of the contemporary post-political condition. Indeed, the political theorists who originally pinpointed the prominence of post-politics in our contemporary era, including Swyngedouw, Chantal Mouffe, Jacques Rancière, and Slavoj Žižek, have all advocated for the obliteration of post-politics. This is due to its perceived entrenchment of political inequality, denial of political agency, and reification of institutional structures that produce a number of injustices in conjunction with neoliberal capitalism (Swyngedouw 2009; Mouffe 2013; Rancière 1999; Žižek 2004). In its place, they call for a return to 'true politics'—one of egalitarian and agonistic confrontations between real political alternatives, including the occupation and reconfiguration of public space (Swyngedouw 2015, 185).

Whilst this chapter accepts that post-political arrangements have indeed taken shape within states across the globe and that such consensual 'common-sense' arrangements do hold back civil society and ordinary citizens from a more egalitarian and unrestricted engagement in the political arena, it takes issue with one key aspect of their work. This is the fact that the theorists of post-politics propose the radical reconquering of public space in efforts to launch a challenge to the norms and principles that underlie the post-political order.

The primary argument that will be made in this chapter is that such an abrupt and event-orientated approach to the transformation of post-political consensus is ill-suited to the political realities of several Southeast Asian polities in which authoritarian or hybrid regimes are either the order of the day or are firmly entrenched. In political arenas such as these, post-political features have been constructed alongside authoritarian ones, rendering any political challenges outside of those designated by the regime a path fraught with risks. As this chapter will demonstrate, challenges to the post-political order in polities such as Singapore and Thailand run the risk of being repressed, confined, and even swallowed up by the legitimacy that has been granted to the post-political order. By employing these case studies, this chapter argues that the 'radical democratic' proposals put forth by Swyngedouw and others are bound to lead to a more precarious situation for these civil societies, particularly when compared to their counterparts residing in liberal democracies.

As a result of this finding, the chapter presents two main recommendations, one relevant to political theory and the other to political practice. On the theoretical side, it will be stated that the theorists of post-politics acknowledged their proposals' reliance on the availability of political rights and the absence of political restrictions. In other words, despite the radical philosophy that informs their project, it ought to be accepted that the proposals are more likely to find footing in liberal democracies. On the side of political practice, civil society activists and concerned citizens in Southeast Asia who wish to see a more politicised and constructively contentious political field cannot be expected to rely on the proposals of the aforementioned theorists to institute a 'return to the political'.

Rather, any chance of getting beyond its narrow confines will require a political struggle of a more sustained and broad-based nature, and one that places political rights and the removal of political restrictions at the heart of its counter-hegemonic project.

The chapter has been organised into two major sections. In the first section, a number of the core theoretical accounts of post-politics will be fleshed out in order to provide a more thorough account of the contemporary post-political condition. Following this, there is a brief exploration of how this theoretical form has found expression in real-world polities, particularly in Western liberal democracies. This will include a discussion of what Swyngedouw and others have documented with regard to the effect of post-politics on policy areas such as sustainability and development. A final area of exploration in this section will present the political prescriptions and counter-measures that have been put forward by the theorists. Doing so will help set the stage for the second section of the chapter.

In this second section, there will be a discussion of the ways in which post-politics has been bolstered by authoritarianism, soft or otherwise, in several Southeast Asian polities. In turn, it will demonstrate how this pairing of post-politics with institutional non-democracy has rendered it difficult for civil society groups and ordinary individuals to go about successfully challenging the post-political consensus in the manner that Swyngedouw and others have proposed. The cases of Singapore and Thailand—polities with varying degrees of restrictions on the political activity of their citizens/residents as well as 'red lines' or 'out-of-bounds (OB) markers' around certain organising principles—are explored to help demonstrate the challenges that civil society groups face when attempting to propose, let alone institute, alternative socio-economic or socio-environmental configurations in their polities. Stemming from this, several conclusions will be formulated regarding the relevance of the theorists' prescriptions in the non-democratic or hybrid regimes in Southeast Asia as well as the potential way forward for civil society activists who wish to engage in a more egalitarian and unrestricted political space.

The contours of the post-political

There have been several attempts in literature to define post-politics and the post-political condition. Before breaking down and elaborating on some of its more central components, it is worth exploring several of these. According to Sangeeta Kamat, the post-political condition describes our current political situation whereby

> the established modes of representative government that allow for contentious politics have been replaced by a new 'art of governance' that relies upon collaboration, coordination, and integration, in which competing interests are harmonised to propose a win-win situation for all.
>
> *(Kamat 2015, 69)*

In a similar line of thought, Erik Swyngedouw, one of the foremost analysts and critics of post-politics, states that the post-political formation is

> one in which dissent is not suppressed but made irrelevant, where all concerned parties have a voice and difference is acknowledged, while conflict and opposition politics are considered redundant.
>
> *(Swyngedouw quoted in Kamat 2015, 68)*

Finally, Wendy Brown, a political theorist who has studied the deep linkages between neoliberalism, the rise of 'governance', and its contemporary political ramifications describes our current post-political condition in the following way:

> the emergence and use of the concept of governance across a range of venues and endeavours (which) signals a dissolving distinction between state, business, non-profit and NGO endeavours—not simply the emergence of private-public partnerships . . . but of significantly altered orientations and identities of each as everything comes to comport increasingly with a business model and business metrics.
>
> *(Brown 2015, 123)*

These statements show that, various theorists and analysts have identified the core components constituting post-politics and the post-political condition. Wendy Larner also lists the following as the most central elements: the reduction of politics to management and administration, the decision-making process being dominated by experts, the particularisation of political demands, states defusing conflict through collaboration with NGOs and other 'responsible' partners, and social movements and other adversarial political actors being co-opted into a framework based on cooperation and dialogue (Larner 2015, 193). To add to Larner's list, many analysts of the post-political condition have also included the end of ideological debates and political antagonism in favour of consensus building and political pragmatism, as well as the ensuing acceptance of the neoliberal market economy (Mouffe 1993, 5; Mouffe 2006, 1, 70; Rancière 1999, 110).

Various analysts have their own understandings of the historical development of post-politics as well as explanations as to why this post-political condition has become prevalent. However, for those who subscribe to its existence as clearly a different way of doing (or not doing) politics compared to times past, there is a general agreement that consensus and pragmatism—two large concepts that can be linked to many of the aforementioned key elements—now form the basis of the ways in which politics is conducted in the contemporary era. As stated previously, many governments and civil societies across the globe agreed to a collaborative approach that avoids conflict between groups (between left and right, state and civil society), thereby accepting the market economy and globalisation as irreversible facts that need to be managed as opposed to being contested, and the application of technocratic knowledge in order to ameliorate social, economic, and environmental problems.

As several analysts have identified, this acceptance of post-politics has found its way into various socio-economic and socio-environmental realms, including those of sustainability and development. As Raco has argued with regard to changes in environmental planning and sustainability, public processes to find solutions to environmental issues have come to be dominated by state technocrats and other partners, including corporations and non-governmental organisations (NGOs), who are seen as the most able to "turn policy agendas into delivery based practice" (Raco 2015, 30). These various agents, as Swyngedouw has added, have engaged with each other through a stakeholder-based arrangement in which "traditional state forms (national, regional, and local) partake together with experts, NGOs and other ... partners in the pursuit of environmentally sustainable socio-economic practice" (Swyngedouw 2009, 608). In order to stay within the contours of the existing social order, including the neoliberal market economy, one common approach adopted by the stakeholders has been ecological modernisation— "technological-managerial conduct that can marry ecological sustainability with economic progress" (Swyngedouw 2009, 605).

Such post-political forms of collaboration leading to a consensus on policy directions have also become increasingly prevalent in the realm of international development. This, in turn, has led to the promulgation of market values such as competitive individualism, norms of active participation, and ideals of empowerment and inclusion into local communities (Kamat 2015, 68). As Kamat explains,

> The post-political operates in multiple registers, from global policy formulation to local community interventions, through which the established divisions between public and private, state and market, individual and community, are dissolved to form a post-ideological global compact on growth and democracy.
>
> *(Kamat 2015, 69)*

Returning to the political

At this point, we need to ask ourselves why many of the theorists of post-politics, including Mouffe, Rancière, and Swyngedouw, are in full agreement with the assertion that post-politics is not a development to be celebrated, but rather to be obliterated. This is particularly necessary when some of the features of the post-political formation have included greater participation from civil society and a greater tendency for all involved parties to engage in fairly constructive compromises. Although each of the theorists present their own rationale based upon their divergent ontological and epistemological starting points, as well as their slightly different political commitments, there are three main reasons that are held in common.

Firstly, there is an understanding that 'the political', as a form of collective action and production of new possibilities, represents a distinct and essential aspect of humanity's being-in-common that should not be buried under 'the social'—the normally accepted distribution of roles and interests in society. This comes hand in hand with a deep commitment to political equality, not as a normative goal that is to be attained at a later date, but as an axiom to be accepted in the here and now, opening the door for anyone and everyone to have an equal voice in the direction of the political community. As Rancière states in *Disagreement*,

> Politics reconfigure the space where parties, parts, or lack of parts have been defined. Political activity is whatever shifts a body from the place assigned to it or changes a place's destination. It makes visible what had no business being seen, and makes heard a discourse where once there was only noise.
> (Rancière 1999, 30)

The post-political arrangement by contrast, which engages individual citizens only according to where they 'fit' within the usual ordering of society—as a student, as a union member, as an NGO worker—hides this possibility of 'stepping out' of one's usual role to engage as a political equal to others. Post-politics' reliance on technocrats and managers, some of which do their work from the private sector, also obscures the possibility of meaningful political engagement from ordinary people.

Secondly, there is a belief that politics proper involves choices between real alternatives. As Brown argues, the properly political—particularly in its historical and philosophical sense—involves the fundamental elements of "deliberation about justice and other common goods", "contestation over values and purposes", "struggles over power", and "pursuits of visions for the good of the whole" (Brown 2015, 127).

This is something, of course, that is foreclosed by post-politics by turning every issue into a matter of management or administration, with government, the private sector, and NGOs all agreeing on the general direction of a whole host of policy decisions. Swyngedouw summarises this problematic aspect of post-politics well when he states that "disagreement is allowed, but only with respect to the choice of technologies, a mix of organisational fixes, the details of managerial adjustments and urgency of their timing and implementation" (Swyngedouw 2009, 611). Furthermore, as Kamat argues, "The interests of all types have a place, but 'politics proper'—that is, any kind of challenge to the existing order—has no space" (Kamat 2015, 79).

Thirdly, there is a shared transformative, anti-capitalist agenda. Post-politics cannot be separated from the workings of neoliberal capitalism as its institutional structures as well as its logic of governance aim to promote non-contentious, market-friendly solutions to prevalent socio-economic and socio-environmental challenges. Yet, in the eyes of the theorists of post-politics, many of these challenges are injustices created by neoliberal capitalism itself. As Kamat argues, in the developing world, post-politics, through which there are said to be no losers, "operates with impunity in the face of staggering levels of poverty, inequality, and dispossession" (Kamat 2015, 69). As a problem facing all polities, Wilson and Swyngedouw point to the fact that the acceptance of neoliberal capitalism and globalisation as the only possible political economy has resulted in the subordination of policy to corporate agendas, leaders following the orders of bond markets and banks, and "socialism for the rich and austerity for the poor", particularly when it has come to large-scale bank bailouts (Wilson and Swyngedouw 2015, 8). The effects of this unconditional acceptance of the market and its needs, as Brown argues, had a dramatic effect on the democratic life of citizens. As she states, "This formulation means that democratic state commitments to equality, liberty, inclusion, and constitutionalism are now subordinate to the project of economic growth, competitive positioning, and capital enhancement" (Brown 2015, 26).

In summary, post-politics is thus understood as foreclosing the possibilities of acting in a truly political manner, of activating a deeply embedded equality, and of imagining and pursuing political and socio-economic alternatives, including to neoliberal capitalism. For these reasons, a 'return to the political' is put forth as the single necessary antidote.

What exactly does this 'return to the political' look like? What Swyngedouw proposes, based on the theoretical interventions of Mouffe and Rancière, is what has been historically referred to in the radical political theory literature as 'radical democracy'—the retaking of public space for the purpose of posing an agonistic challenge to the dominant political order. Rancière calls for radical action when he states that "politics today must be immodest in relation to the modesty forced on it by the logics of consensual management of 'the only thing possible'" (Rancière 1999, 136). Mouffe is more specific in her proposals when she uses the examples of the mass protests of 2011, including the Occupy Movement, the Arab Spring, and other major uprisings as the basis upon which such a challenge to the post-political order can be made. As she states, these types of protests "have to be transformed and new ones established, so as to create the conditions for an agonistic confrontation where the citizens would be offered real alternatives" (Mouffe 2013, 120). However, it is Swyngedouw who goes the furthest when, in applying some of Rancière's key concepts in the context of the 2011 protests, he asks the following:

> Is it not precisely these insurgent architects that brought to the fore the irreducible distance between democracy as the immanence of the presumption of equality and its performative spatialised staging on the one hand, and democracy as an instituted form of regimented oligarchic governing on the other? . . . Is it not the re-emergence of the proto-political in the urban revolts that signals an urgent need to reaffirm the urban, the polis, as a political space, and not just as a space of biopolitically governed city-life?
> (Swyngedouw 2015, 171–172)

His answer is a clear yes. For Swyngedouw, based on what he sees as the hopeful experience of 2011, three steps need to be taken. Firstly, there must be "new imaginaries and the resurrection of thought that has been censored, scripted out, suspended and rendered obscene". Secondly, and most importantly for the next stage of this chapter, there must be a redesigning of the urban "as a democratic field of disagreement". In other words, there must once again be the opening up of "spaces that permit acts that claim and stage a place in the order of things". Finally, there is the need to "transverse the fantasy of the elites" in order to persist with the production of a more egalitarian democratic politics (Swyngedouw 2015, 185).

With the goals of the theorists of post-politics established, it is now time to move on to the more critical and analytical section of the chapter. Once again, although there have been a number of scholars who have taken issue with these proposals from a normative point of view, this chapter will not move in such a direction. Rather, the scrutiny that these proposals will be subject to stems from the belief that such an abrupt break with the current order of things is simply not possible for much of civil society in Southeast Asia, particularly in states in which liberal democratic norms are either not fully embraced or absent altogether.

When theory meets practice

Before we can properly begin a discussion of the limitations that non-democratic regimes, particularly those of Southeast Asia, pose for the 'radical democratic' responses proposed by the theorists of post-politics, it is helpful to identify some of the general limitations that these proposals face regardless of regime. In my doctoral dissertation titled *Agonism and Antagonism: Past and Future Possibilities of Radical Democracy*, I explored the circumstances under which radical democratic politics—namely the occupation of public space for the purpose of posing a challenge to the dominant socio-political order—can be sustained without facing debilitating repression from those in power. These circumstances were established by comparing a series of cases in which such radical democratic challenges occurred, and by identifying the common conditions under which such moments were either (1) sustained or (2) repressed (Matijasevich 2015).

One of the key findings of this study was that even in liberal democratic conditions where citizens are guaranteed a range of political rights such as the right to assembly, such contentious episodes still faced the possibility of repression. To elaborate, those organising in a 'radical democratic' fashion will face potential suppression and persecution if they were perceived as posing too much of a threat to the interests of those in control of the state's coercive apparatus. This was particularly the case when the coercive capacity of those in power had a relative advantage over the 'social capacity' of the protestors or occupiers. In other words, if those contesting the dominant order were unable to pose a sufficiently substantial threat, for example, through building a mass movement and taking control of key nodes of the socio-political sphere that the ruling powers relied on for the usual functioning of their rule (workplaces, schools, media outlets, etc.), then one common result of 'radical democratic' contention was repression. In turn, this also resulted in the inability of the challenges to reconfigure the socio-political arrangement in any lasting way. Only when those contesting the dominant order managed to build up their 'social capacity', strengthening the size of their movement and taking control of certain nodes of the socio-political field, were certain changes able to be instituted that were both outside the policy scope of the usual (post-)political framework and originating from those not typically having a say in the decision-making process (Matijasevich 2015).

As a result of this, one of the key weaknesses of the 'radical democratic' proposals put forth by the theorists of post-politics is that their axiom of equality ignores the stark inequality in resources, available spaces, and overall degree of power that those who claim their equality in the streets face when attempting to take on those in positions of political authority and the dominant socio-political order over which they preside. The following section will demonstrate that these weaknesses are compounded in authoritarian or hybrid regimes whose coercive capacity are almost absolute. In polities such as these, restrictions on political participation combined with the various 'red lines' or 'OB markers' limit what can be contested in the first place. When compared to liberal democracies, this places a straitjacket, of varying degrees of tightness, on those who wish to contest the contemporary post-political order. Under circumstances where post-politics is realised in its entirety, the majority of avenues through which civil society and ordinary citizens can engage in political activity are through the non-conflictual, consensus-based post-political channels themselves. These varying degrees of available space for contesting the post-political order are clearly seen when analysing the interaction between authoritarianism and the post-politics in Singapore and Thailand.

Singapore

In the study of politics, it may be difficult to find two ideas that are more incommensurable than that of the 'radical democratic' retaking of public space, and that of the Singapore government's understanding of the role of civil society. For certain, although the spaces for civil society have gradually grown in the last 50 years, with noticeable changes from the outset of the Goh Chok Tong years and after the 2011 general election, these spaces have typically grown in collaboration or in cooperation with the state in a manner that clearly embodies a post-political arrangement (B. Chua 2017, 100, 160). But for many actors in Singaporean civil society, despite their falling within the rules and bounds firmly set by the ruling People's Action Party (PAP), these new opportunities for engagement mark a far better scenario for activists and NGOs than the conditions they faced in the 1960s to 1980s. As Cheng U Wen Lena, founding member of Singapore's leading women's organization, AWARE, states,

> In the mid-1980s . . . advocacy and activism were almost dirty words in Singapore. While the OB (out of bounds) markers are still there, civil society is today in a much better place to contribute to the continued development of Singapore as an equal and just society.
>
> *(Cheng 2017, 304)*

As Constance Singam, another prominent Singapore women's activist, explains, in the 1960s, when the government turned its attention to political stability and economic development after fighting the anti-colonial battle and securing independence, "with remarkable efficiency, the government silenced all activist groups" (Singam 2017, 3). One of the reasons for this was the fact that civil society groups, including organised labour, radical student groups, and ethnic associations, were seen as potentially exacerbating what the ruling PAP saw as Singapore's key vulnerabilities, including the possibility of economic stagnation, unemployment, racial disharmony, and the threat of communism (B. Chua 2017, 33).

As a result of this, from the 1960s to the 1980s, in the interest of promoting 'social harmony for survival', available spaces for civil society groups were almost non-existent in Singapore. As Cherian George argues, strong measures, such as detention without trial through the Internal Security Act (ISA), were "periodically used like a kill switch or a reboot button to stop an emerging problem in its tracks" (George 2017, 117). After doing so, custom-made constraints, such as new laws or regulations to limit the activities of civil society groups, were installed to ensure that the strongest of measures would not be needed again. Other constraints, such as the establishment of government-sanctioned organisations for labour, students, the media, and the legal profession, were also established to ensure that both the actions of these groups would not be autonomous and that potential challengers could be co-opted (George 2017, 117). For those who stepped outside of these officially sanctioned spaces of activity, a slew of other repressive laws and regulations ensured that the government would not face substantial challenges. As Chua explains, Singapore has historically employed repressive legislation in the areas of labour relations, race relations, media, and civil society, including restrictions on association and assembly (B. Chua 2017, 1). For the purposes of this chapter, one particularly important fact to note is that, until the year 2000 when Hong Lim Park was designated as a legitimate space of public protest, there had been no such space in the country (B. Chua 2017, 161).

Perhaps the most important reason why the PAP government was, and still is, able to delimit spaces for civic engagement in such a minimal manner was the PAP's continued 'performance legitimacy'—the fact that a large majority of Singaporeans were willing to accept heavy limitations on their civil and political rights due to the fact that the government was substantially improving their material quality of life (B. Chua 2017, iv). It also should be noted that, after years of nation building under the PAP government, Singaporeans have also come to internalise the narrative of vulnerability that has continuously informed many of the government's policy decisions. As George argues, Singaporeans have developed a political culture of hypersensitivity to anyone who rocks the boat, including those who engage in confrontational means (George 2017, 104). This, of course, has lent itself to a lack of societal awareness and concern towards the limitations on spaces for civic and political engagements such as protests.

Although social changes since the 1990s have forced the government to cede more space to civil society, the majority of the laws that restrict the crossing of designated 'OB markers', particularly those established around issues related to Singapore's vulnerability, remain enforced. As George states, the 'calibrated coercion' employed by the state—such as defamation suits and the prosecution of activists—that occurs once or twice a year is also enough to keep activists from pushing the boundaries too abruptly (George 2017, 122). In turn, this has resulted in a collaborative approach with the government, despite its post-political limitations, as civil society's best bet for achieving some of its aims. As Singam explains,

> Our political and cultural environment, where the State uses the power of the law when it feels challenged and its policies are questioned, calls for action that is low-keyed and circumspect. It is not so much a question of trying to overturn a system as it is of trying to move it in the desired direction.
>
> *(Singam 2017, 4)*

Thailand

In the case of Singapore, two main factors result in civil society's inability to engage in the 'radical democratic' proposal put forth by Swyngedouw and others. These are (1) restrictions on political rights, such as the right to association and assembly which limit the formation of civil society groups in the first place, and (2) the existence of multiple 'OB markers' or 'red lines'—limitations on acceptable discussion or action that can be used censure the behaviour of groups, even after they have met the requirements to exist. However, unlike the case of Singapore, which has seen post-politics gradually come into being under the half-century rule of the soft authoritarian PAP, the non-democratic protection of a post-political order has been more recent in Thailand.

Since the 2014 coup, the Thai military junta under the leadership of Prime Minister Prayuth has instituted similar restrictions on political rights and limitations on acceptable areas of politics. Whilst the former has certainly assisted the military government—the National Council for Peace and Order (NCPO)—in shoring up its current rule, the latter has helped to forge an authoritarian post-politics that will force Thai civil society groups and other active citizens to engage with the government within the political conditions and rules imposed by the policies set by the military.

The new constitution drafted by the NCPO has ramifications for Thailand's electoral future. Although the constitution promises to hand power to the civilians at a later date, for the immediate future it ensures that the military retains control over the Senate which has the ability to help choose the prime minister after a lower-house election. With the assistance of political parties that the NCPO has made inroads at co-opting, this could also allow the military to have a hand in selecting the prime minister and thus continue to influence the country's political direction (Pongphisoot 2017, 346). As a result of this enduring influence, civil society activists will face limitations on the types of policy changes and other projects that they can pursue. This will particularly be the case vis-à-vis the institutions of the Thai state and state-linked enterprises, as the NCPO has made sure to extend its influence, appointing many of its own members to key institutions and executive boards (Prajak 2018, 366).

These more informal limitations, which will be guaranteed by the mere continuation of the military's presence in politics, will be supported by a series of more formal limitations on what can be pursued, not only by political parties, but also by civil society. These include the incorporation of the '20 year national reform strategic plan' into the constitution, which will bind future Thai governments to the military's current policy direction for 20 years. Amongst the military's plans, are the 'Thailand 4.0' scheme—the development of an economic corridor in Thailand's eastern provinces that will aim to attract investments in biotech, biomedicine, digital technology, and robotics (Prajak 2018, 352). It is also through these initiatives that the current post-political arrangement crafted by the military government was given its authoritarian features. As Phongphisoot Busbarat has argued, "Non-compliance could be interpreted as violating the constitution, leading to motions against the government" (Pongphisoot 2017, 347). Furthermore, future governments' use of the budget will also "be monitored and constrained by independent organisations". Establishing rules for spending—part of the military's quest to discourage 'irresponsible populist' policies—will also lead to restrictions on the types of socio-economic arrangements future governments can pursue (Prajak 2018, 365). This, of course, will also have a direct impact on civil society, whose activism and advocacy, limited by the post-political 'red lines' of the new constitutional arrangement, will be conducted in vain.

There is also concern that the actions of civil society will continue to be severely restricted by repressive policies even after Thai politics returns to 'civilian' government. As Pongphisoot has explained, "The lèse-majesté law and Computer Crime Act have become legal tools used by the military and other political factions to curb the activities of their opponents" (Pongphisoot 2017, 248). Even if these laws are not used to the full extent of their force, however, the new constitution has also "restricted or removed various political and civil rights such as freedom of expression, academic freedom, and environmental rights" (McCargo, Saowanee, and Desatova 2017, 68). As a result, whilst the closure of civil society space is less complete than in Singapore, due to both the short period for which restrictions have been implemented and the continued political divide amongst the population, Thailand represents another case of the trend towards authoritarian post-politics in Southeast Asia.

Opposing post-politics in non-democratic regimes(?)

To conclude the analysis, it is necessary to make a few critical comments regarding the relevance and applicability of the aforementioned 'radical democratic' proposals to combat post-politics in light of what has been demonstrated in the cases of Singapore and Thailand. As stated in the introduction, one of these criticisms is with regard to theory whilst the other is with regard to political practice. Undoubtedly, these two should be taken in tandem, as post-political theory was originally developed not simply as an analytical framing of an empirical political reality but as a call to political action.

In terms of theory, what the authoritarian or hybrid versions of post-politics tell us is that 'radical democratic' responses, although in no way guaranteed by them, rely deeply on liberal democratic norms and even political culture. In cases where 'red lines' and 'OB markers' delimit the official boundaries of political possibility and establish certain contours of the socio-political field as untouchable, including those such as 'the 20 year national reform' and even 'social harmony for survival', those wishing to explode these limits are bound to face regime-led resistance. Although there remains a possibility in liberal democracies where challenging these limits in high-capacity authoritarian or hybrid states—polities in which contenders cannot rely on legally entrenched protections to at least extend their contention—is more likely to be stifled in both a fast and furious manner, when combined with some degree of popular support for these untouchable realms and their unconditional defence, 'radical democratic' opposition is not likely to serve as an effective launching pad for change as it sometimes can be in liberal democratic systems.

One central take-away point, thus, is that the theorists of post-politics, particularly Swyngedouw in his creative appropriation of Rancière, need to more clearly acknowledge the role that liberal democratic norms play in helping to sustain protest politics. There are obvious reasons as to why several of the theorists of post-politics are reluctant to give credit to liberal democracy. For certain, their indebtedness to Marxism (all four aforementioned theorists can be considered post-Marxists) leads them to see liberal democracy as a sort of façade on which lie the real relations of elite domination and capitalist exploitation. Rancière provides a different type of explanation in *Disagreement* when he argues that liberal democracy is one form of parapolitics—one that "neutralises the political energy of the part of those who have no part" by establishing "institutionalised competition for places within an established hierarchy" (Wilson and Swyngedouw 2015, 13; Rancière 1999, 72). In other words, liberal democracy and the representative democracy that accompanies it denies the possibility of citizens to 'step out' of their usual functional role—as a worker, a student, and so on—and engage in politics as an equal to everyone else.

It should be stated, however, that even if we are to agree to the general post-Marxist line or Rancière's alternative critique, this is solely a criticism of the liberal democracy's representational function. It is to say nothing of the political rights that usually accompanies it. It is also to say nothing of the fact that liberal democratic norms are incompatible with people or policies being placed above the political fray, out of bounds and subject to punishment for crossing them. Certainly, the absence of such limitations along with the presence of political rights in liberal democracies is one of the contributing factors as to why an Occupy Wall Street emerged in the United States, whereas an Occupy Singapore or Occupy Beijing did not emerge respectively in Singapore or China. It also partially explains why the eventual crackdown of Occupy Movements across the liberal democratic world was done with tear gas and batons as opposed to live rounds. The same cannot be said for many of the tragic endings of the once hopeful Arab Spring uprisings, which predominantly occurred in hybrid and authoritarian regimes. To turn to the Asian context once more, it is also difficult to imagine transformative moments like

Taiwan's Sunflower Movement—an event that entirely disrupted the consensual patterns of contemporary Taiwanese politics and society—being sustained during the Kuomintang's period of authoritarian rule.

Another key take-away that theorists of post-politics should also more readily acknowledge is the fact that a democratic political culture is one of the necessary requirements for contentious protest politics. As Cherian George has insightfully pointed out about his compatriots, Singaporeans are not simply averse to political confrontation as a result of stringent regulations and tough penalties. Rather, a significant percentage of the population shares the ruling party's belief that those who are too adversarial and too disruptive in their approach are simply causing a ruckus. As George states, "Critics who think that they are acting in the public interest often find that public positively hostile, treating them like troublemakers" (George 2017, 103).

Once again, whilst there are conservative voices in every political community, when such anti-political norms become a central part of the political culture, it becomes extremely difficult to envision how an abrupt and event-centred retaking of the public space could be embraced, let alone sustained. For certain, not only would this political culture have an impact on the number of citizens who would engage in such an action, but it would also affect the likelihood that the authorities will feel justified in cracking down on it, since doing so would be backed by public opinion. The particular lesson from this is that the theorists' return to the political may not be as universally applicable as they assume. Instead, they may need to acknowledge the fact that taking to the streets or squares is not a primordial political impulse of humankind. Rather, it is a behaviour that is profoundly connected to the beliefs that public space is political space and that anyone at all has the right to engage in it. It must be acknowledged that in contemporary Southeast Asia, and perhaps Asia more generally, these beliefs do not currently constitute the dominant understanding of what 'the political' is or ought to be.

What then does this mean for the political practice of civil society groups in authoritarian or hybrid regimes? It is clear that there is no single answer to this question. Much depends on the spaces awarded to civil society, but also on the goals of civil society's constituent groups and movements. As numerous voices from Singaporean civil society have stated, there have been some very notable victories, particularly in terms of progressive policy shifts, by engaging with the government within a collaborative, non-adversarial framework. There is evidence from the recent literature on civil society in Singapore that several organisations have had success working within this forced post-political arrangement, consulting with government and the private sector on needed policy changes, and gradually making headway towards more progressive policies. Examples of these include changes to law or policy with regard to individuals with HIV, the preservation of areas with biodiversity, the preservation of heritage spaces, women's rights, and the treatment of foreign workers (Chan, Banerjee, and Tan 2017; Ho and Lum 2017; A. Chua 2017; Mathi 2017; Gee 2017). As some would have it, post-political engagement has been preferable to the more authoritarian, technocratic model of governance that defined Singapore politics from independence to at least the late 1980s. It is also conceivable that for Thailand, some of civil society's goals can be met in the near future through the adoption of a post-political stakeholder model whilst staying within the boundaries set by the NCPO.

This, of course, will not be acceptable to every advocate or activist. Hence, the critique of the post-political condition remains valid, particularly for those who believe that certain issues and ideas beyond the 'red lines' and 'OB markers', such as a radical rethinking of environmental policy, seeking an alternative to neoliberal capitalism, and democratisation itself, require urgent attention. But by examining the authoritarian and hybrid regimes of Southeast Asia, what this chapter demonstrates is that these larger shifts are unlikely to make inroads without an expansion of political rights, a reduction in the number of issues that are considered untouchable, and even a change in political culture. It is only with the reconfiguration of political attitudes and practices that civil society activists in these polities will have the spaces at their disposal to begin challenging those in power. In short, it means that, in these contexts, a struggle against the post-political order necessitates a struggle for further democratic norms and institutions. This, in turn, would require those interested in civil society to 'play the long game', winning hearts and minds, winning allies to their cause, and honestly acknowledging the great risks that such an approach would entail. As such, whilst it would constitute a more suitable path for overcoming the post-political condition than that proposed by Swyngedouw and others, it is not a path any less difficult.

References

Brown, W. 2015. *Undoing the Demos: Neoliberalism's Stealth Revolution*. New York: Zone Books.
Chan, R., S. Banerjee, and A. Tan. 2017. "Breaking the Barriers in the HIV Response." In *The Art of Advocacy in Singapore*, edited by C. Singam and M. Thomas, 61–67. Singapore: Ethos Books.
Cheng, U. W. L. 2017. "AWARE—The Early Years." In *The Art of Advocacy in Singapore*, edited by C. Singam and M. Thomas, 299–305. Singapore: Ethos Books.
Chua, A. L. 2017. "An Independent Voice for Heritage Conservation." In *The Art of Advocacy in Singapore*, edited by C. Singam and M. Thomas, 97–109. Singapore: Ethos Books.
Chua, B. H. 2017. *Liberalism Disavowed: Communitarianism and State Capitalism in Singapore*. Singapore: NUS Press.
Gee, J. 2017. "Migrant Workers in Singapore: Change Comes Slowly." In *The Art of Advocacy in Singapore*, edited by C. Singam and M. Thomas, 267–273. Singapore: Ethos Books.
George, C. 2017. *Singapore Incomplete: Reflections on a First World Nation's Arrested Political Development*. Singapore: Woodsville News.
Ho, H. C., and S. Lum. 2017. "Protecting Singapore's Natural Heritage." In *The Art of Advocacy in Singapore*, edited by C. Singam and M. Thomas, 75–96. Singapore: Ethos Books.
Kamat, S. 2015. "The New Development Architecture and the Post-Political in the Global South." In *The Post-Political and Its Discontents: Spaces of Depoliticisation, Spectres of Radical Politics*, edited by J. Wilson and E. Swyngedouw, 67–85. Edinburgh: Edinburgh University Press.

Larner, W. 2015. "The Limits of Post-Politics: Rethinking Radical Social Enterprise." In *The Post-Political and Its Discontents: Spaces of Depoliticisation, Spectres of Radical Politics*, edited by J. Wilson and E. Swyngedouw, 189–207. Edinburgh: Edinburgh University Press.

Mathi, B. 2017. "Passion and Experience bring about Change." In *The Art of Advocacy in Singapore*, edited by C. Singam and M. Thomas, 75–96. Singapore: Ethos Books.

Matijasevich, D. 2015. "Agonism and Antagonism: Past and Future Possibilities of Radical Democracy." PhD diss., Carleton University, Ottawa, Canada.

McCargo, D., T. A. Saowanee, and P. Desatova. 2017. "Ordering Peace: Thailand's 2016 Constitutional Referendum." *Contemporary Southeast Asia* 39 (1): 65–95.

Mouffe, C. 1993. *The Return of the Political*. London: Verso.

———. 2006. *On the Political*. London: Verso.

———. 2013. *Agonistics: Thinking the World Politically*. London: Verso.

Pongphisoot, B. 2018. "Thailand in 2017: Stability without Certainties." *Southeast Asian Affairs* (2018): 343–348.

Prajak, K. 2018. "Haunted Past, Uncertain Future: The Fragile Transition to Military-Guided Semi-Authoritarian Rule in Thailand." *Southeast Asian Affairs* (2018): 363–376.

Raco, M. 2015. "The Post-Politics of Sustainability Planning: Privatisation and the Demise of Democratic Government." In *The Post-Political and Its Discontents: Spaces of Depoliticisation, Spectres of Radical Politics*, edited by J. Wilson and E. Swyngedouw, 25–47. Edinburgh: Edinburgh University Press.

Rancière, J. 1999. *Disagreement: Politics and Philosophy*. Minneapolis: University of Minnesota Press.

Singam, C. 2017. "When Ordinary People Do Extraordinary Things." In *The Art of Advocacy in Singapore*, edited by C. Singam and M. Thomas, 1–10. Singapore: Ethos Books.

Swyngedouw, E. 2009. "The Antinomies of the Postpolitical City: In Search of a Democratic Politics of Environmental Production." *International Journal of Urban and Regional Research* 33 (3): 601–620.

———. 2015. "Insurgent Architects and the Promise of the Political." In *The Post-Political and Its Discontents: Spaces of Depoliticisation, Spectres of Radical Politics*, edited by J. Wilson and E. Swyngedouw, 169–188. Edinburgh: Edinburgh University Press.

Wilson, J., and E. Swyngedouw. 2015. "Seeds of Dystopia: Post-Politics and the Return of the Political." In *The Post-Political and Its Discontents: Spaces of Depoliticisation, Spectres of Radical Politics*, edited by J. Wilson and E. Swyngedouw, 1–22. Edinburgh: Edinburgh University Press.

Žižek, S. 2004. "The Ongoing 'Soft Revolution'." *Critical Inquiry* 30 (2): 292–323.

2

MANAGING GRIEVANCES IN THE AGE OF POST-POLITICS

The relocation of communities for the Thilawa Special Economic Zone in Myanmar

Tamas Wells

Introduction

In the last five years, Myanmar's transition away from military governance has garnered much attention from analysts and scholars. Yet this attention has often focussed on the question of *how far* the country has moved from constrained authoritarianism to a new era of open democracy based on international norms. The 2015 election victory of Daw Aung San Suu Kyi's party, the National League for Democracy, and the liberalisation of the economy and media was a remarkable shift from the secretive and violent rule of the Than Shwe government (r. 1992–2011). During the Than Shwe era, government and private-sector development projects—from bridges and roads to irrigation schemes—had been implemented with little regard for the experience of affected populations. After Than Shwe stepped down from power in 2011, his successor, Thein Sein (r. 2011–2016), embarked in a series of political reforms, which resulted in the end of economic sanctions and the injection of new foreign investment into the country. It also enabled the language and practices of 'international standards' to become prominent in the implementation of new development projects. Analysts have largely viewed these transitions through the question of whether or not the Myanmar government is now 'genuinely' democratic. Yet far less consideration has been given to the ways that a new era of 'international standards', and of participation and democracy, might have its own new mechanisms for the constraint, co-option, or defusing of citizen voices.

Theories of post-politics provide a valuable alternative vantage point from which to analyse this new era of 'development', raising different questions about the practices and language of 'international standards' that surround large-scale development projects. Rather than the obvious political struggles between an authoritarian government with citizens and civil society groups, works from Swyngedouw (2011) and Rancière (1999) highlight that modern liberal democracy has become increasingly reduced to a technocratic style of management that eschews deeper political or ideological contests. There is a "suturing of 'the political'" by a mode of governance that is consensual (Swyngedouw 2011, 370). Whilst much scholarship on the 'post-political' condition has been developed in Western contexts, Kamat (2014, 69) importantly highlights that the condition of the post-political may not only be relevant in Europe or North America but also in other parts of the world where the global development architecture, too, can be motivated by a "post-ideological global compact" (Kamat 2014, 69). Yet to what extent can there be the same 'suturing' of 'the political' in a transitional country with limited government resources, such as Myanmar, as there is in Europe or North America? To what extent can theories of post-politics espoused by Swyngedouw (2011) or Rancière (1999) be extended to help make sense of political transition in Myanmar or other contexts in Asia?

The purpose of this chapter is therefore twofold. Firstly, it uses the context of Myanmar, specifically the case study of the Thilawa Special Economic Zone (SEZ), to explore the relevance of theories of post-politics outside their origins in the context of Europe and North America. Secondly, it uses the lens of post-politics to re-examine popular and academic analyses of Myanmar's transition from authoritarianism to democracy. In particular, I draw on the empirical example of the complaints mechanism designed for the Thilawa SEZ project in Myanmar. Its implementers describe this zone, situated close to the country's largest urban centre, as the 'first international standard SEZ of Myanmar' (Thilawa SEZ Management Committee 2018b).

An age of 'post-politics'?

The end of grand ideological contests after the fall of the Berlin Wall has led a number of scholars to observe a new era of 'post-politics' (Swyngedouw 2011; Rancière 1999; Žižek 2002). Rather than contests over political ideologies and structures, modern liberal democracy has become increasingly reduced to a technocratic style of management. Governments, donors, or corporations foster debate and discussion on any number of practical issues, as long as the overarching assumptions of neoliberal economic growth and liberal democracy are not challenged. Political debate continually has its edges clipped in order to ensure that public affairs can be managed through consensual, technically sound, and supposedly objective forms of governance (Swyngedouw 2011). The concern for many scholars, of the era of 'post-politics', is that the managerial function of governance means that society is "deprived of its proper political dimension" (Žižek 2002, 303)—it is 'dissensus' rather than 'consensus' which is a core component of 'the political' (Rancière 1999). By submerging disagreement and contest, those in power are able to prevent the kinds of debates that can precipitate societal change.

In this chapter, I first introduce scholarship on the age of 'post-politics', highlighting four theoretical dimensions of post-politicisation, the integration of democratic principles into post-political forms of governance, the reduction of grievances to the particular rather than the universal, and the reconfiguration of citizen-state relations and the inevitable incompleteness of post-politicisation. I then describe the background of the Thilawa SEZ project, its implementation, and opposition from local residents and civil society groups. Finally, I examine the Thilawa SEZ complaints mechanism through the theoretical dimensions of the 'post-political' outlined in the first section. I conclude that the consensual, technocratic processes of governance described within theories of post-politics are evident in the implementation of the Thilawa SEZ development, though profound and widespread limitations of government capacity, at the local and national levels, undermines the effective 'suturing' of 'the political'. Further I argue that whilst the 'bulldozer consultation' (Wells 2015) of the authoritarian era in Myanmar has given way to a new emphasis—from both government and private sectors—on 'international standards' of liberal democracy, this era presents a different set of constraints which dilute and defuse the voices of citizens and civil society groups in new ways.

The integration of democratic principles into post-political forms of development

The most illuminating analyses of the era of post-politics emphasise the subtleties in the ways in which the parameters of debate are curtailed. Whilst the language of participation and inclusion has undoubtedly been employed by development actors as a façade to cover more predatory forms of engagement with communities, such analyses underestimate the complexities of post-politicisation. The era of post-politics is not characterised so much by repression as it is by dilution and dispersion of disagreement. Kamat (2014) in particular highlights how democratic principles of inclusion and participation are integral parts of the neoliberal vision of development actors. Kamat (2014, 67) argues that there is a "new political formation in which democratic norms and practices have become central to sustaining the ideological complex of neoliberalism". The example of self-help groups in Andhra Pradesh, outlined in Kamat's work, illustrates the way development architecture has shaped a context of political participation and inclusion, and even grassroots advocacy about practical local issues. Yet decisions of broader social or economic significance to rural life and livelihoods are a point of supposed consensus between self-help group members, government, and the private sector.

The example of the Thilawa SEZ, and its complaints mechanism, also illustrates the ways in which democratic principles of inclusion and participation are crucial to the political culture surrounding development actors. Characterising international development actors and government as repressive—and using democratic principles merely as a mask for more profit-driven motives—fails to capture the extent to which certain democratic values and practices are incorporated into systems. Democratic principles are in fact "indispensable to the neoliberal growth strategy", Kamat suggests (2014, 68). International standards of inclusion and participation are often emphasised within statements by all manner of different actors, from advocacy NGOs to multi-lateral institutions and donors. At the same time, the *forms* and *practices* of participation and inclusion, for example, with local communities, are carefully partitioned to minimise contest. For Kamat (2014, 68), the duality of "embodying the democratic ethos while simultaneously repudiating conflict and contradiction is the essence of post-politics". How then is such a duality possible—that processes of post-politicisation both promote participation and inclusion, and at the same time, seemingly curtail opposition to neoliberal development goals?

The reduction of grievances to the particular rather than the universal

The valuing of democratic principles and the constraining of debate can be held together through a particular means of dealing with the grievances and complaints of people who are affected by development programmes. Kamat (2014, 68) argues that it is not the *suppression* of dissent to development programmes, but rather that dissent is made *irrelevant*. In particular, the development architecture and frameworks can allocate grievances to the realm of the local, opinions ascribed to only a limited number of people and therefore addressed only at the level of practical and local intervention. In other words, grievances and complaints of affected people are reduced to the *particular*, whilst they are simultaneously denied any *universal* relevance that they may have. Žižek (2000, 204) argues that "post-politics mobilises the vast apparatus of experts, social workers, and so on, to reduce the overall demand (complaint) of a particular group to just this demand, with its particular content". The larger questions of political ideology or vision are foreclosed. Development actors deal with grievances individually, with the assumption that any opposition must be only particular and isolated. Through participation and communication, all non-governmental organisations (NGOs), local communities, companies, government, and multi-lateral development agencies can 'win'. In this sense, Rancière (1999) argues that all manner of interests and identity groups may 'have a place' in the post-political. Decision makers play the necessary role in arbitration between different interests. This means that the more groups and identities there are, the more scope there is for decision makers to play this role of 'arbitration'. Rather than being challenged by diversity, consensus around neoliberal development is actually 'nourished' by the multiple, in what Rancière describes as "consensus democracy" (Rancière 1999, 95). Anything that falls outside this consensus is irrelevant. There is a 'partition' of what is 'sensible' and what is not (Rancière 1999).

The reconfiguration of citizen-state relations

This consensus democracy is only possible, however, through a reconfiguration of the citizen-state relations with increasing 'governance beyond the state' (Swyngedouw 2011). On the one hand, there is a multiplication of supranational bodies, with development interventions implemented through transnational corporations, international donors, and multi-lateral institutions. On the other hand, sub-national governance bodies are empowered with greater responsibility. It is not just a transfer of power from state to market or to civil society, or contests centring around the role of the state. Rather, there is a diverse array of actors, including multi-sector committees, at various levels, which hold the decision-making power.

SEZ initiatives bring together both elements of the supranational and subnational governance arrangements, thereby reconfiguring the traditional relationships between citizens and the nation-state. By their very nature, SEZs are designed to have a level of independence from domestic laws and procedures. Specific SEZ governance committees have decision-making power and gain concessions from state levels of governance. Within these committees there is often a significant scope for donors, and local and transnational corporations, to engage directly in governance, along with non-profit and community level organisations. The process of post-politicisation is in some ways facilitated by these new multi-scalar and diverse arrangements. The potential for mobilisation of citizens or civil society actors against the national government is curtailed, as responsibility for governing SEZs is dispersed. For example, private-sector actors can take significant roles in governance and yet divert attention to the state's role in governance when necessary. This is important to recognise in that it complicates depictions of development programmes as being simply led by predatory international corporations with local victims. Rather, local and national governments, and even local advocacy groups and religious leaders, are often entwined within the new governance arrangements found in SEZs.

The inevitable incompleteness of post-politicisation

The age of post-politics, however, is not a condition where 'the political' can be indefinitely contained. Swyngedouw (2011, 373) argues that depoliticisation is always "incomplete"—it "leaves a trace and hence, the promise of a return of the political". Scholars point towards new and radical forms of transgressive politics, such as the Occupy Movement, as examples of the "the incompleteness and vulnerability of this process" of post-politicisation (Swyngedouw and Wilson 2014, 300). Whilst the principles of democracy are mobilised, along with a rendering of opposition as local and particular and a dispersion of governance responsibility beyond the state, processes of post-politicisation can never achieve closure (Swyngedouw and Wilson 2014, 301). Even seemingly depoliticised policy areas of science and technology cannot be managed completely through technocratic processes. For example, Reynolds and Szerszynski (2014, 49) trace growing political contests over genetically modified organism (GMO) policies. After initial public opposition to GMOs, governments and corporations used approaches of consumer choice and co-existence to diffuse and manage opposition. Yet whilst technical and expert-led processes can constrain opposition, depoliticised terms themselves can become sites of contest. Reynolds and Szerszynski (2014, 49) highlight how the grounds of science, nature, and technology themselves became politicised in the contests over GMOs. Ultimately, by constraining 'the political', processes of post-politicisation *create* contexts where "outbursts of violence remain one of the few options left to express and stage discontent and dissensus" (Swyngedouw 2011, 371). The consensual procedures of post-democracy are often shot through with antagonisms. The example of Myanmar's Thilawa SEZ is instructive in the ways that terms such as 'international standards', which are often employed by government, donors, or companies to diffuse opposition, can themselves become sites of contest. The battleground of political contest is played out in definitions and evaluations of 'international standards', a point I return to in the final section.

These four theoretical elements of scholarship on post-politics—related to democratic principles, the emphasis on the particular, the reconfiguration of governance, and the incompleteness of post-politicisation—are illustrated in the case of the Thilawa SEZ. However, there are also ways in which scholarship on post-politics is limited in its relevance to the Myanmar context, especially in its assumptions about state capacity to deliver basic services to its citizens. To some degree, the consensual and technocratic processes of post-political democracy—which are well described by Swyngedouw (2011)—are dependent on the sophisticated governance capacity found in wealthy states. As I describe in the final section, if a state cannot provide even basic services to its citizens, then attempts to 'suture' the political through consensual governance processes are inevitably far from complete.

The Thilawa SEZ and the complaints management procedure

This section gives an overview of the Thilawa SEZ before turning to the example of the Thilawa SEZ Complaints Management Procedure (TCMP), which was designed for use by local residents impacted by the SEZ development project.

Background of the Thilawa SEZ

SEZs have become increasingly popular in Asia. They are a means of attracting investment to specific geographical areas by sidestepping challenging legal and economic obstacles that the domestic environment may present. China in particular was an early adopter of the SEZ model, and the widely cited success of the Shenzhen SEZ established in 1980 led other governments in the region to create similar zones with rapid industrial and infrastructure development. From Map Ta Phut in Thailand to hundreds of locations in India, SEZs have continued to be sites of both economic development and intensive community opposition over the last 30 years. Plans for three SEZs in Myanmar were adopted during Than Shwe's era of military government—these SEZs were to be in Kyaukphyu in Rakhine State, Dawei in the Southern Tanintharyi division, and Thilawa, near Yangon. Each of these zones had strategic rationales, with Kyaukphyu serving the specific need of connecting the Chinese economy to the Indian Ocean and Dawei linking the Thai and Myanmar economies. Thilawa, which became operational in 2015, is the SEZ closest to the economic hub of Myanmar.

The ownership and management of the Thilawa SEZ project is diverse, which as the previous section shows, has reconfigured citizen-state relations. Myanmar Japan Thilawa Development Ltd. (MJTD) is responsible for the development, sale, and operation of SEZ lots. The shareholder composition of MJTD is 10 percent for the Myanmar government through the Thilawa SEZ Management Committee (TSEZMC), 10 percent for the Japanese government through the Japan International Cooperation Agency (JICA), 41 percent through a Myanmar private consortium called Myanmar Thilawa SEZ Holdings Public Ltd., and 39 percent through a Japanese private consortium, MMS Thilawa Development Co. Ltd. JICA provides technical assistance to the project, along with Japanese government loans and aid. The aid contribution is to build infrastructure for the zone, particular for power, water, communication, roads, and the port.

Along with the ownership and management of MJTD, the zone is overseen by the TSEZMC, which is made up of Myanmar government representatives. The role of the committee is to ensure (a) "that a favourable, predictable and friendly investment climate is created", (b) "that investors in the Thilawa SEZ are responsible investors", and (c) "that the Thilawa SEZ would not pose any environmental threat to the surrounding areas and communities" (Thilawa SEZ Management Committee 2018b). The TSEZMC encourages investors or private operators who are "having any kind of difficulty" to consult with the Committee (Thilawa SEZ Management Committee 2018b). The governance responsibility for the SEZ project is therefore diffused across foreign and local corporations, the Japanese government, a special sub-national government committee, and the Myanmar national government. As I describe in the next section, governance responsibility is further blurred through the involvement of community-level representatives, local organisations, and religious leaders.

The initial period of development of the zone from 2013 was met with significant community opposition as local residents began to be displaced by the project. Three residents filed a formal complaint to JICA about the negative effects of Japanese investment in the area (Thilawa SEZ Management Committee 2018b). One of the residents, Mya Hlaing, said, "we have tried to tell JICA how things really are in Thilawa by repeatedly submitting letters to JICA requesting appropriate resettlement and compensation measures, as required by their guidelines and international standards. JICA has not listened to our voices" (Associated Press 2014). Another local resident, Tin Hsan, said, "Since we moved here and live in this small place with no space to grow anything, we are living hand to mouth and we are all miserable" (Associated Press 2014).

The Thilawa Social Development Group (TSDG), a local NGO initiated by local leaders to represent relocated communities, argued that JICA's report into the displacement of residents was "overly optimistic" in its portrayal of status of the community in the relocation area of Myaing Tha Yar village (Yen 2014). The damages for relocated families included "loss of farmland and access to farmland, loss of livelihood opportunities, impoverishment, loss of educational opportunities for the villagers' children, sub-standard housing and basic infrastructure in the Myaing

Tha Yar resettlement site and loss of access to clean water" (Yen 2014). The US Campaign for Burma said that 300 people had been moved to "a cramped, flood-prone resettlement site" and that "JICA should not proceed with loan disbursement until . . . impacted communities are provided with resettlement agreements that meet international standards" (US Campaign for Burma 2014, 1).

During this period of disagreement over the conditions for relocated communities, the Myanmar Centre for Responsible Business, a non-government initiative led by a former British ambassador to Myanmar, facilitated the formation of a Multi-Stakeholder Advisory Group (MSAG) which sought to increase dialogue between the government's SEZ committee, MJTD, local communities, and NGOs. The MSAG became a primary point of communication between these stakeholders but was disbanded in late 2016 when an evaluation found that the stakeholders felt that it had "reached its limits" (Zongollowicz 2016, 2), as it could not provide any formal mechanism for grievances to be addressed. At the same time, TSDG—together with the international advocacy NGO Earthrights—began a process of consultation with communities to design a complaints mechanism. This process formed the model of a Community Driven Operation Grievance Mechanism (CDOGM). Between December 2016 and October 2017, the CDOGM model was sent to the private and government stakeholders who had been involved in the MSAG.

In November 2017, however, MJTD and the TSEZMC announced an alternate complaints mechanism to be designed by JICA. This new mechanism was the TCMP. MJTD describes the mechanism as one that aligns with "international good practice in stakeholder management" (Myanmar Japan Thilawa Development Limited 2018a, 3). According to MJTD, the new complaints procedure allows "stakeholders to raise questions or concerns with the Thilawa SEZ and have them addressed in a prompt and respectful manner. The Thilawa SEZ aims to address all complaints received, regardless of whether they stem from real or perceived issues". They go on to suggest that whilst the SEZ project implementers seek to build relationships with communities and "manage the impact" of the project, they recognise that "complaints about its activities may occur from time to time" (Myanmar Japan Thilawa Development Limited 2018a, 3).

Throughout the documents outlining the complaints mechanism, MJTD repeatedly emphasises the principles of 'international standards', 'international good practice', and 'good practice principles'. To support these claims of international standards, MJTD refers to the United Nations Global Compact (UNGC) Ten Principles (of which MJTD has been a signatory since 2015), the UN Guiding Principles on Business and Human Rights (2011), and the International Finance Corporation (IFC) Performance Standard 1: Assessment and Management of Environmental and Social Risks and Impacts (2012). But whilst these principles are named within MJTD documents, there is no specific explanation of how the complaints mechanism actually addresses these principles. With claims of being the "first international standard SEZ of Myanmar" (Myanmar Japan Thilawa Development Limited 2018a, 1), Thilawa is a rich case for analysis of both Myanmar's transition and of the relevance of theories of post-politics. The next section turns to the four elements of theories of post-politics (described in the first section) and examines the specific case of the TCMP.

The TCMP and an age of post-politics

The dynamics of engagement between government, corporations, local populations, and civil society groups have shifted profoundly in Myanmar since the end of the Than Shwe military government in 2011. Than Shwe's reign throughout the 1990s and 2000s was characterised more by forced labour for construction than by the language of grievance mechanisms and international standards. The fact that a grievance mechanism is a focus of analysis here demonstrates the extent of liberalisation and the adoption of international norms in the country. However, in this chapter I seek to explore this shift not as one from 'control' to 'participation', but rather as one from authoritarianism to a condition that reflects many of the dimensions of post-politics which I outlined in the first section. This new era has not led to a dismantling of mechanisms by which government or corporations can exert their influence on development projects, but rather has designed new mechanisms which can be applied within a context of liberal democracy. The blunt instrument of 'bulldozer consultation' (Wells 2015) has been replaced with a more sophisticated array of concepts and practices, including the TMCP. I now turn to the four theoretical elements of post-politics outlined in the first section and argue that there are both similarities and some differences between the elements of post-politics described by Swyngedouw (2011) and the politics surrounding the Thilawa complaints mechanism.

The integration of democratic principles into post-political forms of governance

Crucially, the TMCP cannot be dismissed as simply concealing authoritarianism through a veil of participatory language. It may be tempting for sceptics to dismiss mechanisms such as the TCMP as a façade to cover predatory engagements between the state and civil society. In reality, the design of the TCMP is infused with democratic principles, creating a platform where local residents can engage with those governing Thilawa SEZ. Yet as Kamat (2014, 67) highlights, democratic principles can be central, or even 'indispensable' to a 'neoliberal growth strategy'.

The TCMP mechanism claims "to enhance overall project outcomes by giving project stakeholders satisfaction that their voices are being heard and that their issue or concern has been subject to formal consideration by the TSEZ". Communities who are affected by the SEZ implementation are invited to participate and share their concerns. In promoting the TCMP and the project's engagement with communities, JICA's chief representative in Myanmar, Keiichiro Nakazawa, said that "the new [Myanmar] government was very much caring about the people's voice and trying to be inclusive for making decision or for making development planning (sic)" (Kean 2017). JICA is "trying to be inclusive and hear the people's voice". He concluded that "we have to be very careful particularly for the vulnerable people who are affected by the project" but optimistically suggested that "overall the assessment by the people in the region I believe is quite positive" (Kean 2017). MJTD— the implementers of the project—have not sought to repress the voices of affected communities, in a way that was common in the Than Shwe era. Rather, they have actively created channels for affected citizens to communicate to the SEZ governance. The evaluation of the MSAG reflected this tone of optimism about the possibility of building consensus in project implementation. The evaluation argues for shifts in the interaction between communities, NGOs, companies, and government around the Thilawa SEZ. These proposed shifts are from negotiation as "power driven" to "mutual gains" driven, from "win-lose" to "win-win", from "tactics and tricks" to "openness", and from "manipulating information" to "searching solutions together" (Zongollowicz 2016, 5).

The documentation and discourse around the complaints procedure is thoroughly infused with democratic language of participation, and assumptions about a consensual management of the project which can integrate the views of all stakeholders. How then might a complaint mechanism designed around principles of participation at the same time dilute or defuse opposition to the SEZ project?

The reduction of grievances to the particular rather than the universal

One means of managing grievances in a managerial or technocratic context of governance is by reducing each complaint to its particular context. The particular complaint is not dismissed or rejected, but rather stripped of any relevance to the universal so that it does not allude to wider structural and ideological inequalities that exists between the SEZ governing bodies and ordinary citizens. Kamat (2014, 68) argues that it is not the *suppression* of wide dissent to development programmes, but rather that such dissent is made *irrelevant*. The TCMP is structured to deal with grievances, for example, from a family or community, on an individual basis focussing on practical situations. Through the complaints mechanism the Thilawa SEZ "reserves the right not to address a complaint that it reasonably considers amounts to no more than general, unspecified and therefore un-actionable dissatisfaction with the SEZ" (Myanmar Japan Thilawa Development Limited 2018a, 3). The validity of a complaint is dependent on it being specific and actionable. Wider opposition to the project or to the manner of its implementation is deemed to be irrelevant to the TCMP. Therefore, only certain kinds of complaints are allowable and delimited to the practical and the specific.

Meanwhile, MJTD documents assume overarching stakeholder support for the benefits of the project. Referring to the relocation of affected communities known in official government discourse as project-affected persons (PAPs), the Thilawa SEZ website states that "the majority of PAPs are fine with the new relocation place as they accept that they now get (at the new place, i.e., after the relocation) what they could not get in the past (i.e., in the old place)". This is followed by an acknowledgement that "some PAPs are still complaining by saying that the situation after the relocation gets worse". The website then provides a table outlining the many improvements in the new site as compared to the previous site (Thilawa SEZ Management Committee 2018a). This assessment of improvements in relocated communities is disputed by reports from advocacy groups (Earthrights International 2017). Yet for the purpose of this chapter, what is important is the consistent characterisation of complaints as isolated to *particular* people or contexts, rather than the possibility that there may be more fundamental opposition to the project.

A diverse range of practical grievances is not a threat to the project. Rather, as Rancière suggests, multiple, different kinds of practical feedback mean that the project implementers can take a role as arbitrator. Neoliberal development is in fact 'nourished' by this multiplicity (Rancière 1999, 95). The complaints mechanism operates by taking into account multiple experiences and interests, and dealing with them tangibly and individually, rather than in ideological or overarching terms. Thus, it serves to diversify opposition, casting grievances as those from the individual dissenter who, through negotiation, can be brought into a sensible consensus—a consensus which inevitably involves the ongoing implementation of the planned project.

The reconfiguration of citizen-state relations

This form of grievance management is also facilitated through a reconfiguration of citizen-state relations and institutions of governance. Myanmar's political context of the 1990s and 2000s was a blunt example of a highly centralised military government—bolstered by both the armed forces and its associated military-owned corporations—that repressed the political rights of the citizenry and civil society. In contrast, the age of the post-politics is characterised by governance *beyond* the state (Swyngedouw 2011). Rather than a highly centralised form of government control, there are complex governance arrangements, embracing supranational governance bodies, decentralised local governance arrangements, private corporations, NGOs, and even religious leaders, as in the case of Thilawa SEZ.

The Thilawa SEZ is on one hand governed by the Thilawa SEZ committee as a special sub-national government body. Importantly though, the TCMP is not administered by the government's SEZ management committee, but by MJTD, which involves the Japanese government through JICA, along with both international and local private corporations. Thus, the complaints mechanism sits outside of Myanmar legal processes. The TCMP states that it "does not replace existing Myanmar legal processes, or TSEZ administrative processes already in use". The TCMP also "does not impede access to other judicial or administrative remedies that might be available through domestic law or through existing arbitration procedures" (Myanmar Japan Thilawa Development Limited 2018a, 2). This complicates questions of where the responsibility lies for different kinds of grievances, and whether grievances are the responsibility of the TSEZMC, the MJTD, or the local-level government. Responsibility is deflected between these groups. For example, when asked about specific grievances of the first group of relocated residents, JICA advisor Takuro Takeuchi said that he understood that resettled communities are facing difficulties in Thilawa, but that ultimately "it's the Myanmar government that has to settle the situation" (Associated Press 2014). Similarly, one of the investors in MJTD, Mitsubishi Corporation, said that the 'ultimate responsibility . . . rests with the government of Myanmar' (Mitsubishi Corporation 2014). Whilst MJTD takes clear responsibility for managing the TCMP, the diversity of actors involved in governance means that it is unclear who holds responsibility for addressing specific grievances.

The uncertainty about responsibility for support for affected people was reflected in a field visit to one of the relocated communities near Thilawa SEZ. As part of the agreement of relocation, MJTD was to build a health clinic for the new village. Although MJTD did construct a multi-roomed concrete building in a central part of the village, the building remained little more than a concrete shell, lacking in medical equipment, staff, and medicine. MJTD had fulfilled its responsibility for constructing the health clinic, yet local-level governance capacity and resourcing was insufficient to staff or equip the centre. Whilst I have sought in this section to highlight how theories of post-politics are relevant to the emerging forms of governance in Thilawa SEZ, this issue of government capacity also raises significant questions about the applicability from the context of European or North American governance. Shifts to consensual and technocratic post-political forms of democratic government require a certain degree of government capacity to deliver basic services to stifle societal discontent and dissent. In the case of communities relocated from Thilawa, MJTD and JICA's statements about managing complaints reflect a desire for technocratic management. Yet this is undermined if local levels of government are unable to, for example, staff or supply a local health centre. The diffused mode of governance found at Thilawa SEZ supports post-politicisation, as it deflects responsibility from any one actor tasked with the management of the site. Yet a consensual and technocratic practice of governance requires all governance actors to have at least certain levels of resources and capacity, which potentially opens up spaces for contestations amongst ordinary citizens. MJTD may be able to build a health centre, yet they cannot staff and maintain it. Theories of post-politics—and the shift to consensual technocratic governance—may falter in their applicability to situations where even a basic level of governance capacity cannot be fulfilled.

Beyond governance responsibility lying with either corporations or with different layers of the Myanmar government, the reconfiguration of citizen-state relations also involved the communities, religious leaders, and NGOs. At the community level, there was significant competition over claims to representation. The relocated communities had formal representation through the Myanmar local government system of representatives that spoke on behalf of a certain number of households. However, the aforementioned TSDG was partly formed in response to a lack of confidence in formal community representation. Amongst local advocacy groups and the TSGD, there were concerns about whether the interests of formal representatives were aligned with those of the community, or if they had been co-opted by MJTD. The leaders of the TSDG were elected through an alternate process and claimed to be more genuine representatives of the community. This, however, was disputed by other stakeholders. The evaluation of the MSAG highlighted that some members of the group questioned whether TSDG representatives were in fact "community gate keepers" who presented a barrier to those "most in need" (Zongollowicz 2016, 4).

Further complicating the citizen-state relationship was the role of religious leaders as intermediaries. A local monk played an active role within the MSAG and was invited by MJTD to be an interlocutor with the relocated communities. His role in the development of the complaints mechanism was, however, questioned by local and international advocacy groups. Criticism was made first about the monk's lack of skills and training to engage in negotiation and mediation processes. Furthermore, due to the religious and social role of Buddhist religious leaders within local communities, activists felt that community members would be reluctant to openly present their grievances to the monk. Whilst the role of a religious leader as an intermediary further broadened the range of stakeholders involved in governance arrangements, it also constrained the voices of affected citizens.

Similarly, in its negotiations with affected communities, MJTD also enlisted the support of 'third-party organisations'—which were local development organisations—who could witness meetings and act as an external monitor. But this also sparked debate over whether local development organisations should play this 'third-party' role. The activist organisations most engaged with the Thilawa SEZ project were invited to be 'third-party organisations' but refused, arguing that it would legitimise what they deem to be the problematic approach of MJTD. MJTD then approached another two other local organisations who agreed to be 'third-party organisations'. Rather than a binary governance relationship between citizens and the state—as was more evident in the authoritarian era—the governance of the Thilawa SEZ is dispersed across a sub-national government committee, local and international corporations, the Japanese government, local community representatives, religious leaders, and local 'third-party' organisations.

The dispersed nature of governance arrangements serves to defuse opposition to the project. The development of the Thilawa SEZ cannot be characterised as just the predatory engagement of international corporations. Rather, local and national governments, local corporations and even local communities, religious leaders, and development organisations are also incorporated within new governance practices and procedures. Grievances are not only rendered *particular* rather than *universal*, but they are also managed with interlocking governance arrangements where the state both takes, but also abrogates, responsibility. But as I have described, the dynamics of this consensual style of governance are different from Swyngedouw's (2011) reflections on Europe or North America. The technocratic discourse of the SEZ committee and MJTD is undermined by the local government's inability to provide basic services to the relocated communities. The citizen-state relationship may have been reconfigured since the end of Myanmar's authoritarian era, yet the stark realities of basic community needs for services remain.

The inevitable incompleteness of post-politicisation

The incorporation of democratic principles, the categorisation of grievances as the particular over the universal, and the reconfiguration and diffusion of relations of governance have served to bolster the process of post-politicisation around the Thilawa SEZ project. Yet as Swyngedouw (2011, 373) highlights, this process is always 'incomplete', there can never be closure, and counter-moments or re-politicisation will inevitably emerge. In the example of the Thilawa SEZ, the TCMP has itself become a site of political contest.

As described earlier, there were competing processes for the design of complaints mechanism for affected communities, with TSDG and Earthrights championing for the CDOGM, and MJTD and JICA initiating an alternate process to design the TCMP. After the alternate process was announced in late 2017, Earthrights International responded with a report stating that

> we are disappointed that the Thilawa SEZ (TSEZ) parties have elected to reject three years' worth of requests from community members to collaborate on a multi-stakeholder grievance process. Rather, in the face of consistent efforts from the Thilawa community towards meaningful dialogue, the TSEZ parties chose to spend time and money to create a competing complaints procedure.
>
> *(Earthrights International 2018, 1)*

The report went on to suggest that "international good practice requires grievance mechanisms to be accessible, predictable, equitable, legitimate, rights-compatible, and transparent. The TCMP meets none of these criteria, ignoring the most basic and well-accepted elements of good practice" (Earthrights International 2018, 1). The implementers of the Thilawa SEZ, MJTD, in turn responded—though without mentioning the Earthrights report—by arguing that "we welcome discourse aimed at improving our operations, supporting access to financial and vocational assistance for affected people and continuing our policy of transparency in compliance with international best practice" (Myanmar Japan Thilawa Development Limited 2018b).

The language of 'international standards' in governance, as seen in processes pertaining to the management of grievances, are part of the mechanics of post-politicisation, rendering opposition irrelevant unless it complies with a managerial and technical agenda. Yet local and international opposition to the SEZ project has politicised both the language of international standards and the seemingly technocratic mechanism of a complaints procedure. There is now an emergent struggle over who has claim to 'international standards'—there are claims and counter-claims over whether or not the project is complying with 'international best practice'.

These new struggles over 'international standards' could, on one hand, be viewed as part of the incompleteness of post-politicisation. There is an inevitable re-politicisation, with ideological contests seeping into mechanisms as seemingly benign and technocratic as a complaints procedure. Yet on the other hand, the struggle over claims to following 'international standards' itself reinforces the centrality of those 'standards'. There is a paradox for local and international civil society groups, where their resistance to the implementers of the project and their efforts to amplify the voices of affected residents, at the same time, reinforces the very mechanisms that are used in the process of post-politicisation. Returning to Rancière and the 'partition of sensible', (Rancière 1999) the challenge for affected citizens and activists is that they face a 'reigning configuration'. Groups such as TSDG or Earthrights can play by the language and discourse of that configuration—in this case the language of 'international best practice'—and be heard, and yet because of this, their voices become absorbed into the consensual and technocratic processes. Local and international civil society groups in this case are at once both opponents to and participants in the process of post-politicisation. Or alternatively, citizens and activists can challenge the reigning configuration itself and yet risk being dismissed as radical or irrelevant, as one particular identity group or interest group who are 'unreasonable'.

Conclusion

In the 1990s and 2000s, Myanmar's political context had been the example *par excellence* of overt political struggle, a period of repressive authoritarianism punctuated by street protests. It is, therefore, at one level an unlikely context to be examining the age of post-politics. Yet rapid political and economic liberalisation in the nation since 2011 has meant that there has been a stark shift in the culture of governance—particularly around the implementation of new development projects including the Thilawa SEZ. This rapid shift has revealed a new context where the government and private-sector actors seek to manage the grievances of communities who are affected by development projects. The example of the Thilawa SEZ complaints mechanism demonstrates the rapid infusion of consensual and technocratic forms of governance into Myanmar's urban development.

This study of the Thilawa SEZ reveals key dimensions of post-politicisation: the integration of democratic principles into post-political forms of governance, the reduction of grievances to the *particular* rather than the *universal*, and the reconfiguration of citizen-state relations. Yet the context is also characterised not by the elimination of political and ideological struggle, but rather by its emergence in new and unexpected sites or contest. In this case, the seemingly technocratic mechanism of the complaints procedure has been a central focus of contest as private-sector implementers, the local government, affected communities, and civil society groups struggle over who has claim to 'international standards'. However, in resisting the process of implementation of the SEZ, citizens and activists also serve to bolster the possibility of a consensual democracy and the mechanics of technocratic management. Paradoxically, they are both challenging and reinforcing the emerging system of developmental decision-making in Myanmar. Theories of post-politics are valuable in challenging recent popular and scholarly representations of Myanmar's political transition.

Beyond a re-evaluation of Myanmar's political transition within the past decade, the second purpose of this chapter has been to use the lens of the Thilawa SEZ complaints procedure to explore the relevance of theories of post-politics outside their origins of Europe and North America. I described how the consensual, technocratic processes of governance described within theories of post-politics are evident in the implementation of the Thilawa SEZ development. Yet at the same time, profound limitations of government capacity, at all levels, undermine the effective 'suturing' of 'the political' in the same way that Swyngedouw (2011) and Rancière (1999) describe. As Myanmar's new political configurations continue to emerge from decades of authoritarianism, scholars must be attentive to the ways in which these configurations both reflect and also diverge from notions of post-politicisation that have emerged in Europe and North America.

References

Associated Press. 2014. "Farmers versus Factories a Dilemma for Japan Aid Group in Myanmar's Showcase Economic Zone." May 29. www.foxnews.com/world/2014/05/29/farmers-versus-factories-dilemma-for-japan-aid-group-in-myanmar-showcase.html

Earthrights International. 2017. "Thilawa SEZ Access to Remedy Denied." https://earthrights.org/wp-content/uploads/ERI_Thilawa-Handout.pdf

———. 2018. "Analysis of the Thilawa SEZ Complaints Management Procedure." 8 February. https://earthrights.org/wp-content/uploads/180206_ERI-Analysis-of-TCMP.pdf

Kamat, S. 2014. "The New Development Architecture and the Post-Political in the Global South." In *The Post-Political and Its Discontents: Spaces of Depoliticisation, Spectres of Radical Politics*, edited by J. Wilson and E. Swyngedouw, 67–85. Edinburgh: Edinburgh University Press.

Kean, T. 2017. "JICA Chief: 'We Are Also Trying to Be Inclusive and Hear the People's Voice'." *Frontier Myanmar*, January 25. https://frontiermyanmar.net/en/jica-chief-we-are-also-trying-to-be-inclusive-and-hear-the-peoples-voice

Mitsubishi Corporation. 2014. "Signing of Joint Venture Agreement for 2nd Zone of Thilawa SEZ in Myanmar." Press Release, October 21, 2016. www.business-humanrights.org/sites/default/files/media/mitsubishi-response-jun-2014.pdf

Myanmar Japan Thilawa Development Limited. 2018a. "Thilawa SEZ Complaints Management Procedure (TCMP) Thilawa Special Economic Zone (TSEZ)." https://www.mjtd.com.mm/sites/default/files/TCMP%20Version%203%20%28Eng%29.pdf

———. 2018b. "Myanmar Japan Thilawa Development Limited response to concerns expressed about the Thilawa Complaints Management Procedure (TCMP)." 28 February. https://www.business-humanrights.org/sites/default/files/documents/MJTD%20response_28%20Feb%202018.pdf

Rancière, J. 1999. *Disagreement: Politics and Philosophy*. Minnesota: University of Minnesota Press.

Reynolds, L., and B. Szerszynski. 2014. "The Post-Political and the End of Nature: The Genetically Modified Organism." In *The Post-Political and Its Discontents: Spaces of Depoliticization, Spectres of Radical Politics*, edited by J. Wilson and E. Swyngedouw, 48–66. Edinburgh: Edinburgh University Press.

Swyngedouw, E. 2011. "Interrogating Post-Democratization: Reclaiming Egalitarian Political Spaces." *Political Geography* 30 (7): 370–380.

Swyngedouw, E., and J. Wilson. 2014. "There Is No Alternative." In *The Post-Political and Its Discontents: Spaces of Depoliticisation, Spectres of Radical Politics*, edited by J. Wilson and E. Swyngedouw, 299–312. Edinburgh: Edinburgh University Press.

Thilawa SEZ Management Committee. 2018a. "Thilawa SEZ Management Committee: Conditions after Relocation." www.myanmarthilawa.gov.mm/conditions-after-relocation

———. 2018b. "Role and Functions of the Thilawa SEZ Management Committee." Thilawa Special Economic Zone Website. https://www.myanmarthilawa.gov.mm/role-and-function

US Campaign for Burma. 2014. "U.S. Campaign for Burma—Press Release: Japan Must Postpone Thilawa SEZ Financing Until Forced Displacement Reviewed." April 1. www.burmapartnership.org/2014/04/press-release-japan-must-postpone-thilawa-sez-financing-until-forced-displacement-reviewed/

Wells, T. 2015. "Quality Talk?" *The Irrawaddy*, February 27. www.irrawaddy.com/news/burma/quality-talk.html.

Yen, S. 2014. "Myanmar's Thilawa Residents Formally Complain to Tokyo." *The Irrawaddy*, June 3. www.irrawaddy.com/news/burma/thilawa-residents-formally-complain-tokyo.html

Žižek, S. 2000. *The Ticklish Subject: The Absent Centre of Political Ontology*. London: Verso.

———. 2002. *Revolution at the Gates—Žižek on Lenin: The 1917 Writings*. London: Verso.

Zongollowicz, A. 2016. "Thilawa Multi-Stakeholder Advsory Group (MSAG) Evaluation." www.myanmar-responsiblebusiness.org/pdf/2016-10-21-Thilawa-MSAG-Evaluation_en.pdf

3
EMERGING POST-POLITICAL CITY IN SEOUL

U-Seok Seo

Introduction

In the introduction of their edited book *Post-political and Its Discontents*, Wilson and Swyngedouw (2014) refer to the novel *Seeing* by José Saramago as a critical description on the current state of Western democracy. In *Seeing*, an allegory about a general election in a city is told where 83 percent of the citizens casted a blank vote. With this parable, the disaffection of voters within a supposedly representative democracy is satirised by Saramago, who argues that there exists only the appearance of democracy, like a simulation. Paralleling this story, the local election in Korea held in May 2018 provides an opportunity to think about the state of democracy in an urban setting. As a heuristic approach, a question could be raised about whether Saramago's criticism bears any relevance to urban politics in Korea. Through a study of Seoul, this chapter argues that this post-political syndrome is increasingly observed in the urban politics of the capital city, against the background of the distinctive developmental trajectory of politics in South Korea. After the political eruption against the neoliberal urban redevelopment policy, the regime change into the liberal urban government brought forth the post-political inclination based on the governance building incorporating the critical forces. The diagnosis of Seoul as a post-political case is applicable to local politics throughout South Korea, in a sense that the substance of democracy is questionable in spite of the emphasis on governance and civic participation.

Whilst the significance of the post-political city debates regarding the realm of South Korean urban politics is not evident at first glance, this chapter shows that discourses on post-politics and its depoliticisation provides a valuable theoretical tool to critically diagnose and reflect upon the current state of democracy in an Asian context (Crouch 2004; Swyngedouw 2009, 2014), especially since democracy in South Korea is believed to have expanded at the national and local levels since the 1980s. Attempting to discuss the urban realities in East Asian countries through the notion of the post-political city poses difficulties because there is little empirical research featuring post-politics or post-democracy discourses based in the region (Beveridge and Koch 2017), and because overall, the concept and characteristics of the 'post-political city' remains nebulous.

This discussion will help us understand the contingencies of the 'post-political city' by taking into account historical differences between the Asian and Western contexts, taking into consideration the path-dependent development of East Asian cities.[1] For example, the historical emergence of neoliberalism in East Asia departs from the West. Whilst post-politics in Western countries is related to processes of depoliticisation after the decline of the welfare state and social democracy, few East Asian countries implemented welfare states and democratic practices to the same extent as the West. Irrespective of these differences, in the case of Seoul, the city exhibits characteristics of the post-political city. Over the past several years, the city has experienced "the dynamics of de-politicisation and the disappearance of the political" (Swyngedouw 2014, 123), through the emergence of consensual politics and the fading of political debates over urban policy issues. The question this chapter seeks to address is how post-politics came to manifest in this Asian city.

This chapter begins by outlining how the post-political condition has emerged in South Korea, evidenced through differing levels of voter engagement with national and local politics, noting that the interscalar dimension in South Korea is quite a complex issue. The next section then provides the understanding of the backgrounds for the underdeveloped urban politics in Korea and the genuine features of Seoul. This will then be followed by a discussion regarding two contrasting stages in terms of 'the political' that will be described in chronological order.

Current divisions between local and national politics in South Korea

At first glance, voter participation in the May 2018 local election was the highest in the past 23 years, at 60.2 percent (*Chosun Ilbo* 2018). However, the level of political participation obfuscates the extent in which citizens actually engage with local politics. This local election espoused post-political symptoms and should be recognised as a mid-term evaluation of the national government, rather than as a desire for citizens to be involved with the decision-making about local issues. Above all, voters were hardly aware of the differences amongst political parties involved with local political issues. According to the post-poll survey, only 52 percent of voters knew the name of local council members. Whilst 90 percent of voters knew the name of the local governor or mayor, only 53 percent knew the election pledges of these governors and mayors.[2]

Whilst the legal institutional procedures for local politics and local democracy have undoubtedly improved over the past decades, for a greater part of voters, local election functions as an expression of their political attitudes towards national politics, rather than as a means of voting for local issues. The Korean voters voting in local elections do so without much consideration and awareness about local politics, such that their political participation is no better than the voters in *Seeing* who cast a blank vote.

There are several reasons behind citizen disinterest in local elections. The indifference voters express towards local politics in Korea results partly from the complicated voting system. During the 2018 local election, each voter received seven ballot papers asking them to choose a (1) wide-area provincial governor/metropolitan mayor, (2) local governor/local city mayor, (3) superintendent for educational affairs, (4) wide-area/metropolitan council member, (5) local council member, (6) proportional wide-area provincial/metropolitan council member, and (7) proportional local council member. Most voters hear the names of local politicians for the first time only at local elections, so it is not surprising that voters hardly discern the differences amongst local political candidates beyond their respective party affiliations. Furthermore, the disinterest of voters in local politics is not featured or discussed in media coverage of local issues, which only serves to reinforce the pervasiveness of this disinterest. Particularly, the 2018 local election was overshadowed by the historic summit between US president Donald Trump (2018–present) and North Korean supreme leader Kim Jong-un (2012–present), held in Singapore on 12 May that same year, one day before the South Korean local elections.

Yet, there is a structural and historically embedded reason for this political disinterest and the underdevelopment of urban politics. This political disinterest in local urban politics amongst voters forms the underlying condition for the post-political city, as illustrated in the next section.

Historical background for the underdevelopment of urban politics

The underdevelopment and weakness of urban politics in Korea stems from the historical development of the nation, specifically its long history of political centralisation and lack of feudal polities. The historical origins for this centralisation dates back to the unification dates back to the seventh century, when the Silla Dynasty (57 BC–935 AD) unified the "Three Kingdoms—Koguryo in the north, Paekche in the southwest, and Silla in the southeast" (Ahn 2006, 75). Since then, one political power ruled over the Korean peninsula, interrupted briefly by an exceptional transition period during the Joseon dynasty (1392–1897), which governed the country through public officials who were disseminated from the central political power. Under these circumstances, individual provinces were unable to develop political autonomy of long continuance.

It was only in 1952, four years after the founding of the new government under the first Republic of Korea (r. 1948–1960), that the centralised governing power and political system allowed for localised autonomy to emerge; its short history forms an important element for the weak development of local politics. Furthermore, this system allowing for localised political autonomy was not stable, and was temporarily ceased under the authoritarian regime that emerged after the 1961 military coup (Yoo 1993). It was not until the 1990s that the local autonomy system in Korea was re-established, as a part of the democratisation process from 1987 onwards. The local autonomy system is implemented through the direct election of local councilmen and the executive heads of local governments as mandated through the 1988 and 1994 Local Autonomy Act, complemented by the "introduction of information disclosure (1996), petitioning (2000), local referendum (2004) and resident recall system (2006)" acts (Bae 2013, 767). This process of devolution was far from a smooth passage. Even under the Roh administration (2003–2008) that actively strived for more devolution, the central government resisted against devolution to maintain its own jurisdiction and influence over the country (Sonn 2010). Although the building of democratic institutions for local governments was legally accomplished in the end, there remains a large discrepancy between the ideal of the constitution and the reality that exists with regard to local autonomy (S-T. Kim 2016).

The politics surrounding the urbanisation process has also impacted the shaping of urban politics in Korea. Weber (1969) frames the features of the Occidental city as its own distinctive politico-administrative concept and a creation of new forms of community. No comparable tradition existed in Korea, as the formation of the city-state or the free city was not found in the traditional Korean history of city building (S-T. Kim 2016). In the Japanese colonial era, city growth was facilitated mainly through the implementation of modern transportation and administrative apparatus, which all contributed to the exploitation of the Korean peninsula.

Yet this does not mean that city building in Korea is neither related to political changes nor has any political significance. Urbanisation has provided a critical spatial condition for the development of democracy, especially in association with the growth of the educated middle-class. Whereas the conservative Liberty Korea Party (the ruling party of the country until 2016) is more popular in the rural area, the opposition party gains more votes in urban areas, where there are large concentrations of the educated middle-class who supported democratisation during the authoritarian regime. As much as the urban middle-class plays a great role in the process of democratisation at every election, the public spaces in the city have functioned as a locus of the people's democratic struggle and fight for democratisation, as seen from Seoul's Spring in 1980 to the Great Citizen's Democratic Fight in 1987, and recently, the Candlelight Protest in 2016 and 2017 leading to the impeachment of the former president Park Geun-hye (2013–2017). However, it should be noted that such public spaces in the city cover mainly national issues rather than local problems.

The features of ideological conflicts in Korean history also crippled the development of local urban politics. The major political ideological clashes in South Korea have historically been rooted in the confrontation against the communist regime of North Korea, and more recently against the United states, which manifested as anti-American sentiments; in turn, most urban policy issues seem to be distanced from the ideological conflict of Korean politics. Furthermore, the enduring regionalism of Korean politics results quite often in a political landscape where different geographical areas experience one-party dominance. For instance, the metropolitan councils of Gwangju, the epicentre of the left liberal party, and Daegu, the heartland of the conservative party, tend to be occupied by over 90 percent of their preferred party. One-party dominance in local politics clearly hinders the mechanism of checks and balances through parliamentary oversight, which then exacerbates public scepticism towards the accountability of the local government, subsequently driving public demand for an alternative critical perspective through a locally autonomous system.

An underdeveloped interest and engagement with local urban politics prevails throughout South Korean cities, including the capital of Seoul; at the same time, the distinct political situation in Seoul should be emphasised. The uniqueness of Seoul stems from the concentration of political power, human resources, and financial capital around the capital city region during a period of "compressed" urban development since the 1960s, whereby urbanisation occurs at a rapid rate within a short time frame (M. Kang 1998, 100–101). Its privileged status as the capital city for nearly six centuries from the onset of the Joseon dynasty was extended after the founding of the Korean republic, when the city received the designation of 'Seoul Special City'. Furthermore, economic growth by the developmental state strengthened the dominant status of Seoul in nearly every social dimension. Thus, Korea is even cynically called the 'Seoul Republic' (Ahn 2006). The unbalanced development and the concentration of socio-political and economic power into the Seoul metropolitan area emerged as an important political agenda in terms of the management of national land. As a result, the urban economy in Seoul is often not distinguished nor differentiated from the national economy. Seoul appears to be exempt from competing for capital investment with other Korean cities. Improving the economic situation in Seoul tends to be regarded less as a task of the city government than as that of national government, except for local area development. Since many citizens regard the economic condition in Seoul as a matter of national politics and not of urban politics, the endeavours of attracting investment or the population seldom emerge as local election issues in Seoul. This distinctiveness of Seoul explains in part the disinterest of citizens in urban politics.

The history of political centralisation and concentration does not mean that Seoul has more autonomy than other cities against the central government. On the contrary, Seoul has always been subject to strong control by the national government, serving as the location of the presidential residence, the government, and the parliament, even though most government ministries moved to Sejong City since the mid-2000s. However, Seoul holds a strong potential to develop its own autonomy. The enormous political importance of Seoul in Korea stems not only from its population size, as the biggest city, but also from the diversity of its population from their regional origin. The increase of Seoul's population from 1.6 million to 10.6 million between 1955 and 1990 resulted from rural-urban migration, as well as migration from other cities. Whilst the influence of regionalism on political attitudes reveals itself less evidently in Seoul, the political attitude of Seoul's citizens has symbolic importance as a representation of the political attitudes for the whole country. Moreover, the likelihood of the mayor of Seoul becoming the next presidential candidate positions the political interest and discourses being formed about the city within national political concerns. In sum, whilst the political outcomes in Seoul gain great importance with regard to its dominant position to central and national politics, the urban politics of Seoul remain underdeveloped due to the city's neglect of its urban problems and local issues as political agendas. Here emerges the imbalance between Seoul's huge outer growth compared to Seoul's own political immaturity towards its urban politics.

Political antagonism against the neoliberal power

The rise of political antagonism through Cheonggyecheon project

The previous section illustrated the inter-related historical features that have led to the underdevelopment of urban politics and the prevalence of depoliticising conditions, such that the rise of the political in Seoul in recent years was hardly expected. As this section shows, the politicisation of local urban politics occurred in the first decade of the 21st century, when Lee Myung-bak (2002–2006) and Oh Se-hoon (2006–2011) served as the mayors of the Seoul Metropolitan Government. Lee and Oh are both affiliated with the conservative Grand National Party supporting free trade and neoliberal ideologies, and have implemented ambitious mega-projects for urban (re-)development driven by economic growth (Table 3.1), which in turn enabled the emergence of the political within local urban politics. With the rise of criticism against these neoliberal urban programmes, this has allowed for an anti-urban redevelopment movement to emerge and strengthen the alliance between left liberal political parties and civic groups.

One important feature of the political climate during the terms of Lee Myung-bak and Oh Se-hoon was the growing concern about the spatial disparity within the Seoul area, which had its roots in the successful development of Gangnam from the mid-1970s to the 1980s. The growing spatial inequality seems to be rather paradoxical; Gangnam was deliberately developed to make the area attractive to the middle-class, who had initially been apathetic to such new towns and hardly moved into the new residential area. The development of Gangnam succeeded at least in its outer appearance and on an infrastructural level, and Gangnam eventually became the locus of the middle-class in Seoul. The forces driving rapid industrialisation and economic growth in Gangnam caused unbalanced development within Seoul. The divergence between modern and affluent Gangnam located to the south of the Han River and the aging historical Gangbuk area located to the north of the Han River manifests itself not just in the realm of material wealth but also in cultural tastes and lifestyles that the singer Psy describes in his 2012 mega hit song 'Gangnam Style'. The successful development of Gangnam is further demonstrated by the area's lucrative investment performance in the real estate market. The speculative desire to accumulate property assets leads to the positive perception

TABLE 3.1 The elected mayors of Seoul

Mayor	Local Election	Period	Party	Political Ideology	Relation with National Government
Cho Soon	First	1 July 1995 to 9 September 1997	National Congress for New Politics	liberal	opposition
Goh Kun	Second	1 July 1998 to 30 June 2002	National Congress for New Politics	liberal	ruling
Lee Myung-bak	Third	1 July 2002 to 30 June 2006	Grand National	conservative	opposition
Oh Se-hoon	Fourth	1 July 2006 to 30 June 2010	Grand National	conservative	opposition
Oh Se-hoon	Fifth	1 July 2010 to 26 August 2011	Grand National	conservative	ruling
Park Won-soon	Complimentary	27 October 2011 to 30 June 2014	Democratic United (elected as an independent)	liberal	opposition
Park Won-soon	Sixth	1 July 2014 to 30 June 2018	Democratic Party of Korea	liberal	opposition
Park Won-soon	Seventh	1 July 2018 to the present	Democratic Party of Korea	liberal	ruling

of redevelopment as societal progress, and the growing gap between Gangnam and Gangbuk became an important political agenda, helping to bring broader support for the redevelopment projects in Gangbuk. In addition, the production of surplus capital in the mid-1980s facilitated property-based urban redevelopment, functioning as a substantial source of investment in real estate and the built environment (Shin 2009). Hence, both mayors were able to undertake large-scale redevelopment projects in Gangbuk.

Moreover, a post- or neodevelopment paradigm based on capitalistic ideas emerged with the increasing interest in quality-of-life issues amongst the population, which led to a critical view towards the outcomes of compressed economic development (Cho 2010). There emerged a demand to develop remedies for the negative consequences resulting from rapid urban expansion, and the narrow focus on economic rationality is increasingly questioned, accompanied by a growing desire to pursue different lifestyle values based on an environmental, cultural, and more humane orientation. As popular interest in the ecological rehabilitation of Seoul has grown in the early 2000s, the restoration of Cheonggyecheon, meaning 'Clean Valley Stream', emerged as the hottest issue during the 2002 Seoul mayoral election. Lee Myung-bak, the former CEO of Hyundai Construction Company between 1977 and 1988, promised the restoration of Cheonggyecheon as a flagship electoral commitment which would bring economic and environmental vitality to the deteriorated inner city. The core feature of this project was the demolition of the multi-storied road that once covered the Cheonggyecheon, inducing the creation of a new landscape with modern office and commercial buildings along the stream as a waterfront redevelopment (H. Kim and Han 2012).

Although the Cheonggyecheon project claimed to address issues of growing public interest such as environmental values and historical preservation, in actuality, it evoked much public criticism. This is because the project was implemented through the same developmentalist methods used in the past, methods oriented towards efficiency at the expense of proper deliberation and characterised by weak citizen participation with limited consideration for the voices of the socially underprivileged. Whilst the Cheonggyecheon Restoration Citizens Committee was to provide a link between the city government and the public, with its membership comprised of NGOs, academics, businessmen, and journalists, the committee had little actual influence in steering the project, and the technocrat group in charge of civil engineering affairs was apathetic about the voices oriented towards ecological concerns and democracy (Cho 2010). In particular, Lee Myung-bak's outcome-oriented manner of project management brought forth outcries against the project, claiming that it violated promises of environmental restoration and historic preservation. The opposing forces developed into a network with four types of action groups, including (1) the Green Seoul Citizens Committee; (2) academic groups such as the Environmental Sociology Association, Korea Planners Association, and Environmental Impact Assessment Society; (3) a non-governmental organization (NGO) coalition movement such as the Citizen's Coalition for Correct Cheonggyecheon Restoration; and (4) merchant groups of shopkeepers, as well as a large number of illegal street vendors, operating along Cheonggyecheon (Cho 2010). Even though their criticism was nearly omitted when confronted with enthusiasm over the completion of the Cheonggyecheon project within the planned time period, critical awareness of urban redevelopment projects began to grow and spread amongst citizens, with networks and mobilisation amongst divergent civil society groups being made.

The explosion of political antagonism against the New Town Programme and the Yongsan disaster

The New Town Programme (NTP), introduced by Lee Myung-bak and later expanded by Oh Se-hoon, has an enormous importance on the shaping of local urban politics. NTP replaced the Joint Redevelopment Programme (JRP), which had been introduced in 1984 to transform informal settlements into high-rise housing estates (Shin 2009). The NTP is legitimised as an effective measure to reduce the gap between Gangnam and Gangbuk by compensating for the weakness in old redevelopment schemes. The NTP had been expected to emphasise publicness, by providing public facilities and creating spaces for public access, incorporating public consultations and inspections in the planning and construction process, and providing proper infrastructure and to execute projects more efficiently (Byeon 2008, 2014). The alleged publicness of the NTP can be affirmed through its comparison with the JRP. Whilst the JRP had often been implemented without considering the need to provide additional public infrastructure for the population, in turn, the NTP accounts for the provision of the necessary public infrastructure based on its large-scale planning practices.

At the initial stage, the NTP designation was made for three areas, these being Eunpyeong, Ahyeon, and Jangwi. The rapid rise of housing prices in these areas after they received NTP designation led to a rapid increase in the number of designations to 35 other areas, which covered 27.6 percent of the whole residential area in Seoul (Byeon 2013). Seoul's urban redevelopment to transform high-density, low-rise residential areas into high-rise flats has reached the climax with this project. Led by the municipal government from its birth, the NTP gained popularity in other regions and even with the central government, which despite being a different political party from the Seoul Metropolitan Government at the time, similarly believed that the NTP was the solution to enacting more balanced development within cities. The NTP later turned out to be a policy failure (with the exception of some minor cases) for many reasons beyond the scope of this chapter, including the global economic downturn, leaving enormous negative consequences for a number of local neighbourhoods and residents.

Besides the later collapse of NTP projects in their entirety, it is worthwhile to note that the NTP is part of the new-build gentrification effort, embedded in Korea's highly speculative urban development processes from the 1980s (Shin and S-H. Kim 2016). Property owners, construction firms, and the local and central governments coalesced and successfully enabled the extraction of exchange value by closing the rent gap, and wholesale redevelopment became a dominant approach causing redevelopment-induced gentrification (Shin 2009). With 80 percent of original residents displaced in the redevelopment process (Ha 2004), the biggest problem created by redevelopment projects has been the resettlement of residents and tenants. Particularly, the compensation for tenants had been a critical issue that has been gradually improved. Whilst there had been no compensation arrangement for tenants upon the introduction of the JRP in 1983, some concessions for tenants have since been introduced, and by mid-1989 tenants were offered cash compensation equivalent to three months' living costs, and there is now the mandatory requirement for the provision of 'redevelopment rental housing' to rehouse willing and eligible tenants. These kinds of progress only became possible due to the tenants' struggle against their forced eviction and their call for housing rights (Shin and S-H. Kim 2016). Although the NTP did not lead to the emergence of 'the political' within urban politics in an explicit way, the tenants' movement against eviction and the housing rights movement empowered residents, civic groups, and critical urban scholars.

Oh Se-hoon, succeeding Lee as the fourth and fifth elected mayor of Seoul, was inspired by the international fever of creating the 'creative city' (Lee and Hwang 2012). As the 'creative city' has become a buzzword in urban policy for many cities across the world in the 21st century, Oh Se-hoon styled his governing of Seoul Metropolitan Government as the 'Creative Urban Administration'. Oh also incorporated the concept of 'culturenomics'—originally introduced by Peter Duelund, a professor at the University of Copenhagen, Denmark—into his own political brand, arguing that valourising cultural assets is the most effective way to reinforce the city's competitiveness. Considering that Korean cities had strived mainly for a quantitative expansion during the period of fast economic growth in the 1970s and 1980s, Oh's policy focus on culture and creativity represents a profound change in urban governance. The creative city policy was coupled with urban development projects, enlarging its magnitude and influence. For example, Oh's city government launched several urban development projects across Seoul dubbed as 'renaissance' projects influenced by a logic of culturenomics, as embodied by Oh's Creative Urban policies that encourage the framing of Seoul as a 'design city'. Amongst these initiatives, the Han River Renaissance Project is the most important and controversial one, given its sheer size and because of its complex nature.

The Han River Renaissance Project contains a diverse range of initiatives that form a part the Yongsan Redevelopment Project, and has the capacity to redefine the scope and nature of these schemes. Despite its proximity to the central business district, Yongsan experienced deterioration in the 1990s, when it was announced that the rail yards and US Army station in the area would be relocated. Yongsan has since became the locus of many urban redevelopment projects, including the construction of Yongsan International Business District. These huge urban redevelopment projects have been underpinned by an expectation to provide better amenities for citizens, and to produce an internationally renowned city image. However, the coupling of an amenity model with developmental policy, as embodied by the Yongsan Redevelopment Project, turned out to be the greatest failure of urban redevelopment in Korea (Lee and Anderson 2012). The main reason for the failure of the project lies in stagnated redevelopment of Seobu Icheon-dong, where Yongsan is located, which in turn arises from the inability of the government to achieve consensus amongst residents regarding how redevelopment was to be implemented. However, the decisive symbolic moment in the collapse of the Yongsan Redevelopment Project was the 2009 Yongsan disaster, which became the pivotal event evoking the wider struggle against the urban redevelopment. As new high-rise flats had already been constructed in Yongsan since the early 2000s, Yongsan grew into the epicentre of the anti-urban redevelopment movement (Lee 2017). On 20 January 2009, a number of Yongsan tenants, dissatisfied with what they deemed to be inadequate compensation, occupied and protested on the rooftop of an office building in Yongsan. As a result of police actions, a fire broke out in the building, with five protesters and a policeman killed and a number of people injured.

The repression of the protest against the redevelopment of Yongsan that cost the lives of several people acted as the catalyst for the public dissatisfaction towards widespread urban redevelopment to break out. A variety of civic groups, political fractions, as well as religious groups were unified to fight for the Yongsan disaster victims and their families. The funeral was postponed for nearly one year, as the families of the deceased and the redevelopment association negotiated to reach a settlement claim. During that time, the anti-redevelopment struggle was sustained in various ways. For instance, a mass for the victims was held every day at the black spot of the accident by Catholic priests, with cultural activists and artists also participating to express their solidarity and as a means of protest. Even five years after the disaster, 3,000 people from the victims' families, civil society, and businesses gather to memorialise the event. Yongsan International Business District projects have been postponed indefinitely, and most of the Han River Renaissance projects were also cancelled. Even though the Yongsan Redevelopment and Han River Renaissance projects had various weaknesses, the Yongsan disaster clearly formed a watershed within the political movement against neodevelopmental urban redevelopment and the profit-driven urban growth machine. This tragic accident led to the formation of a counter-hegemonic bloc against the neoliberal urban development bloc in Seoul. Issues of urban development dominated the following local metropolitan council elections, eventually prompting a change in mayor and mode of urban governance.

A post-political city with 'good governance'

The neoliberal regime of Seoul has retreated in quite a dramatic way. In 2010, Oh Se-hoon succeeded in the re-election campaign only with a marginal gain, but the majority of the metropolitan council lost to the opposition Democratic Party. With more than two-thirds of council seats now possessed by the opposition party, Oh even lost the right to veto against the city council. Subsequently, most major mega-projects initiated by Oh were heavily criticised by the city council, and lost much of their funding. To overcome this stalemate and his political inertia, Oh implored citizens to vote on the Seoul Free Lunch Referendum, whereby Oh wanted to provided free school meals only to impoverished schoolchildren, whereas the Democratic Party wanted to provide free meals for all schoolchildren, which Oh discounted as a populist measure. The turnout rate for this referendum did not reach the necessary criterion, so the vote was invalidated and, consequently, Oh resigned. At the consequent by-election of 2011, Park Won-soon, at the time an independent politician but who received support from the Democratic Party, was elected as mayor.

Park, once a mogul in the civil activist community, implemented diverse policy changes to create a more inclusive city, which substantially dissolved the political antagonism that emerged under the administrations of Lee and Oh (Byeon 2014). The orientation and method of urban planning has changed considerably. First of all, the Seoul city government attempted to remedy the 'side effects' of the previous profit-driven (re-)development practices. Based on decision-making by the civic committees concerned, the city government curtailed the building of large-scale infrastructure, such as the Han River Renaissance Project which lacked a detailed management plan and caused an enormous financial burden. Exit strategies for the NTP and urban renewal projects were implemented, including cancelling NTP designation and subsidising the sunk costs of the housing redevelopment association (Chung 2014). It is also worth mentioning that the city government commissioned comprehensive research on the Yongsan disaster and published the white paper on the eve of the incident's eighth anniversary promising a memorial hall to commemorate the victims (S-J. Kim 2017). Instead of large-scale urban redevelopment, emphasis was placed on urban regeneration policies as an alternative scheme of urban space management, addressing issues such as community building and historic preservation. This change includes a shift in the nature of urban planning, from the narrow focus on the design of urban infrastructure, to accounting for more diverse social dimensions. In the process of urban planning, civic participation is emphasised to avoid unilateral decision-making. When preparing for the comprehensive urban planning framework of Seoul 2016, 170 representative citizens from across the demographic spectrum were involved, including youths (Seoul Metropolitan Government 2016). Besides the management of urban space, Park embraces the sharing of economic and social innovation to boost social economy and to foster communal relationships in neighbourhoods through diverse projects of community building.

This paradigm shift in urban policy led to the expansion of urban governance that accompanied the change of the city's political landscape as well. Initially, Park governed with the support from the majority in the city council that remained affiliated with the Grand National party, along with support from civic organisation groups. After the 2018 local election, the city administration became even more consolidated, with the Democratic Party increasing its lead over the opposition Grand National Party, taking 102 (92.7 percent) of 110 seats, up from 77

(72.6 percent) of 106 seats from the 2014 local election. In the city council, the opposition party nearly disappeared, as one-party dominance emerged. Furthermore, under Park's government, the growth in the number of citizen committees is remarkable, rising from 130 in 2011 to 194 in 2017 (Figure 3.1). As many critical scholars and leaders of NGOs are invited to various kinds of committees, critical opinions from leaders in a variety of civic groups have been incorporated into urban governance. Influential urban researchers were also appointed to important posts in city agencies and think tanks.

But with the Seoul Metropolitan Government essentially under a one-party rule, and the current left liberal urban regime incorporating critical voices from civil society into its governance, the politics involved with the implementation of urban policies has become hollowed out. The oppositional forces shrunk substantially, whilst civic groups seem to hardly express any more dissent apart from some diffused attacks of the conservative political forces at the national level. From this constellation a post-political city emerges with the formation of urban governance. The emergence of the post-political city in Seoul is observed in two recent cases: the opening of Seoullo 7017, and the 'Air Pollution Roundtable' that both took place in May 2017.

The Seoullo 7017 project involves the transformation of the Seoul Station overpass, which was built in 1970, into a 1.7-kilometre-long walkway for pedestrians, echoing New York's High Line Park. The goal of this project is to create the walkable city, through the connection of 17 passageways. Designed by Dutch architect Winy Mass, winner of Seoul Metropolitan Government's 2015 international design competition, Seoullo 7017 comprises of more than 24,000 trees and 228 plant species, a series of small cafés, performance stages, and shops. Whilst Seoullo 7017 has

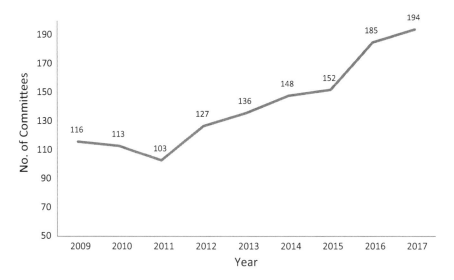

FIGURE 3.1 Changes in the number of citizen committees

many similarities with the mega-projects of Cheonggyecheon and Dongdaemun Design Plaza, serving as a new tool of urban boosterism to bring a new dimension to Seoul, it differs from these previous projects with regard to the weight given to the civic voice.[3] A citizen committee of 35 members was formed for the Seoullo 7017 project, being comprised of professors, experts, residents speakers, and city councillors. The committee convened at least five times, though only the minutes to the second session were disclosed to the public on the Seoul Metropolitan Government homepage. A live broadcast, streamed through the official web TV channel of the city government, began with a speech from Park before showing the architect Winy Mass respond to every question and suggestion from committee members during a two-and-a-half-hour meeting. Considerable efforts were made to persuade nearby merchants and residents concerned about the traffic congestion to support Seoullo 7017, and to disseminate and promote plans for Seoullo 7017 to citizens by organising a working group such as the '7017 observatory', which was managed by civic activists to play a role as a mediator between citizens and the Seoul government.[4]

Despite the city government making great progress in establishing communication with citizens, civic participation in the planning of Seoullo 7017 is still viewed by civil society groups and citizens as insufficient, particularly when compared to the level of citizen involvement with the New York High Line (H-J. Kim 2015). In New York, the 'Friends of the High Line', a civic organisation founded in a community board meeting, played a leading role in staging a marketing campaign, raising funds, and gaining support from the city council (Ascher and Uffer 2015). In contrast, a top-down approach run by the city government dominated the Seoullo 7017 project, resulting in the marginalisation of stakeholders and citizens during the project.[5] This comparison is well expressed in the dialogue between two architects who were familiar with public architecture in Korea, stating that "whereas Highline Park is formed by citizen's initiative, in case of Seoullo, from the beginning city government made a decision and changed its usage . . . This is somewhat 'old fashioned'".[6] After crucial decisions were made by the leadership and city officials, civic participation was encouraged only in a limited scope and in the expected direction. Whilst the effectiveness and sustainability of Seoullo 7017 is still controversial,[7] the critical voices were not organised into a collective dissenting body, and the lack of the political is evident.

Another example of Seoul becoming a post-political city is found in the case of the 'Air Pollution Roundtable', a large-scale outdoor event organised by the Seoul Metropolitan Government which took place on 27 May 2017; 3,000 citizens, including experts, environmental groups, and the media, filled the Gwanghwamun Square and sat around 244 tables to discuss the development of air quality policies. The topics of discussion were pre-determined by the roundtable organisers and presented to roundtable participants on a big screen, and the participants were asked to engage in a timed debate on each topic, with their moderated responses subsequently presented on the screen as well (H. Kang 2017). As the timetable for the roundtable shows (Table 3.2), the tightly organised time plan contained civic

TABLE 3.2 Timetable of the 'Air Pollution Roundtable'

Time	Programme	Details
16:00–17:00 (60 minutes)	Registration	Watch pre-event performances, show video clips, provide information about discussion
17:00–17:15 (15 minutes)	Introduction	Introduce VIPs, explain what causes particulate matter and the efforts taken to improve air quality
17:15–18:40 (85 minutes)	Discussions	• Have roundtable discussions on diagnosis and resolutions (per table, 30 minutes) • Interview and discuss with main opinion providers (all, 25 minutes) • Vote on major agenda items, wrap up discussions (per table, 30 minutes)
18:40–19:00 (20 minutes)	Review and group photo	• Review from the mayor of Seoul, announce future roadmap, watch performances

Source: Material from the Seoul Metropolitan Government.

participation. Discussions comprised three parts, with (1) roundtable discussions on diagnosis and resolutions (30 minutes), (2) interviews and discussions with the main opinion providers (25 minutes), and (3) a brief vote on major agenda items and a wrap-up of discussions (30 minutes). The limited time allocated for the roundtable did not make genuine discussion and deliberation about air pollution feasible. Furthermore, after citizen discussions, the mayor of Seoul was supposed to conclude the roundtable with the announcement of a future roadmap for the city. Faced with this tight time plan, such a mayoral proclamation would be only possible if consensus from the discussions was already foreseen and established before the roundtable was organised. Adhering to the perspective of the post-political city discourses, the possibility of any dissent and the need for deliberation is not taken into serious consideration in plans of participatory democracy, as seen in the roundtable. As the restored Cheonggyecheon was viewed as no more than a space of spectacle at the expense of historical and environmental values (Cho 2010), the massive scale of the roundtable at Gwanghwamun Plaza would be described as a spectacle of civic participation without any sincere consideration of dissent.

Conclusion

The previously discussed weakness of civic participation could be treated as a momentary feature, as South Korea continues to transition from an authoritarian to a civic participatory regime. However, it is important to acknowledge the structural conditions which enforce post-political ideologies in the urban setting. Above all, the centralisation of power within the political landscape lowers the interest in urban politics, deterring the emergence of a critical oppositional force towards the local government, except amongst some academics and NGOs which remain keenly interested in the negative consequences from neoliberal urban policy. Accordingly, criticism from academics and civic groups is much weaker during Park's administration than for the former mayors' projects, as the main counter-hegemonic bloc against neoliberal power (as embodied by the administrations of former mayors such as Lee and Oh) has seized power and now controls the Seoul city government. This is the reason why discourses on the post-political city are now relevant; the post-politics in Seoul does not simply manifest as the submission of civil society to "hegemonic consensus that no alternative to liberal-global hegemony is possible" (Swyngedouw 2009, 608). Rather, the Seoul Metropolitan Government emphasises the importance of civic participation, though the admittance of the alternative scheme to previous neoliberal malaise seems to enforce an arranged consensus. Furthermore, time pressure plays an important role in the emergence of the post-political condition in Seoul. To facilitate their re-election into the mayoral office every four years, or to facilitate their participation in the national presidential election, the mayors of Seoul can hardly afford to increase the processing and implementation time for urban projects and policies, which will inevitably result in an uncertainty of the bottom-up deliberative approach. Preference tends to be given to visible outcomes in a short time period which would gain media attention. Under such circumstances, even the continuous expansion of citizen participation would lead to the anticipated results conforming to the leadership of the Seoul Metropolitan Government, thereby reinforcing the emergence of the post-political city. Following the political shift from conservative to liberal ideologies after the 2017 impeachment of Park, notions of inclusivity and public participation in matters of governance have been implemented not only within the Seoul Metropolitan Government but also across the nation, which makes the emergence of post-political conditions within the wider political domains of South Korea a likely outcome for the future.

Notes

1 In this chapter, 'politics' is defined as the presence of political antagonism in addressing socio-political or economic problems and issues. In contrast, 'post-politics' represents the lack of such contentions dynamics.
2 "2명 중 1명이 "黨만 보고 시도지사 찍었다, 공약 모른다" [One in Two say they 'Voted for the Party, Not the Governor'] (*Chosun Ilbo*, 22 June 2018). http://news.chosun.com/site/data/html_dir/2018/06/21/2018062104421.html.
3 Although the Cheonggyecheon project did allow for civic participation during the planning process, civic involvement was still considered inadequate and insufficient. Similarly, plans for the Dongdaemun Design Plaza were criticised for their lack of collaboration with the merchants in the surrounding areas, even though the project claimed to boost the vibrancy of the Dongdaemun Market.
4 See www.seoulcity.co.kr/news/articleView.html?idxno=121534.
5 "A Heartfelt and Valuable Gift" (*Dong-A Ilbo*, 13 June 2017). http://www.donga.com/en/Search/article/all/20170613/951456/1/A-heartfelt-and-valuable.
6 See *Remark Press*. 2017. "What Seoullo 7017 Left Behind." [Interview with Lee Jae Jun, Lee Seok-tae, and Lee Jae-jun]. https://remarkpress.kr/boardPost/104834/8.
7 For example, "Seoullo 7017, Mayor Park's Choenggye Stream?" (Dunbar 2017).

References

Ahn, Y. 2006. "A Preliminary Review on the Causes of Central Concentration in the Capital Region of Korea." *Geographical Journal of Korea* 40 (1): 69–81. [In Korean]
Ascher, K., and S. Uffer. 2015. "The High Line Effect." *Council on Tall Buildings and Urban Habitat, New York*, p. 227.
Bae, Y. 2013. "Decentralized Urban Governance and Environmental Collaboration in South Korea: The Case of Hyundai City." *Pacific Affairs* 86 (4): 759–783.
Beveridge, R., and P. Koch. 2017. "The Post-Political Trap? Reflections on Politics, Agency and the City." *Urban Studies* 54 (1): 31–43.
Byeon, C. 2008. "Critical Evaluation on the Policy Decision-Making Process and Policy Effects of the New Town Projects as Urban Regeneration Methods." *Space and Society* 29: 176–208. [In Korean]
———. 2013. "Analysis of Vicious Cycle of Policy Failure: Case Study on the New Town Project in Seoul." *Space & Environment* 44: 85–128. [In Korean]
———. 2014. "Structural Attributes and Legacies of Neo-Developmentalism and Policy. Suggestions to Overcome Its Challenges: Case Study on the Mayorships of Lee Myung-bak and Oh Se-hoon." *Democratic Society and Policy Studies* 25: 13–50. [In Korean]
Cho, M. R. 2010. "The Politics of Urban Nature Restoration: The Case of Cheonggyecheon Restoration in Seoul, Korea." *International Development Planning Review* 32 (2): 145–165. [In Korean]
Chosun Ilbo. 2018. "Voter Turnout Highest in 23 Years." June 14. http://english.chosun.com/site/data/html_dir/2018/06/14/2018061401043.html
Chung, J. 2014. "The Issues and Improvements on the Exit Strategies of Newtown and Urban Renewal Projects." *Korea Real Estate Review* 24 (4): 7–24.
Crouch, C. 2004. *Post-Democracy*. Cambridge: Polity Press.
Dunbar, J. 2017. "Seoullo 7017, Mayor Park's Cheonggye Stream?" *The Korea Times*, May 11. www.koreatimes.co.kr/www/opinion/2017/05/197_229179.html
Ha, S-K. 2004. "Housing Renewal and Neighborhood Change as a Gentrification Process in Seoul." *Cities* 21 (5): 381–389.
Kang, H. 2017. "Gwanghwamun Democracy 2.0: Air Pollution Roundtables." *Korea Exposé* 29 May. https://www.koreaexpose.com/gwanghwamun-democracy-air-pollution-roundtables/
Kang, M-G. 1998. "Understanding Urban Problems in Korea: Continuity and Change." *Development and Society* 27 (1): 99–120.
Kim, H-J. 2015. "Launch of the Seoul Station 7017 Project: Significance and Future Challenges." National Assembly Research Service Report 952: 1–4. (In Korean).
Kim, H-M., and S-S. Han. 2012. "Seoul." *Cities* 29 (2): 142–154.
Kim, S-T. 2016. "Thoughts on The Decentralization and Korean Local Autonomy." *Korean Journal of Local Government Studies* 19 (4): 1–24. [In Korean]
Kim, S-J. 2017. "White Paper on 2009 Yongsan Disaster Out." *The Korea Times*, January 19. www.koreatimes.co.kr/www/nation/2017/01/113_222441.html
Lee, J. Y., and C. Anderson. 2012. "Cultural Policy and the State of Urban Development in the Capital of South Korea." In *The Politics of Urban Cultural Policy*, edited by C. Grodach and D. Silver, 85–96. London and New York: Routledge.
Lee, S. Y. 2017. "Cities for Profit: Profit-Driven Gentrification in Seoul, South Korea." *Urban Studies* 55 (12): 2603–2617.
Lee, Y-S., and E-J. Hwang. 2012. "Global Urban Frontiers through Policy Transfer? Unpacking Seoul's Creative City Programmes." *Urban Studies* 49 (13): 2817–2837.

Shin, H. B. 2009. "Property-Based Redevelopment and Gentrification: The Case of Seoul, South Korea." *Geoforum* 40 (5): 906–917.

Shin, H. B., and S-H. Kim. 2016. "The Developmental State, Speculative Urbanisation and the Politics of Displacement in Gentrifying Seoul." *Urban Studies* 53 (3): 540–559.

Sonn, J. W. 2010. "Contesting State Rescaling: An Analysis of the South Korean State's Discursive Strategy against Devolution." *Antipode* 42 (5): 1200–1224.

Swyngedouw, E. 2009. "The Antinomies of the Postpolitical City: In Search of a Democratic Politics of Environmental Production." *International Journal of Urban and Regional Research* 33 (3): 601–620.

———. 2014. "Where Is the Political? Insurgent Mobilisations and the Incipient 'Return of the political'." *Space and Polity* 18 (2): 122–136.

Seoul Metropolitan Government. 2016. *Urban Planning of Seoul*. Seoul: Seoul Metropolitan Government. https://seoulsolution.kr/sites/default/files/gettoknowus/%5BBrochure_En%5D%20Urban%20Planning%20of%20Seoul_2016.pdf

Yoo, J. H. 1993. "A Study on the Local Autonomy System in Korea: The Politics of Decentralization." *Korea Observer* 24 (2): 151–167.

Weber, M. 1969. "The Nature of the City." In *Classic Essays on the Culture of Cities*, edited by R. Sennett, 23–46. New York: Appleton-Century-Crofts.

Wilson, J., and E. Swyngedouw. 2014. "Seeds of Dystopia: Post-Politics and the Return of the Political." In *The Post-Political and Its Discontents: Spaces of Depoliticization, Spectres of Radical Politics*, edited by J. Wilson and E. Swyngedouw, 1–22. Edinburgh: Edinburgh University Press.

4
BACK TO THE LAND
Post-political utopias of organic living

Karl Beelen

Introduction: back to the land

I am ploughing my way through remote agricultural plots and fields close to the South Indian town of Tiruvannamalai. It is late morning, and I have taken an autorickshaw looking for the new farmstead of Gouthami and Suresh, located some ten kilometres out of town. Although the sun is reaching its zenith, there is still a fresh and pleasant breeze in the air in these weeks following onto the end of monsoon season. The exact location of the farmstead proves hard to find, as we turn left and right looking for the right direction. I point my driver onto a dirt track. When we pass by some local farmers on the road, the driver asks them where to find the new farmhouse of Gouthami and Suresh, but we only received some quizzical looks. Finally, the question seems to dawn on the man: "*Aiyar vidhaa?!* You mean the Brahmin's house?" Once we rephrase our destination in such terms, we get prompt and accurate directions.

I was searching for Gouthami and Suresh's house whilst visiting Saritha, another back-to-the-land farmer who had just resettled here from Chennai. As a town, Tiruvannamalai is entirely organised around the hallowed presence of Annamalai Hill, an outlier of the Eastern Ghats mountain range that dominates every view in town. Culturally, the town is best known for its splendid and ancient Arunachaleswarar Temple and for the ashrams that grafted themselves deeply into the town's spiritual and globally connected economic landscape. This landscape of new age ideas and farming opportunities also acts as a magnet for aspiring back-to-the-land farmers in Chennai, such as Suresh, Gouthami, and Saritha.[1]

I am here to join a weekend meetup of aspiring farmers in pursuit of a more organic, natural, and sustainable lifestyle. This is a fairly spontaneous gathering, and much like myself and my host Saritha,[2] all of the participants have travelled close to 200 kilometres from the state capital Chennai down to this three-story residential house in Tiruvannamalai, which acts as the venue for this gathering. None of the participants are formally farmers; some of them did convert to farming recently, but did so starting from more affluent and educated backgrounds. Most of them, however, work as software engineers, act as consultants, own private businesses, or run shops down in Chennai; typically, they would have met at earlier meetings and talks over in Chennai, where they work and live.

This 'back-to-the-land' movement is widely entangled and interconnected, and extends beyond Chennai's immediate sphere of influence. The term 'back to the land' refers to middle-class urbanites with no farming backgrounds who are looking for land outside the city to start new farms. Typically, these farms would be based on organic principles of cultivation (to be discussed in detail in the following sections). Apart from Tiruvannamalai, the movement's advocates and supporters can be found throughout the entire southern Tamil Nadu State. Yet in spite of this seeming distance, Chennai remains the city where most of their lives seem to converge. It is the place where they make their living, the fount of their budding farming knowledge, and historically one of the main hubs where the back-to-the-land movement in South India has emerged. As India's fourth most populous city, and the capital to one of the country's most urbanised states (Census of India 2011),[3] Chennai figures centrally within the movement's grassroots networks of knowledge circulation. More crucially perhaps, the city is also the hub where most of the imaginations and aspirations of the movement seem to emerge, including exasperations towards city life.

The concurrence of the two—evading the city whilst remaining rooted in it—is no matter of circumstance. This liminal position of being both in and out of the city, both out on the land and tied up in town, is in fact indicative, I argue, of reconfigured state-civil society relations emerging in the cities of South India. It is symptomatic of the fact that the city's rural hinterland represents vital points of contention (and potential allegiance) between civil society and the state—even whilst the city's hinterland is rapidly being built up and urbanised, exacerbating its disappearance.

In this chapter I am lining up my fieldwork with back-to-the-land protagonists in Chennai to retrieve their dispersed legacy as a (post-)political space. This legacy is strung politically between the expansion of the city and its unwieldy institutions of urban (state) governance, on the one hand, and the continuing efforts of a growing number of individuals and groups, on the other, who are seeking to carve out an alternative within the time span and the possibilities of their own (middle-class) lives.

'Back to the land' is a term whose roots lie in the English Romantic movement of the 19th century. Having been adapted to different regions and time periods over time, back-to-the-land genealogies may appear to advocate for a move away from the city and into the land, but in reality contain many contradictory motives and aspirations. I am repurposing the term here to refer to a diverse group of people, ranging from organic farmers and aspiring agriculturists to vegetable shop owners, retirees, and software engineers with a penchant for farming. Their motivations and ideas revolve around organic smallholder farming, no-input cultivation, self-reliance, indigenous crop varieties or native cattle breeds, and a retreat from city life—all of which amount to 'farming' lifestyles that try to break away from their earlier middle-class backgrounds and careers in the city. I argue that they mobilise and advocate particular ideas about the environment and heritage, whilst looking for alternatives to the future(s) bestowed on them by urbanisation, the city or the state, and its institutions. But a weakness in the back-to-the-land movement lies in the ambiguity and incompleteness of the back-to-the-land participants' actions and motives. Back-to-the-land farmers seek to vacate the city and restart their lives on the land. At the same time, the means, networks, and motivations that might allow them to do so also keep them rooted in urban soil.

On the one hand, back-to-the-land motives are clearly evasive in that they seek rural farm land, healthier living standards, higher standards of education, or other forms of fulfilment outside the limits of the 'mechanical' city and its rather restrictive institutions. This escape often happens in defiance of prevailing policies, or in the absence of more established channels to influence and envisage developments in their own immediate (urban) environment. Yet on the other hand, back-to-the-land motives remain inevitably grounded in their frequent middle-class belongings. Although the prospects of a future life on the land beckon strongly and set a horizon for action, back-to-the-land protagonists remain trapped in two ways. Firstly, they are trapped by the city and the moorings that it offers them in terms of income, aspirations, capital, and means. Secondly, they are trapped by their middle-class status. As they return to the land, their distinct lifestyle—whether it is a new age, organic, or consumerist one—inherently throws them back onto long-standing social hierarchies of caste, land tenure, and day labour, as in the case of Suresh and Gouthami. Unless back-to-the-land aspirants fully move out to the land and subscribe to all the risks and discomforts that this move entails, the trappings of a perceived *jamīndār*-like status awaits them with every watchman, or labourer, that they hire.[4]

It is this liminal position of back-to-the-land farmers that I seek to explore in this chapter. Back-to-the-land ideals are 'peripheral' in more than one sense, positioned in between city and land, future and heritage, and on the border of the urban and the rural. As will be shown throughout this chapter, back-to-the-land logics piggyback on urban infrastructures that not only pull farming plots and ranches geographically within reach of the city, but also help vacate these lands in the first place (as their previous owners and tenants move off the farm). Thus, the 'peripheral' quality in back-to-the-land ideals in this context also refers to one of the most dominant and persistent tropes in the Indian political imagination since the country's independence from British colonial rule in 1947: that of the 'village'. In a country that is still largely rural in spite of the massive urban transformations it has witnessed over the last few decades, the nation's political imagination and agenda continues to be informed by notions of villages, farmers, and farmer distress.

In this context, it may seem counter-intuitive to focus on a relatively 'marginal' group of back-to-the-land farmers whilst perceivably 'real', low-income farmers and their enduring state of economic duress continue to rule the national political agenda. In a country where farmer suicide is rife, and where election campaigns are built on distributing state money to hundreds of millions of mainstream 'chemical' farmers,[5] the motivations and inspirations of back-to-the-land farmers could not possibly be more contradictory.[6]

To address these contradictions, I take inspiration from James C. Scott's work (2009) to argue that there is relevance in describing state-making and governance from the decentred perspective of its margins.[7] The main argument of this chapter is, therefore, at least in part, also methodological. If the post-political is to gain analytic traction in describing emerging forms of urban environmental governance in South Asia, it will need to factor in those who are moving 'the other way' as well, either because they seek refuge from the status quo, or because they remain too unorganised to be co-opted into any such formal consensus building. To this end, the chapter will make use of interviews conducted from 2015 to 2016 with a group of approximately 20 farmers and other relevant individuals. Although the quotes in this text may not necessarily reflect this, I have also continued following some of these back-to-the-land farmers over subsequent years.

Decentring environmental post-politics

Environmentalist debates in India, Guha argues, originated in the environmental actions that marginalised groups took up to fight deforestation and environmental degradation caused by mineral extraction and large hydro-development projects (Guha 1994, 2000; Guha and Martinez-Alier 1997). This focus gradually shifted to cities in the wake of India's 1990s economic liberalisation and the staggering urban growth in the aftermath of those reforms. Writers like Baviskar (2011) in particular, shifted the inherently socio-environmental focus of earlier debates towards the country's new urban middle-class lifestyles, and their interconnections with (bourgeois) environmental consciousness, nature conservation, and the position of the urban poor (Follmann 2016, 123).

Following economic liberalisation, the Tamilnadu state and Chennai's municipal administrations started to adopt such 'global' ambitions, bringing into play discourses of 'modernisation', 'world class cities' (Beelen, Gerritsen, and Srivathsan 2010), 'beautification' (Coelho and Raman 2013), and 'resilience' (GCC 2017; Roul 2017), in their urban planning and development policies. As Chennai turned into a city of business process outsourcing services, IT companies, and global car manufacturers, engineers from the middle classes began to make up a sizeable part of the city's population of 4.7 million (a figure that rises to 8.7 million within the larger Chennai Metropolitan Area [CMA]; see Government of India 2011). To accommodate its sprawling industries and residential developments, Chennai's municipal city limits were repeatedly expanded to incorporate almost twice the city's area; in a similar vein, the CMA expects to expand its jurisdiction to roughly eight times its current size.[8]

Post-liberalisation developments like these were typically marked by a concurrent and conspicuous rise in middle-class consumption. Glitzy malls, cafés, residential complexes, gated communities, and flyovers index Chennai's spread-out urban landscape, serving as tokens of its middle-class citizenry and their new global consumerist belonging (e.g., Brosius 2014). Such evolutions, plans, aspirations, or policies cannot be viewed in isolation from recent environmental contestations. From the environmental degradation over coal-fired energy plants in the northern Ennore wetlands (Govindarajan 2017), Tamil Nadu state's clampdown on farmer oppositions against the construction of new greenfield expressways (Kumar 2018), to the political contestation over the Tamil Nadu police's violent crackdown on anti-Sterlite protesters in Thoothukudi[9] and the city's catastrophic floods of 2015 attributed to illicit, state-condoned infilling of the city's wetlands and lakebeds for residential constructions (Arabindoo 2016). All these cases signal an underlying trend that urban India is developing primarily at the expense of the natural and social environment (Balakrishnan 2019).

Parallel to these contestations against environmental degradation—though typically not in direct opposition to it—middle-class aspirations in Chennai have retained, or reclaimed, a strong penchant for authenticity, for localness, and for the natural (Gerritsen 2015). This is evident and has been observed in the trope of farming and back-to-the-land desires. I argue that back-to-the-land motives offer an adjustment to the tropes of bourgeois environmentalism and neoliberal consumerist aspirations because they highlight rising powerful undertones of nativist belonging, heritage, and authenticity, as witnessed both in majoritarian state politics and in middle-class consumerist desires. For example, the issue of native Indian cattle breeds seems to resonate with popular desires to protect native (Tamil) breeds from foreign imports,[10] and triggers widespread political protests such as the 2017 pro-Jallikattu street protests in Chennai that opposed the Indian Supreme Court's ruling to uphold a national ban on traditional Tamil bullfighting.[11]

However, to factor in back-to-the-land farmers as part of the environmental debates in India, the question of how they are organised plays a significant role. In their assessment of environmental post-political practices, Oosterlynck and Swyngedouw (2010, 1579) signal that "research on urban and environmental change has been concerned primarily with policies/politics but has been strangely silent about 'the political'". They argue that opposing (environmental) political questions and demands cannot be reduced to classes, groups, or indeed movements, but that participation in (post-)politics is conditional upon opposing such demands or interests assembling themselves as groups.[12] So far, I have been labelling the back-to-the-land farmers as a 'movement', but that is somewhat disputable given the participants' lack of formal organisation as social actors. Moreover, the farmers self-identify through a range of other identities, including organic farmers, new age farmers, and agriculturists.

Rather than focussing on the various forms of governmentality that farmers might be involved in, this chapter works from the ontological question back-to-the-land farming poses to the framework of the post-political. In particular, can the post-political framework influence the spectrum of everyday environmental aspirations in the Indian or South Asian context? Back-to-the-land farmers aspire to bring about change, yet they lack the kind of unified organisation that is presupposed under post-political conditions. To help bring the disarrayed nature of back-to-the-land actions within a more analytical frame, the following section underlines three modes of interaction that back-to-the-land farmers bring to the environmental debates in India. These include their resistance to state capture and atomised desire for breaking away, their belief in the organic as an achievable part of everyday utopia (be it as part of a market-based endeavour), and their belief in the authentic and the rural as an integral part of urban middle-class belonging.

Atomised desire for breaking away

Back-to-the-land discourses have a long genealogy of acting both with and against the state. Its farmers seek to act against uniformisation, and against state capture. They present a frontier in the periphery of the city-state and its institutions, from which initiatives continue to sprout. That frontier typically materialises in the notion of the 'organic'. 'Going organic' is not only a matter of leading a healthier life free from pesticides, stressful work conditions, and other problems associated with urban living, such as air pollution. Organic farming is also a way of antagonising dominant 'chemical' farming methods advocated by the State through its many schemes (of offering electricity, water pumps, pesticides, fertilisers, etc.) to mainstream its farmers or to win over their votes. In moving back to the 'village', organic back-to-the-land aspirants hope to learn from their farmer-neighbors whilst gradually converting them into the more sustainable and self-sufficient lifestyle of the organic. This kind of transition tends to be conceived as a self-replicating process, spreading from farmer to farmer, until finally it gathers enough momentum to sway the opinion of the state.

The organic as part of an every (market) utopia

The back-to-the-land movement offers a rather confusing landscape of lifestyle aspirations, blended with strong beliefs in alternative ways of cultivation and living. These beliefs tend to conform to the shibboleths of organic smallholder farming, whilst at the same time sustaining its members' entrepreneurial (IT-based) preoccupations with up-scaling and business expansion. Back to the land processes are not absolutely utopic, nor do they represent a very consolidated set of ideas, but rather follow Davina Cooper's (2013) description of a loosely interactive landscape of 'everyday utopias'. Cooper frames everyday utopias as the anticipatory space between the everyday and the future that capture what is doable, feasible, and worth pursuing in view of the present. But they also anticipate something more, something beyond the horizon of what can realised in the present (Cooper 2013, 4). The everyday utopias established by back-to-the-land farming often revolve around particular readings of the organic, whose principles are moulded to meet the farmer's needs.

Farming as heritage

Ideas driving the back-to-the-land movement are predicated on the implicit notion of farming as the quintessential representation of an Indian authenticity, heritage, and identity (that demands active involvement and maintenance). The back-to-the-land movement (re)presents a mixture of heterodox knowledges and aspirations, circulating practices and exasperations, which are partially non-conformist in stance and partially reinforcing of the status quo.

From the Gandhian era up to the present, the future of India has typically been portrayed as belonging in its villages (cf., e.g., Khilnani 1999; Nandy 2001, 16; Prakash 2002). The figure of the village underscores a constitutive tension in Indian conceptions of the modern city (Gandy 2008). This tension continues to play out in Indian and Tamil Nadu state policies on urban governmentality and urbanisation, even in the current era after India's 'urban turn' in the 1990s (Prakash 2002).

After the 73rd and 74th Constitutional Amendments were passed by the Indian Parliament in 1992, governance in India was decentralised, giving decision-making power to the local municipal bodies and rural panchayats.[13] The panchayat raj—a millennia-old system of political representation—refers to a strongly decentralised form of local self-governance. Mahatma Gandhi (1869–1948), leader of the Indian independence movement, advocated for this process of decentralisation as the foundation of India's post-independence political system.[14] The 73rd and 74th Amendments were efforts to wed India's highly centralised ideal of administration as enshrined in the country's constitution of 1950 with Gandhi's much more decentralised idea of self-governance at the village level (*gram swaraj*).

The back-to-the-land movement is clearly influenced by that intellectual heritage, as it geographically and institutionally resonates with the decentralising legacy of the 73rd and 74th Amendments. As the city's municipal boundaries expand, its regulatory framework for taxation and land-use redevelopment pushes farmland further away from the core urban area. Back-to-the-land geographies also piggyback on this transformation, seeking out opportunities to experiment with alternative non-urban farming lifestyles and self-governance in farther-off places like Tiruvannamalai. Yet, the expanding frontier of roads, highways, and other state infrastructures also continues to push into rural lands as a consequence of CMA expansion.

Empirically speaking, to talk of back-to-the-land farming in the context of Chennai may thus seem contradictory at first: on the one hand, media accounts, popular discourse, and casual conversations in the city convey the impression that Chennai has a deep-rooted nostalgia and desire for village life, authentic food, and farming. On the other hand, CMA government statistics (CMDA 2019), looming political reforms, and a glance at the larger city map reveal that there is very little (if any) space in the city for practices such as farming.

On the whole, this section has attempted to see individual 'heritage farmers' as the product of, and as intrinsically shaped by, urbanisation and India's changing landscape of the urban. In short, it sees them as a particular embodiment of contemporary citizen-activists who are both urged on and repelled by the opportunities and misgivings of the city's fast-changing geographies of mass-produced food, health hazards, and environmental degradation.

Breaking away—Tiruvannamalai

> *The urban community has forgotten the [farmers'] language—they're not speaking it, they'd have forgotten the lot. [. . .] What puts us off on the urban front is the total disappearance of this [farming] community from the urban community's radar. That is something that really turns us off.*
>
> —Gouthami

It is early 2016. After an extremely wet and dramatic monsoon season, life in Tamil Nadu has gradually returned to normal. With public bus connections being restored, I met up with Saritha, one of the back-to-the-land farmers mentioned at the beginning of the chapter. Saritha has recently moved back to Tiruvannamalai, and her house is in a recently developed housing area, only a few hundred metres behind the main road. Loud cries of peacocks on a mandapa rooftop betray an ashram's presence immediately behind the compound wall at the end of the street.

This is Tiruvannamalai, a dusty inland town of temples and ashrams strung out along a busy road at the foot of Mount Arunachala.[15] Once a year, thousands of pilgrims gather here to walk along the foot of the mountain. Yet, at only half a day's bus ride west of Chennai, the town also acts as a stronghold of organic farming. The town's arid, upcountry climate doesn't put off farmers, and the town's organic community has been thriving. Over the years it has seen smallholder farming initiatives, community-run organic farming schools, and larger farming start-ups and investment schemes specialising in new agricultural products such as lemon grass oils.

Saritha's house is a two-story dwelling, which doubles as an informal community venue and a community training centre. On this particular occasion, it also serves as a collective dormitory for people from Chennai. The house is filled with aspiring farmers who have travelled to the town for the weekend, eager to learn about their host's experiences. Over the following two days I listened to their stories and heard about the vicissitudes of life and work in the city, the demands of working in the IT sector, and the dubious benefits of leading a modern working-day life in the city.

Switching to farming—especially organic farming—is not an easy path, and many of the guests are hesitant about making the switch. But these are not existing farmers. In fact, they are not farmers at all, and continue to juggle life, work, and family in the city—a hand-to-mouth existence that, according to some of these individuals, only leads to a vicious cycle of work and expenses without any prospects for life outside 'the machine of the city'. They are looking for a life outside the system, but they wonder whether organic farming will allow for that alternative.

Tiruvannamalai acts as one hub in a growing network of places where people come to look for cheaper agricultural land in pursuit of a more 'natural' lifestyle away from 'the city'. Tiruvannamalai seems to meet these requirements, offering a more balanced and simpler lifestyle that is off the grid, out of town, and outside of mainstream ideologies and practices for contemporary living. As we meet and talk over the weekend, people talk of sustainable food practices (natural, organic, or otherwise) and invoke heritage lifestyles of 'traditional farming' to give shape to their rather personalised imaginations of a better future—one that is off the grid and located outside of the confines of the urban. In sum, these individuals at Tiruvannamalai imagine the 'future' as going 'back to the land'.

The weekend segues into further encounters. Gopal, Krishnan, Gouthami, and Suresh recently made the switch from city careers to a farming life. Their children now visit the private Marudam school nearby,[16] one of the more palpable links tying the Tiruvannamalai network together. Gopal is an affluent city professional who has recently built a house in Tiruvannamalai. The ecological construction techniques that he used on his house are those taught by the same foundation that built the school. Krishnan is a self-confessed 'high school dropout' from Chennai who specialises in forestry, and gradually turned himself into a self-trained consultant in organic farming and organic licencing. I knew Krishnan and Gopal from earlier events over at Restore, a collectively run organic farming shop in Chennai. Gouthami and Suresh, on the other hand, were new to me. When I ask which place they had moved to Tiruvannamalai from, Gouthami chuckles and says,

> *All of us are from Chennai. My husband and I are from Chennai, traditionally doing our software engineering jobs and things like that. I was working with a professor in physics. It was always nagging us inside that this is not how you do it. We had been contemplating for long years [how to move to farming]. Then we understood that we had to move—but how to design it? Once we decided that we had to move out of Chennai . . . we didn't move as a community. It is just the two of us.*

Gouthami and Suresh bought four acres of land, on which they do 'very low labour intensive' farming. This type of smallholder farming is premised on the use of a motorised tiller, a farming tool condemned by most of the organic farming community for compressing the soil and killing its natural aeration. After their very first yield of organically produced paddy rice last year ("we were lucky" they add), they are now planning on restructuring their land into small cultivation beds. Moving out from Chennai to Tiruvannamalai, Gouthami and Suresh decided against 'remote farming' and the tensions that it could bring. 'Remote farming' is when the owner of the farm hires someone to live on the farm site and look after the farm's day-to-day affairs. This allows the farmer-owner to farm 'remotely', commuting between his farmstead and his Chennai abode, but also creates tensions for the farmers. Many back-to-the-land farmers that I spoke to relate stories of disappearing yields, absenteeism, and other difficulties in finding 'honest' managers and workers. The culprit of their complaints is often the rural employment scheme known as the Mahatma Gandhi National Rural Employment Guarantee Act (MGNEGA), which some back-to-the-land farmers credit for pushing up wages and bringing down motivation amongst day labourers.[17] Such complaints reinforce the stratifications between conventional farmers, labourers, and the middle-class urbanites, highlighting the persistent rifts underneath their back-to-land trappings.

Gouthami and Suresh soon determined that, rather than hiring someone else to look after their farm, they themselves would be tilling their land and residing on it right from the start. They resolved to give up their Chennai address, relocating to Tiruvannamalai, where they built their own house.[18] Although they continue to travel to Chennai for work, they cite '(Chennai) city hypocrisy' as being one of their main motives to move, stating that "hypocrisy is something that we couldn't take in Chennai. That is what kickstarted us. The hypocrisy of 'just because I wanted to do physics having to be associated with an institute'—that was killing me". For them, back-to-the-land farming is a delicate balancing act between the autarky of living directly off the land, retaining employment in Chennai, and maintaining the ability to carve out some remaining time for study and reading. Gouthami recognises the middle-class elements in their farming lifestyle, and admits "we don't actually call ourselves farmers", claiming that this "just wouldn't be fair on those who are". As she elaborated,

> *I don't want to call myself a farmer, nor does my husband, because that's not a wise thing to do. Because with submitting yourself to such a "neglected" thing of society you're going to incur yourself many issues. I enter into their vicious circle of battling, battling, battling. Both of us are very clear that, yes, this is a lifestyle. This farming is our lifestyle, that's all. We're willing to work with the soil, we're willing to work with nature, we are going to do our best. But beyond that, all of us aspire for something a little beyond, where you finetune your mind.*

On the village frontier

Back-to-the-land farmers present a rather dispersed but well-networked group of people typically from middle-class urban settings, who seek to step out of the mould of standard city-based careers and lifestyles. They do so by adopting radically divergent lifestyle practices by returning to farming, or by contemplating such kinds of futures that represent a radical departure from their current urban conditions. The alternative pathway of going 'back to the land' promises self-reliance and a breakaway from unhealthy models of consumption; it refutes normative, unilinear visions of engineering careers in 'the city', and promises a rupture with the perceived 'hypocrisies' of fashionable modern city living.

Such back-to-the-land movements are not unique to this corner of India, nor to this particular juncture in time. They have emerged at various locations and moments throughout the 20th and 21st centuries.[19] Recently published books like *Moong over Microchips: Adventures of a Techie-Turned-Farmer* (Iyer 2018) underscore the extent to which back-to-the-land narratives have currently caught the wider imagination of audiences throughout present-day India. In the book, Iyer relates his rational transformation from being a manager swamped in IT work, and plagued by Mumbai's persistent air pollution, to being a farmer tilling legumes (*moong*) in upland Maharashtra. However, the epistemologies and ideas of back-to-the-land ideas are rather polygenous and go far beyond such books. According to Ramachandra Guha (2000), the origins of the movement dates back to English Romantic environmentalists such as Edward Carpenter, whose 1889 *Civilization, Its Cause and Cure* served as a kind of textbook for the back-to-the-land movement,[20] as well as to the ideas of the Gujarati saint-politician Mahatma Gandhi. This suggests that back-to-the-land doctrines are underpinned mostly by figureheads of national or international standing, but pioneers such as G. Nammālvār or Subhash Palekar point to the vital specificity of the regional (Tamil) context—a point I will return to.

Like no other, Gandhi represents the extent to which Indian cultural principles are enshrined in the Indian village (Nandy 2001). Essentially a back-to-the-land figure himself (Guha 2000), Gandhi's intellectual heritage denotes a deep ideological attachment to rural life:

> *An ideal village [. . .] It will have cottages with sufficient light and ventilation, built of a material obtainable within a radius of five miles of it. The cottages will have courtyards enabling householders to plant vegetables for domestic use and to house their cattle. The village lanes and streets will be free of all avoidable dust. It will have wells according to its needs and accessible to all. It will have houses of worship for al, also a common meeting place, a village common for grazing its cattle, a co-operative dairy, primary and secondary schools in which industrial education [i.e., vocational] education will be the central fact, and it will have Panchayats [village councils] for settling disputes. It will produce its own grains, vegetables and fruit, and its own Khadi [hand-spun cotton]. This is roughly my idea of a model village.*
> (Mahatma Gandhi quoted in Guha 2000, 23)

Born in an urban family, Gandhi only began to rework his political framework after his late 40s, when he began to seriously explore rural India (Ibid.). His attachment to rural life is still reflected, one could argue, in the epistemological underpinnings of the back-to-the-land movement. This can be observed on two levels. On the one hand, Gandhian ideas seem to be echoed in the movement's penchant for rural land, and in its attraction to environmental forms of farming that are typically organic, soil-friendly, natural, and self-reliant, and do not require external inputs or genetic modification (Münster 2014). Instead of seeing farmland as being inert, inefficient, and in need of additives, Gandhian ideas see soils as being 'built', 'liberalised', and brought to life again by relying on the cow for tilling, and on growing different crops that require less labour costs and less irrigation.

On the other hand, the same discourse can also be observed in the back-to-the-land movement's concern to salvage soil cultivation as a relevant material and socio-cultural practice towards preserving the nation's agrarian heritage in the context of rapid urbanisation,[21] including the city's anxieties over securing food supplies and healthy living. Half a century after the start of India's Green Revolution, I suggest that this growing concern for authenticity (Gerritsen 2019) and health is now mobilised through the notion of 'the organic', and is being reinforced as an *urban* concern.[22] However, the requirements for engaging in organic farming paradoxically position back-to-the-land initiatives into distinct geographies that are strongly coproduced by urbanisation, urban governance, and the ensuing urban land speculation.

Organic utopias—'We don't speak the organic language, we speak money to them'

Back-to-the-land concerns graft themselves on this evolving landscape of urbanisation in India and on the anxieties and opportunities that emerge in tandem with this transformation, as seen from the rise of organic farms near cities. Here the notion of the 'organic' also seems to split the back-to-the-land movement along a deep-seated rural-urban divide. For back-to-the-land farmers, going organic means to fulfil desires about tilling and dwelling on land and actively proselytising that idea among local farming communities. In contrast, for existing local farmers, however, this fixation on the organic appears primarily as a fancy preoccupation of city-dwellers, with little relevance or potential for their own livelihoods and futures. The back-to-the-land aspirations of these middle-class farmers may be projected onto the rural landscape, but smallholder farm aspirations still project onto the city as a space that can fulfil desires for a better livelihood and future.

Certainly where land gains value in relation to economic speculation and development in urbanising regions, 'going organic' does not seem to bestow the best future potential for most farmers. With organic rice priced at 65 rupees (£0.72) per kilo, as opposed to 'chemical' rice being available free of charge in Tamil Nadu State food banks or priced at 45 rupees (£0.40) in Chennai food stores, the consumption of organic produce is far beyond the reach for the average smallholder farmer. Yet, this is also the case for organic production, as smallholder farms could never afford the temporary lack of income and the amount of extra labour that converting to organic farming typically involves. In light of these considerations, the question then becomes, how do back-to-the-land farmers imagine this transition to be viable or sustainable? Many of the back-to-the-land farmers have put a lot of thought into this question, and as Gouthami says,

> We have to come down and sit with them. We have to speak their language and work with them for several years to go. Our intentions are not to change them. We are nobody to change them. They have been doing this [farming work] for several decades. We want to work as a community with them. [. . .] We don't speak the organic language to them. We are letting them observe us. We tell them: you actually spent 3,000 rupees [£33] on your pesticides. I spent zilch on pesticides. We speak money to them.

There are strong ties between the organic movement and the back-to-the-land farmers in India. The organic movement within Tamil Nadu has a long history, mostly revolving around key figures like the late G. Nammālvār, agronomist and organic farming activist who had been active since the 1970s until his death in 2013.[23] Organic farming activism also has a long history within the country, especially in advancing the concerns of low-income farmers vis-à-vis the concerns of the state, and in opposing larger industrial initiatives and so-called chemical farming at large. I argue that the back-to-the-land movement is firmly rooted in the organic movement, with both movements sharing similar aspirations, arguments, and ideas. But it remains crucial to give credit to the imaginations and memories of ancestral farming and of living on the land, which serve as powerful motivations in how urban dwellers construct and carry out alternative livelihood pathways.

This genealogy ties Tamil Nadu's 'going-organic' movement into discourses surrounding environmental heritage conservation and urbanisation. Understanding the strong ecological undertones of back-to-the-land strategies in Indian cities like Chennai would require a re-reading of the history of the environmental movement in India in relation to the Green Revolution (see Shiva 1991),[24] organic farming, and the persistent notion of agrarian crisis that has shaped environmental debates since the Gandhian era (see Reddy and Mishra 2009). The outcome and implications of the Green Revolution continue to inform prevailing policy measures towards urban food production as devised by the Indian central and regional states today. Its long-lasting legacy continues to cast dark shadows into the future, offering a dystopian canvas that the back-to-the-land movement is partly predicated upon. 'Chemical farming' and its perceived social, environmental, and health side effects are recurrent features in shaping the instincts, dispositions, and aspirations of back-to-the-land farmers, motivating them to consider a new—and typically organic—mode of life outside of the city and free of chemicals.

On the whole, what is astounding about the back-to-the-land movement is not the extent or the strength of the networks it has established, but rather the variegated assembly of aspirations, practices, followers, and beliefs that it assembles. Most of these divergent beliefs and aspirations do share one common factor, in that they revolve around the figure of the 'farmer'. The farmer figure seems to evoke both one's own rural family lineage (and that of India more broadly) and beliefs about how consumption, social life, or knowledge should be re-organised 'sustainably' in Indian society. This starts from making radical changes in one's livelihood, most notably by moving back to the land and embracing the creed of the 'organic' or the 'natural'.

Back-to-the-land farmers seem to fit with that interpretation of reimagining a different way of life than that offered by mainstream forms of consumption and living. They strive for a more natural or organic alternatives (similar to other movements like eco-*swaraj*, natural farming, and so on). Starting a farm is in part a private, small-scale utopia; it is where an individual engages in a lifestyle makeover by adopting an alternative 'good-life' way of living to circumvent the realities of urban living. Antagonisms between farmers still emerge, but tend to be narrated through the topic of organic conversion—how existing farmers can be encouraged to switch to organic production practices. However, when turned into reality, many individual utopias that emerge from back-to-the-land farming clash with the harsh realities of agrarian living. Apart from crop insecurity, a risk of bodily harm, and a lack of economic profitability, realising one's organic farm utopia also brings in deep-seated caste distinctions that have to be circumnavigated throughout everyday life, as seen in the case of Gouthami and Suresh (see Gill 2009). To Gouthami and Suresh, their current lifestyle may be about sustainable farming techniques, but to their neighbours they remain upper-caste city folk with the freedom to return to Chennai on any given day. They are aware of this caste-based tension, admitting that the back-to-the-land farm can remain exclusionary and is not a dream attainable by all, which is something the movement will need to rectify in the future:

> *The organic world serves the elite mass. I can't afford it. Forget the farmer. Even a normal, middle-class man in Chennai city can't afford it. If it's going to be that kind of a thing I don't want to be a part of that kind of a movement. I want to be part of a movement where I am able to talk real sustainability. Labour is not a sustainable thing—that is a fact. We need to come to grips with that fact that labour is not a sustainable thing, even in a country like India. Even if you're going to confine yourself to a corner of the world like Tiruvannamalai.*

Back-to-the-land politics?

Perhaps the most paradoxical feature of the back-to-the-land movement in Chennai remains its ambivalent position to commercialism, capitalism, and consumerism. Back-to-the-land farmers typically depict their own newly adopted agrarian lifestyle in commercial terms, rather than through their concerns for sustainable production. To outsiders like me or fellow farmers, organic farming is pitched as a code that needs cracking, centring their own input as newly converted farmers on logistical intuitions, stubborn experimentation, or meticulous financial accounting. This may be an expression of predominant curricula in India—the farmers I met would typically have backgrounds in supply chain management, economics, or engineering. But this dominant pitch is also in blatant contradiction to their own deep-seated desires for change, and the alternative farming principles that they subscribe to when labelling themselves organic.

My argument about the post-political in this chapter has been to show that atomised, individual urban lifestyle choices like those witnessed by the back-to-the-land movement should not be put down as being 'apolitical' simply because they don't aggregate politically, or because they are inherently consumerist and only superficially committed to socio-environmental engagements (Barendregt and Jaffe 2014). Rather, I have argued that back-to-the-land motivations are deeply political, but that they are organised in non-confrontational and almost atomised ways that reject wholesale ideological conversion. I lifted out three aspects of back-to-the-land farmers to illustrate this point: the aspiring farmers' atomised desire to break away, their resort to organic farming as an everyday utopia, and their sustained belief in farming as a dwindling heritage in need of restoration. The latter in particular is symptomatic of a larger trend in Indian urban middle-class society embracing narratives of nativist belonging, heritage, and authenticity.

This does not relieve back-to-the-land ideas of due criticism, more particularly of back-to-the-land's implicit premise that social justice and sustainability could be organised through the marketplace (Ibid.). In this article I have sought to show that the back-to-the-land's reliance on organic food, and technically reconfigured supply chains, does not wed easily with sustainable principles of organic farming and locally supported production, but that they certainly can't be reduced to consumerist lifestyles either.

Instead, the case of the back-to-the-land farmers suggests that there is a middle ground between middle-class consumerism and activism when it comes to post-political environmental organisation. Methodologically this chapter has built a case for widening the scope of the post-political to include voices that carve out alternatives through collaboration and alliance, yet back away from more formal political organisation.

Acknowledgements

I would like to thank the Indo-German Center for Sustainability at IIT-Madras, Chennai, for funding most of the fieldwork that this article is based on. I am equally grateful for the comments of the participants and organisers of the ARI conference that led to this book. Most importantly, I would like to thank all the back-to-the-land farmers—aspiring or real—for generously sharing their time and insights with me whenever I showed up in town. I hope this chapter does justice to their cause.

Notes

1 I use the term 'new age' here to refer to a specific subset of back-to-the-land farmers in Tiruvannamalai who were attracted to the town both due to its local availability and cost of land. Moreover, the presence of alternative schools like Marudam, a collectively run organic farming school for children that works entirely outside the formal Indian schooling system (which is another attraction factor as well).
2 Saritha is part of the collective organic shop Restore on the East Coast Road. Restore and the Organic Farmer's Market both stem from the same group of people who ostensibly initiated the organic movement in Chennai.
3 In the 2011 Census of India, an area is considered 'urban' if it is either governed by a corporation, municipality, or town panchayat, or when 75 percent of the area's male population is found working in non-agricultural occupations (provided such 'census towns' have over 5,000 inhabitants and a density of 400 inhabitants per square kilometre or more).
4 I am using the Tamil word of *jamīndārs* to broadly refer to landlords (*zamindars*) who depend on peasant workers to carry out cultivation work in the fields.
5 'Chemical' is a catchword used by organic farmers. It refers to the standard, mainstream, state-subsidised farming practices which depend heavily on the use of pesticides, fertilisers, water, and fast-growing rice varieties. 'Chemical' inputs allow mainstream paddy

farmers to achieve the two to three harvests per season, which farmers critically depend on for their livelihood.
6 Cf. the concurrent schemes of Krushak Assistance for Livelihood and Income Augmentation and Pradhan Mantri Kisan Samman Nidhi, introduced respectively by the Biju Janata Dal–led Odisha State government and by their rival, the Bharatiya Janata Party (BJP)-led central Indian State Government, in the run-up to the upcoming 2019 General Lok Sabha elections. The BJP's scheme financial assistance of up to 6,000 rupees (GBP£66) for each of the approximately 120 million smallholder farmers owning land of two hectares or less in size (Krishnan 2019).
7 In his book *The Art of Not Being Governed*, James C. Scott argues that "the huge literature on state-making, contemporary and historic, pays virtually no attention to its obverse: the history of deliberate and reactive statelessness. This is the history of those who got away, and state-making cannot be understood apart from it" (2009, x).
8 Like all metropolitan authorities in India, Chennai's Metropolitan Development Authority (CMDA) is administered by federated state authorities. CMDA is a nodal planning agency which falls under the Tamil Nadu State's Ministry of Housing and Urban Development. This is in contrast to the Greater Chennai Corporation, the city's municipal administration which is considered a civic body.
9 Sterlite is a UK-owned mining company, whose copper smelting plant in Thoothukodi (Tuticorin) is linked to widespread environmental degradation and health concerns (such as cancer) in the Thoothukodi District of southern Tamil Nadu.
10 Similar policies can be witnessed on the level of national legislation. See the BJP Finance Minister Piyush Goyal's 2018–2019 budget announcement of launching the Rashtriya Gokul Mission, an initiative to allocate 7.5 billion rupees (GBP£82.8 million) to support farmers who promote indigenous breeds of cattle (Koshy 2019).
11 The Jallikattu protests emerged after the Indian Supreme Court in New Delhi ruled to uphold a ban on the sport, which was itself the result of an earlier legal case filed by animal rights organisations. Tamil historian A. R. Venkatachalapathy writes that "Jallikattu partisans have much to thank the animal lovers for" and that as a result of their legal action, "Jallikattu now stands enshrined as *the* symbol of Tamil cultural pride" (2018, 276).
12 "The field of politics/the political is thus split into two: on the one hand, the political which stands for the constitutive lack, the ontological condition of society's absent ground or, in other words, the impossibility of securing a stable ground/basis on which to found society (like 'community', 'class', 'the people', 'the nation'); whereas politics stands for the ontic, the always contingent, precarious, and incomplete attempt to institutionalise the social, to offer closure, to suture the social field, to let society coincide with community" (Oosterlynck and Swyngedouw 2010, 1581).
13 The 73rd Amendment created village councils at the *gram* (village), *taluk* (county), and *zilla* (district) levels of administration. However, decisions on assigning actual powers and budgets to those panchayats are left up to Indian federated state legislatures.
14 Gandhi's idealised conception is typically referred to as *gram swaraj* (village self-governance).
15 The Arunachala Mountain goes by various other names, including Arunagiri and Annamalai, after which the town itself is named.
16 "Marudam Farm School is run by The Forest Way—a registered non-profit charitable trust involved in education, afforestation, environmental education, organic farming and more. Marudam Farm School receives no funding from the government. The school is registered under the rules & regulations in force in the Indian state of Tamil Nadu". Accessed 20 July 2018 at www.marudamfarmschool.org/.
17 The Mahatma Gandhi National Rural Employment Guarantee Act (2006) guarantees a minimum of 100 days of unskilled manual work to households in rural India.
18 In constructing their house, Gouthami and Suresh avoid 'countrylike constructions' such as thatched roofs, which are popular amongst other back-to-the-land farmers like Gopal. Gouthami and Suresh hired a local traditional craftsman as their mason. 'Traditional' here

refers to ruling construction industry conventions, such as armoured concrete floors and reinforced concrete cement finishing.
19 In contemporary (South) India, one of the main motivations that back-to-the-land farmers subscribe to is organic food production and the advancement of organic farming tenets through the conversion of smallholder farms.
20 Edward Carpenter was an associate of William Morris, another mainstay in the English back-to-the-land movement, and founder of the arts and crafts movement. Edward Carpenter eventually founded a commune and farm, growing its own food and vegetables and baking its own bread, described as a true Arcadia (Guha 2000, 15–16).
21 "Indeed, the very idea of the modern city has for much of the post-colonial era played an ambiguous role within Indian conceptions of national identity with its deep ideological attachment to rural life" (Gandy 2008, 126).
22 The Green Revolution began in the 1960s to boost agricultural food production, but led to environmental problems with pesticide pollution and unsustainable soil practices,
23 Others include Thalaanmai Uzhavar Iyakkam (Self-Reliant Farmers Movement).
24 Also referred to by back-to-the-land protagonists as 'chemical farming'.

References

Arabindoo, P. 2016. "Unprecedented Natures? An Anatomy of the Chennai Floods." *City* 20 (6): 800–821.
Balakrishnan, P. 2019. "Governing India's Many Spaces." *The Hindu*, February 8. www.thehindu.com/opinion/lead/governing-indias-many-spaces/article26206909.ece
Barendregt, B., and R. Jaffe. 2014. *Green Consumption: The Global Rise of Eco-Chic*. London: Bloomsbury.
Baviskar, A. 2011. "Cows, Cars and Cycle-Rickshaws: Bourgeois Environmentalism and the Battle for Delhi's Streets." In *Elite and Everyman: The Cultural Politics of the Indian Middle Classes*, edited by A. Baviskar and R. Ray, 391–418. New Delhi: Routledge.
Beelen, K., R. Gerritsen, & A. Srivathsan. 2010. "Climbing up the Rank Ladder: Imagining Chennai as a World-Class City." *Monu Magazine* 13: 97–105.
Brosius, C. 2014. *India's Middle Class: New Forms of Urban Leisure, Consumption and Prosperity*. London: Routledge.
CMDA (Chennai Metropolitan Development Authority). 2019. "Masterplan Land Use Maps." http://cmdalayout.com/landusemaps/landusemaps.aspx.
Coelho, K., and N. V. Raman. 2013. "From the Frying Pan to the Floodplain: Negotiating Land, Water, and Fire in Chennai's Development." In *Ecologies of Urbanism in India: Metropolitan Civility and Sustainability*, edited by A. Rademacher and K. Sivaramakrishnan, 145–168. Hongkong: Hongkong University Press.
Cooper, D. 2013. *Everyday Utopias: The Conceptual Life of Promising Spaces*. Chicago: Duke University Press.
Census of India. 2011. Office of the Registrar General of India. http://www.censusindia.gov.in/2011-Common/CensusData2011.html
Follmann, A. 2016. "Delhi's Changing Riverfront: Bourgeois Environmentalism and the Reclamation of Yamuna's Floodplain for a World-Class City in the Making." In *Ville et Fleuve En Asie Du Sud*, edited by H. Joshi and A. Viguier, 169–194. Paris: Presses de l'Inalco.
Gandy, M. 2008. "Landscapes of Disaster: Water, Modernity, and Urban Fragmentation in Mumbai." *Environment and Planning A: Economy and Space* 40 (1): 108–130.
GCC (Greater Chennai Corporation). 2017. *GDC Disaster Management Plan 2017*. Chennai: GCC. www.chennaicorporation.gov.in/NorthMonSoon2017/cdmcb.pdf

Gerritsen, R. 2019. "Food Walks and Street Doctors: Health and Culinary Nostalgia in a South Indian City." In *Food Identities at Home and on the Move: Explorations at the Intersection of Food, Belonging and Dwelling*, edited by D. Crenn, C. Desuremain and R. Matta. London: Bloomsbury Academic Press.

Gerritsen, R. 2015. "Chennai Beautiful: Shifting Urban Landscapes and the Unanticipated City." In *Visual Homes, Image Worlds: Essays from Tasveer Ghar*, edited by C. Brosius, S. Ramaswamy and Y. Saeed. New Delhi: Yoda Press.

Gill, K. 2009. *Of Poverty and Plastic: Scavenging and Scrap Trading Entrepreneurs in India's Urban Informal Economy*. New Delhi: Oxford University Press.

Govindarajan, V. 2017. "Activists Claim Tamil Nadu Hid a Key Coastal Plan to Facilitate Ennore Creek Encroachments." *Scroll.in*, June 21. https://scroll.in/article/840922/activists-claim-tn-hid-a-critical-coastal-plan-in-order-to-facilitate-ennore-creek-encroachments

Guha, R., ed. 1994. *Social Ecology*. Delhi and New York: Oxford University Press.

———. 2000. *Environmentalism: A Global History*. New Delhi: Oxford University Press.

Guha, R., and J. Martinez-Alier. 1997. *Varieties of Environmentalism: Essays North and South*. London: Earthscan.

Iyer, V. 2018. *Moong over Microchips: Adventures of a Techie-Turned-Farmer*. Penguin Books India.

Khilnani, S. 1999. *The Idea of India*. London: Penguin.

Koshy, J. 2019. "Not Really Bullish on Native Cow Breeds." *The Hindu*, February 2. www.thehindu.com/business/budget/750-crore-to-nurture-native-cow-breeds/article26155987.ece

Krishnan, V. 2019. "Everybody Loves a Farmer." *The Hindu*, April 12. https://frontline.thehindu.com/cover-story/article26643343.ece

Kumar, B. A. 2018. "Why Are There Protests over a Highway?" *The Hindu*, June 30. www.thehindu.com/news/national/tamil-nadu/why-are-there-protests-over-a-highway/article24301276.ece

Münster, D. 2014. "A Letter to Subhash Palekar, Natural Farmer." *RCC Perspectives* 6: 23–26.

Nandy, A. 2001. *An Ambiguous Journey to the City: The Village and Other Odd Ruins of the Self in the Indian Imagination*. New Delhi: Oxford University Press.

Oosterlynck, S., and E. Swyngedouw. 2010. "Noise Reduction: The Postpolitical Quandary of Night Flights at Brussels Airport." *Environment and Planning A: Economy and Space* 42 (7): 1577–1594.

Prakash, G. 2002. "The Urban Turn." In *Sarai Reader 02: The Cities of Everyday Life*, edited by R. S. Vasudevan, J. Bagchi, R. Sundaram, M. Narula, G. Lovink, and S. Sengupta, 2–7. Sarai: The New Media Initiative.

Reddy, D. N., and S. Mishra., eds. 2009. *Agrarian Crisis in India*. New Delhi and New York: Oxford University Press.

Roul, A. 2017. "Can Chennai's City Disaster Plan Ensure Resilient Future?" *Down To Earth*, December 2. www.downtoearth.org.in/news/natural-disasters/can-chennai-s-city-disaster-plan-ensure-resilient-future-59268

Scott, J. C. 2009. *The Art of Not Being Governed*. Singapore: NUS Press.

Shiva, V. 1991. *The Violence of the Green Revolution: Third World Agriculture, Ecology, and Politics*. London: Third World Network.

Venkatachalapathy, A. R. 2018. *Tamil Characters: Personalities, Politics, Culture*. New Delhi: Pan Macmillan India.

PART II

Post-politics in heritage governance

5
BETWEEN STATE AND SOCIETY
Heritage politics in urban China

Yujie Zhu

Introduction

The interaction between state and society in urban Chinese heritage practices can be usefully examined through the insights of post-political scholarship, which draws attention to the lack of dissent between the state and civil society in Europe and America. With the shift to an Asian context, however, the concept of 'civil society' warrants further examination, particularly with regard to the relation between the state and society. Scholars, especially historians (Kuhn 1994; Strand 1990), often question the origin and nature of the term 'civil society' and its effectiveness, particularly in non-Western contexts, in analyses regarding the relation between the state and society. This chapter does not intend to define or question the concept of 'civil society' and how it is practised in China. Nor do I intend to celebrate the Western narrative of democratic development or argue that China is an exceptional social environment, completely separate from Western discourse. Instead, the notion of 'civil society' in this study serves as a device to analyse certain forms of communication between the state and society that can offer insight into how different Chinese societies function. Specifically, the chapter examines various examples of recent city developments and civic activities in Xi'an to understand how cultural heritage has been used as a soft but powerful tool for urban governance, whereby disagreements between societal actors and governing bodies have become obfuscated.[1]

Heritage in contemporary Chinese cities

Today, China has become one of the focal points in cultural heritage and urban governance. Its rapid economic development in cities has had a profound impact upon its heritage landscape. Since the start of the 21st century, local governments have formed alliances with heritage experts to facilitate the urban renewal of historic cities for the purpose of city branding and theming (Zhang 2006). The booming heritage tourism industry in historical cities plays a significant role in processes of historical branding, which stimulates both the regional and national economy (Oakes 1993; Zhu 2018b).

Major cities throughout China are redesigning themselves as exemplary architectural and cultural examples of key periods in their past (Zhu 2018a). These cities have become both the focus of a global 'tourist gaze' (Urry 1990) and a prominent stage for socio-cultural representations of hegemonic discourses of Chinese nationalism (Oakes 1993). Xi'an, a major city centre in the northwest of China, is following a similar pattern of urban renewal. The capital of Shaanxi province, a prominent region for cultural development, Xi'an is regarded as the cradle of Chinese civilisation, and this national mythos is an important component in Chinese identity formation. As the former capital of 13 dynasties and the eastern end of the Silk Road, the city (known as Chang'an in the Tang dynasty) was the most spacious, and often the most populous and civilised urban centre during China's imperial eras (Xiong 2000).

In response to national policies of the Western Development Plan (*xibu dakaifa*)[2] launched in 2000, Xi'an has capitalised on its historic heritage as a cultural resource for tourism consumption (Zhu and Yang 2017). In 2017, 180 million international and domestic tourists visited Xi'an, creating 163.3 billion Yuan (ca. £18.7 billion) in tourism revenue—this accounted for 21.8 percent of the local GDP (Xi'an Bureau of Statistics 2017). It is not an exaggeration to say that the development of this city, in particular its modernisation and globalisation, relies heavily on heritage tourism.

Heritage is used by the Xi'an government as a strategy to interpret the past though dominant historical narratives in order to justify commercial development. I argue that in contrast to other countries in Asia where local social groups and organisations might use transnational organisations to bypass local governments, local authorities in China use heritage discourses (of beauty, pride, and fun) as an effective tool to influence urban governance for renewal and development. These heritage values of beauty and pride being evoked by the official discourses encouraged an emerging consensus between the state and society. This burgeoning consensus positions voices of contestation as temporary and fragmented with civil groups lacking sustained political strategies to counter the power and extent of dominant modes of city redevelopment. The ability of the state to dominate urban space and the ways in which it is interpreted and experienced, essentially locking out effective contestation, has led to a situation that falls into the logic of post-politics within the context of heritage.

Yet at the same time, this chapter illustrates that local organisations and social groups have alternative ways of interpreting their social and cultural life of their native city, using various traditional and modern social media to increase their bargaining power and negotiate the dominant structures of authorised heritage discourse espoused by the state. Based on case studies of various cultural activities in

Xi'an, this chapter examines (a) how different social groups assert their own meaning and sense of place as a response to the rapid changes of the urban landscape and official regulations and (b) how personal and private needs are fulfilled through public channels such as social gatherings, religious education, and social media.

Rethinking civil society in China

The idea of 'civil society' comes out of a particular historical context when European society underwent rapid commercialisation and industrialisation which led to the growth of capitalism. The notion of 'civil society' initially appeared in the 16th century to describe a group of educated elites who operated as an unofficial counter-poise to the state. Civil society gained prominence in 18th-century Europe, when society sought a new relationship with the state which could offer an alternative definition of social order. This led to the emergence of the public sphere (*Öffentlichkeit*), designed to be a realm of rational, critical debate.

Since the 20th century, the concept of 'civil society' and its influence has expanded widely. Civil organisations now have distinctive and influential roles in modern society, although in practice their influence and makeup vary substantially across the world. Depending on their social and geographic context, some civil societies provide social welfare and community services, as exemplified by the Evangelical Lutheran Church in East Germany, whilst others serve on the consultative bodies of governments by offering advice on the formation of policy, such as The Compact in England, the Polish Solidarity movement from the 1980s, and the range of non-profit organisations (NPOs) in Japan. Citizens, especially from Eastern Europe, interpreted 'civil society' as an "arena of independent associational activity, free from state interference" (Perry and Fuller 1991, 663). It consisted of the "utilitarian, contractual relationships characteristic of a bourgeois society created by a modern market economy" (Madsen 1993, 188). At the same time, the state fostered the emergence of a public sphere, since the new state bureaucracies needed financial resources from free trade as well as communication channels to publicise policies (Habermas 1991). Under the growing power of the media, capitalism, and bureaucracies of the modern state, public space, initially envisioned as a platform for society to engage in deliberation and political participation, came to serve corporate and state interests. Public space increasingly transitioned to a platform for the circulation of advertisements and propaganda, a more insidious space where state, capital, and civil influence were blurred.

When we attempt to reconceptualise 'civil society' in an Asian context, we need to shift from an exclusively Western culturally bound term to a concept which takes into consideration the specificities of the regional context. As Sinologist Philip Kuhn (1994) argued, 'civil society' is a model, not a reality. China has a unique historical and cultural background. There has been no linguistic borrowing from Western social and political thought about the subject of 'civil society' in China; nor is the notion present in traditional Chinese thought. However, scholars of China studies, especially historians (see Rowe 1990; Strand 1990; Wakeman

1993; Duara 1996), use certain historical examples of 'civil society' to question the relevance of the term for the study of Chinese society.

Using the example of 'professional associations' (*fatuan*) from the late Qing and early Republican period during the 20th century, David Strand (1990) illustrates that these non-governmental bodies (such as chambers of commerce, bankers, and lawyers' associations composed of local elites) acted as independent and autonomous communities. Similarly, as William Rowe argued in his seminal work on the same period in Chinese history, *Hankow: Commerce and Society in a Chinese City*, "a substantial degree of de-facto autonomy had emerged with real power balanced between officials and the leaders of local society" (1984, 339). Most of the urban non-governmental associations appeared at the local level in the hands of gentry managers (*shen-tuan*) and gentry deputies (*weiyuan*) (Rowe 1984, 120). As Rowe (1990, 3–5) summarised, the city of Hankow had a lot in common with early modern European cities, including "the steady development of organised, corporate-style civic action and the proliferation of a wide range of philanthropic and public service institutions, designed to meet the unprecedented and specifically urban social problems faced by cities in the early modern period".

The development of the Chinese market economy and the open policy in the 1990s and 2000s have bought about rapid growth in China's civil society. There has been a large variety of civil organisations in Chinese cities and rural areas, such as NPOs registered with the state administrations for industry and commerce purposes, urban community organisations, village community public welfare or mutual assistance organisations, farmers' cooperative organisations, foreign financial aid organisations, and religious groups (Yu 2011). Terms such as *gongmin shehui*, *minjian shehui*, and *shimin shehui* have been used to refer to this nationwide phenomenon in Chinese scholarship, and all come close to being the Chinese-language equivalent of 'civil society' as espoused in the West. According to Yu Keping (2011, 65), the translations of each of these terms offer different perspectives on the notion of 'civil society'.[3] The term *shimin shehui* is the most widely used and originates from the Chinese translation of the classical Marxist text. The term *minjian shehui* was translated from Taiwanese and later adapted by mainland historians in China, whilst *gongmin shehui* was recently adopted after Deng Xiaoping's reform emphasising the 'political science aspects of the term'.

In the past decade, China has experienced dramatic and rapid changes politically, culturally, and socially. Politically, the country has continued to develop as an authoritarian country. Consequently, the state offers little space between itself and society, with the former closely monitoring the actions of the latter. State and local governments have continuously taken "the dominant position in the power distributions, controlling the public fields and all resources for collective behaviour" (Kang and Han 2011, 117). The emergence of civil society, as understood in the Western sense, has been suppressed by the power of the state. Socially, the decline of transnational institutions in China, such as environmental organisations or the 'green public sphere' (Yang and Calhoun 2007), combined with new state regulations and techniques of control, offer the state a more powerful way of governance than ever before (Zhu 2016). Along with the dramatic decline of non-governmental organisations (NGOs) and the increase of other forms of extra-governmental organisations, such as government-organised non-government organisations (GONGOs), there are no purely autonomous organisations in China that reflect the Western narratives of democratic development.

Culturally, China inherited a dynamic blend of Confucianism, capitalism, and neoliberalism that has had a strong impact on the country's recent social transition from socialism to market economy (Ikels 2006). Its modern, consumer-driven society does not offer a suitable ground for social mobilisation to fulfil the need for a public space or 'civil society' as understood in the Habermasian sense. At the same time, Chinese people are increasingly exposed to a plurality of information via multiple channels and platforms. The rapid development of new mass media, mainly blogs (*weibo*); self-led apps like WeChat; and the World Wide Web generally offer new spaces for individuals to interact with the society.

However, the question of whether the development of Chinese mass media reveals a tendency towards the loosening of political control and a trend of commercialisation is questionable. The Internet is not only used for resistance by a small number of social groups but also becomes a tool of regulation, since the state, through various government agencies, uses the Internet to increase surveillance and supervision in various ways. As a consequence of increasing online intervention by the state, the Internet has become a space where it is difficult to create genuine public debate and deliberation. Consequently, the growth of digital space is not so different from that of traditional public spaces that are heavily influenced by the state.[4] The Internet and new media serve a new supervisory tool in Chinese politics and prevent people from mobilising. A censored and surveyed virtual space does not offer individuals fertile ground for the development of autonomy and civic association. Due to the power of search engines and the increasing awareness of self-censorship, it is difficult for virtual communities to mobilise in order to make rational decisions or act towards influencing matters of urban governance or to realise notions of the common good. Instead, the formation of virtual communities often leads to temporary gatherings based on personal matters and networks, such as through shared travel, or friendship, family, and alumni networks.

Heritage governance and Urban renewal in Xi'an

Echoing national campaigns of urbanisation across the country, the current master plan (2008–2020) of Xi'an was approved by the Ministry of Housing and Urban-Rural Development in 2014. As part of this master plan, the Xi'an municipal government focusses on the promotion of heritage, in line with national policies emphasising heritage tourism as a pillar industry. Accordingly, the mayor of Xi'an city announced the launch of the Imperial City Restoration Plan in the 'Government Working Report in February 2005' (Feighery 2011; Zhu 2018a). According to the 12th Five Year Plan of Xi'an (2011–2015), the government is endeavouring to reconstruct the old city for the sake of reviving the "prosperous age" of

Xi'an as an ancient capital and the heart of Chinese civilisation (Xi'an Municipality 2005, 25). Within this umbrella project of urban renewal, three popular heritage discourses—emphasising beauty, pride, and fun—have emerged out of a series of urban renewal and heritage activities.

Xi'an's Imperial City Restoration Plan legitimises a new, distinctly urban desire for *city beautification*, which in the context of this chapter, refers specifically to improving the physical appearance of the urban landscape. Since the 1950s, Shaan'xi has been the top producer and consumer of coal in the country, and the local coal industry has left the region highly polluted. As a consequence, Xi'an became a dusty and industrial mid-western city with a high density of inhabitants and factories. To transform such an industrial centre into a tourism-friendly city, a widespread urban renewal strategy to promote the aesthetication of the urban landscape has been underway since 2000. A city planning committee, composed mainly of urban planners, heritage experts, and government officials, was created to decide the new appearance and form the urban landscape would take on, in order to reinforce the theme of cultural heritage.

For the planning committee, the beautification of Xi'an was to be realised through the selective and idealised recreation of imperial landscapes of the past, an idea that was applied throughout the city. As I have presented elsewhere (Zhu 2018a; Zhu and Yang 2017), it is material heritage that is highlighted, reconstructed, and sometimes invented so as to create an urban landscape that adheres to the theme of the Tang Imperial City. Narrow streets of the inner city have been extended to mimic the wide boulevards that divided the Tang capital in the sixth century. The demolition and revamping of these residential areas meant that a large number of local residents have been relocated to other parts of the city.

The ideology underpinning these heritage spaces is not political, but rather capitalistic and materialistic. Xi'an has gone through a process of museumification in which the function and form of public spaces and buildings have been transformed into heritage objects on display to visitors for their consumption (Zhu 2015). Such transformation does not only narrowly refer to shopping in the souvenir markets, but also to the 'romantic consumption' of affective and emotional experiences (Zhu 2018b). Visitors can walk or cycle on the city wall, purchase copies of relics in the souvenir shops, taste traditional food in the local food court, and watch cultural performances in the city's entertainment parks.

Finally, the urban regeneration of Xi'an fosters and facilitates the development of national pride amongst the Chinese population. During the Tang dynasty, Xi'an was the capital of the most distinctive and glorious dynastic period in China. The Tang dynasty saw the city reach a climax of cosmopolitanism and cultural development as a result of the city's connection with the world through regular cultural and business exchanges. The official narrative created by the newly constructed or invented heritage sites references this glorious historical period in order to articulate and reinforce the city's goal of cultural resurgence and the restoration of national confidence.

In this process, the historic narrative displayed through public space offers a visual representation that acts as a form of political propaganda to help the contemporary Chinese population establish a connection with a past associated with state-oriented forms of Chinese civilisation. The physicality of recreated heritage environments (mostly an imagined and simplistic version of Tang cityscapes) in urban space evokes within the population feelings of permanence, eternity, and authenticity attached to the past. For citizens inhabiting and visiting these heritage landscapes created by the contemporary Chinese state, to be 'good' residents in the city not only means following codes of good behaviour in public space, but also entails developing a mental and emotional connection with the history of the nation. The newly established heritage landscape in Xi'an becomes an affective practice to evoke people's national pride. The association of Xi'an's heritage spaces with positive sentiments of pride and affection compels ordinary citizens to embrace and accept such landscapes, also making it difficult for people to criticise and challenge these landscapes, thereby echoing post-political conditions whereby consensus between the state and society is enforced. Yet as the next section shows, such post-political consensus is not absolute, because whilst societal dissent may be difficult in the Chinese context, it is not non-existent nor impossible.

Contested landscape

The development of Xi'an's urban landscape has led to the rearrangement of its spatial environment and the loss of many old traditional neighbourhoods. A number of social groups residing in the city, especially the middle-class, express concerns and frustrations about the dramatic changes that have happened in Xi'an, such as the increasing cost of living, increasing pollution, heavy traffic due to mass reconstruction, and social displacement and gentrification. Various social groups such as religious communities and intellectual reading groups have spoken out in the city to highlight and address these concerns, albeit by using different methods to open up public spaces where dissent is possible and that resulted with different outcomes, as illustrated here.

Religious education

Xi'an's Muslim Quarter is a square-mile district that is home to 30,000 Chinese Muslims known as the Hui, which is about half of the city's Hui population. Muslims first arrived in Xi'an through the Silk Road networks from Central Asia and became powerful merchants that facilitated trade between Xi'an, China, and Central Asia. Xi'an's Muslim Quarter has grown over the centuries into a collection of densely populated streets packed with shops, restaurants, and residential buildings. The area has 12 mosques located within 13 streets and alleys. The Ming-era Great Mosque, the earliest landmark in the Muslim Quarter, is a highly significant cultural centre and tourist destination.

Xi'an's initial urban renewal project in the early 2000s included a massive redevelopment of Muslim Quarter that requires the relocation of the local Hui residents. Faced with an official request of mass relocation, the Muslim community argued that this would threaten the community's religious and cultural identity. A self-organised religious community (*siguanhui*) was formed, and became instrumental in leading and strengthening the community to resist the city's renewal project. Mosques become the centre of public debate and social mobilisation, resembling the public spaces as envisioned by Habermas (1974). Through daily gathering and discussion, the community maintained a strong sense of ethnic and religious cohesion, which supported them through their fight for recognition and status (Zhai and Ng 2013).

The Hui community's strength and persistence in opposing their relocation eventually led the municipal government to alter their plans for the Muslim Quarter's renovation. Xi'an's government had initially intended to turn the area into a tourist destination that centred on its architecture, especially its mosques. The residents' fight to stay forced officials to redesign their plans such that the presence of the Muslim community is acknowledged, and to enable the Muslim community's involvement in shaping the urban landscape. As a consequence, the local government allows the Muslim communities to develop business within the Muslim Quarter on their own terms, without intervention from external investors.

The local government further proposed that Hui residents could participate in the development of a Muslim food street as a popular tourist destination in Xi'an. The popularity of this food street, and the money it draws from tourists, has motivated many Hui families to open businesses in the area. Today, the area is named the 'Hui Food Street' and has become a mass of neon-lit restaurants and shops packed around the Great Mosque. The dramatic development of the area has caused a huge shift in the cultural practices of the local community. Large portions of the Hui community, especially the younger generations, have increasingly focussed on their businesses, and neglected other aspects of community life.

The development of a community-managed food street celebrating Hui culture was initially treated as a victory by residents of the Muslim Quarter in the early 2000s, but although the community was able to stay in the neighbourhood, there has been a long-term loss of social cohesion and religious belonging. This loss is particularly concerning because the resistance against relocation, and the fight for inclusion in the urban planning process, was originally driven by the Akhunds, the religious leaders of the Great Mosques, who now find themselves not only having to fight to preserve the right of the Hui to remain in the area, but also having to fight against the dissolution of their communities' foundation. The Hui campaigned to seek state recognition, which led to their becoming absorbed and incorporated into state models of urban governance that emphasises economic gain. Adhering to government encouragement for the Hui to partake in the tourism development of the Muslim Quarter by opening shops and restaurants, some members of the Hui have emulated the government in embracing economic values over societal and religious values, thereby putting the internal community cohesion amongst the Hui at risk.

Cultural salon and social media

Founded by a local intellectual by the name of Prof Chen in 2015, *Zhiwuzhi* is a cultural salon located in the centre of Xi'an. Through frequent reading groups, public lectures, and workshops, the cultural salon establishes a public space where a group of local intellectuals have the opportunity to address ideas and attitudes towards the city's culture and recent urban development. Popular topics of discussion at *Zhiwuzhi* include the efficiency of urban governance, the roles of heritage in gentrification, the attitudes towards heritage tourism, and how community participation engages with city development. These discussions echo those appearing online in WeChat accounts not only in Xi'an but throughout China.[5] Intellectuals across the country use the app to post articles and discuss social and cultural issues concerning their home cities. The people in Xi'an who attend the cultural salon might be the same people who read the WeChat posts, although given the relative ease of attaining Internet access, it is likely that the audience and readership of these WeChat discussions is actually much larger than those who attend *Zhiwuzhi* meetings.

The formations of public spaces where debates can circulate are significant counter-points to the dominant political nationalistic ideologies embedded within the heritage narratives that the city and state are attempting to impose on civic space. As the heterogeneous landscape of the lived city space is rapidly transformed through government-initiated urban theming and reconstruction, alternative spaces like the cultural salon and WeChat become important platforms for discussion and potential resistance. These public spaces, both physical and online, are not only places of indulgence, freedom, pleasure, and recreation, but also places where the middle-class can develop a community that shares similar symbolic forms, morals, values, and visions of their home cities. Such community building enables people to be recognised and valued by groups of like-minded people.

However, the influence of voices from channels such as the café and social media are still limited in their ability to bring about sustained movements towards resistance. Even though new media has provided these intellectuals innovative platforms for social mobilisation, such forms potentially exclude and alienate the working-class, who are the people most affected by the city's rapid urbanisation. More importantly, the pervasive and ostensibly positive nature of the new heritage spaces produced by the state avoids attracting open opposition by diffusing images of affluence, progress, and beauty into the regeneration of urban space. The new modes of living and narratives of cultural supremacy offered by Xi'an's recent development attract many people, especially tourists and residents that have just migrated to the city, who subscribe to state discourses that associate such heritage sites with values of beauty and fun for the purpose of their own gratification (including some of the middle-class who are involved with the cultural salon activities). In addition, both the cultural salon and social media require external financial support from private donors and corporations to maintain their daily operations and management; this means that the autonomy of these spaces, and whether these spaces are truly representative of the aforementioned notions of *Öffentlichkeit*, becomes questionable.

Discussion

The different cultural landscapes outlined previously reflect a complex and contested picture of the recent urban developments in Xi'an. Throughout the municipals government's urban redevelopment projects, the discourse of cultural heritage based around notions of beauty and nationalistic pride has been embraced by the local authorities, as a means to depoliticise and unbalance the relationship between the nation-state and the daily life of ordinary citizens. Yet various social groups throughout Xi'an have displayed individual and collective responses to changes in their social and living environments in the city. These civic groups, comprising the middle-class, intellectuals, and religious groups, are working on various forms of negotiation and resistance to reshape the relationship between the state and society. The nature and organisational forms of these civil activities vary. Some of these civic groups are social organisations (*minjian zuzhi*) such as NGOs and grassroots groups, which are registered and subject to regulation by the state, and their numbers have been dramatically decreasing since 2010. Other civil society actors and organisations are associated with universities or religious associations (*zongjiao tuanti*).

These civic groups, inclusive of NGOs, private business associations, cultural groups, and grassroots associations, exercise varying degrees of autonomy depending on their registration status, funding sources, and the issue addressed in their projects. In addition to their organisational forms, the mobilisation techniques these civil groups use also vary. Places like streets, along with spaces of commercial activity like intellectual cafés, bars, karaoke centres, and even restaurants, are recognised as part of a 'public sphere'. Such public realms of life result in an expansion of civic power against the state. This situation is not unique to Xi'an; cafés similar to *Zhiwuzhi* exist in many Chinese cities, organised around their own unique ways of facilitating critical debates of local issues. These types of cafés are often popular and remain autonomous from the government, although in some instances, certain cafés are considered local government projects and receive state funding.

Recently, the decline of traditional newspapers and the development of the Internet has introduced new elements into the dynamics of resistance (Yang 2003), allowing new forms of public debate and techniques for social mobilisation. As shown in the case of *Zhiwuzhi*, there is an emergence of a virtual community where similar common interests can be mobilised to gather a temporary, issue-specific group. The rise of online media and its unique format means people are able to use it to disseminate information, formulate goals and strategies, identify opponents, and organise events without gathering at a physical place. More importantly, online platforms potentially enable society to criticise and express dissent against state schemes, thereby bringing the political into the state-society dynamic in China.

It is certainly true that the forms of community-led resistance under discussion in this chapter have bought about important, and in some cases dramatic, change for communities. However, the impetus behind their acts of resistance is temporary, and largely concerned with immediate interests and goals. Community resistance does not engage with, or directly resist, heritage stewardship and patrimonialism; nor do these movements reject or distance themselves from notions of beauty, fun, and pride—framed by the state as the products arising from their heritage spaces— that urban renewal offers. In other words, the positive elements of beauty, fun, and pride in Xi'an's heritage discourse structures both resistance and support; it successfully evokes a set of shared and supposedly desirable values, which encourage the emergence of consensus on a national level, making it difficult for civil groups or individuals to articulate dissent or resistance.

The subtle power of Xi'an's heritage discourse has similar effects to what Erik Swyngedouw (2009) described as the condition of post-politics. As Swyngedouw (2009) argued through examining climate change politics, a post-political consensus is formed when people become a 'united humanity' to confront a common predicament or threat. The discourse of cultural heritage differs from the discourse of climate change because whilst the latter emphasises a shared threat, the former evokes values that are pleasant and celebratory. Yet the rise and acceptance of shared values in narratives of cultural heritage also lead to a similar outcome of political consensus that makes it difficult for people to resist the authorised ideologies embedded in heritage discourses, and to search for alternative meanings and values. As a consequence of the post-political condition combined with increased censorship in China, it is hard for people and groups to develop and articulate an understanding of the common good that exists beyond their own conception of a good and prosperous life. The manifestations of a public sphere as illustrated in this chapter can then be more accurately described as being composed of temporary, fragmentary, and self-interested groups without a sustainable sense of community building.

Conclusion

Recent scholarship on 'civil society' in China has shifted from a focus from examining the degree of autonomy civic actors and organisations possess, and towards acknowledging and exploring the dynamic relationship between the state and society in the form of partnership and collaboration (Teets 2009). By examining different civil groups and their relationship to heritage governance in Xi'an, this chapter moves away from conventional portrayals of state-society relationships as being solely characterised by dominance and resistance. Although the civil groups featured in this chapter did resist aspects of Xi'an's heritage schemes, especially in the early stages of gentrification and forced relocation, the chapter shows that ultimately, heritage discourses of beauty, fun, and pride serve to legitimise urban redevelopment projects, particularly when they benefit people economically. The manifestations of public spheres in Xi'an have transformed from being sites of resistance to becoming spaces of private self-interested activities. Whilst state-led practices of city transformation can be regarded as social engineering projects aimed at managing and modelling urban populations, they still allow for multiple unofficial channels to contest the hegemonic urbanism of the state. In this sense, although the term 'civil society' only exists as a conceptual apparatus, it affects the way we think about society and the authoritarian state, and continues to contribute to the hope that certain spaces might exist for different groups of people to engage with society in an experimental manner.

Notes

1 Ethnographic fieldwork was conducted in the city of Xi'an in August 2011, July to August 2014, and March 2015. Fieldwork included participant observation whilst living in the Muslim Quarter and visiting most of the heritage sites, parks, and museums of Xi'an.
2 The China Western Development Plan is a comprehensive regional development plan to boost the economies of western provinces.
3 *Shimin* focuses on the relation between citizen and the civil society. *Gongmin* focuses on the role of the public, whilst *minjian* illustrates the idea that civil society co-exists with the state and is not directly regulated. However, none of these definitions offers a perfect solution for translation of the English term, since the term 'society' should refer to *xiehui* 'associations' or *zuzhi* 'organisations'. All of the them emphasise the word *min* (the ordinary people), indicating that these organisations are groups composed of 'the people'.
4 See broader debates about the Internet as the 'new' political public sphere in Rasmussen (2014).
5 WeChat is a popular Chinese mobile app used for sending messages and payments, and is used as a social media tool to connect people.

References

Duara, P. 1996. *Rescuing History from the Nation: Questioning Narratives of Modern China*. Chicago: University of Chicago Press.
Feighery, W. 2011. "Contested Heritage in the Ancient City of Peace." *Historic Environment* 23 (1): 38–47.
Habermas, J. 1974. "The Public Sphere: An Encyclopedia Article (1964)." *New German Critique* 3: 49–55.
———. 1991. *The Structural Transformation of the Public Sphere: An Inquiry into a Category of Bourgeois Society*. Cambridge: MIT press.
Ikels, C. 2006. "Economic Reform and Intergenerational Relationships in China." *Oxford Development Studies* 34 (4): 387–400.
Kang, X., and H. Han. 2011. "Graduated Control: Research on State-Society Relationship in Contemporary Mainland China." In *State and Civil Society: The Chinese Perspective*, edited by Z. Deng, 97–120. Singapore: World Scientific.
Kuhn, P. A. 1994. *La société civile face à l'État* [Civil Society and Constitutional Development]. Paris: École française d'Extrême-Orient.
Madsen, R. 1993. "The Public Sphere, Civil Society and Moral Community: A Research Agenda for Contemporary China Studies." *Modern China* 19 (2): 183–198.
Oakes, T. 1993. "The Cultural Space of Modernity: Ethnic Tourism and Place Identity in China." *Environment and Planning C: Society and Space* 11 (1): 47–66.

Perry, E. J., and E. V. Fuller. 1991. "China's Long March to Democracy." *World Policy Journal* 8 (4): 663–685.
Rasmussen, T. 2014. "Internet and the Political Public Sphere." *Sociology Compass* 8 (12): 1315–1329.
Rowe, W. T. 1984. *Hankow: Commerce and Society in a Chinese City, 1796–1889*. Stanford, CA: Stanford University Press.
———. 1990. "The Public Sphere in Modern China." *Modern China* 16 (3): 309–329.
Strand, D. 1990. *'Civil Society' and 'Public Sphere' in Modern China: A Perspective on Popular Movements in Beijing, 1919–1989*. Asian/Pacific Studies 90 (1). Durham: Asian/Pacific Studies Institute, Duke University.
Swyngedouw, E. 2009. "The Antinomies of the Postpolitical City: In Search of a Democratic Politics of Environmental Production." *International Journal of Urban and Regional Research* 33 (3): 601–620.
Teets, J. C. 2009. "Post-Earthquake Relief and Reconstruction Efforts: The Emergence of Civil Society in China?" *The China Quarterly* 198: 330–347.
Urry, J. 1990. *The Tourist Gaze: Leisure and Travel in Contemporary Societies*. 1st ed. London: Sage Publications.
Wakeman, F., Jr. 1993. "The Civil Society and Public Sphere Debate: Western Reflections on Chinese Political Culture." *Modern China* 19 (2): 108–138.
Xi'an Bureau of Statistics. 2017. *Xi'an Statistical Yearbook 2017*. Xi'an, China: Xi'an Bureau of Statistics.
Xi'an Municipality. 2005. *The Twelfth Five-Year Plan of Xi'an (2011–2015)*. Xi'an, China: Municipality of Xi'An.
Xiong, V. 2000. *Sui-Tang Chang'an (583–904): A Study in the Urban History of Medieval China*. Ann Arbor, MI: University of Michigan.
Yang, G. 2003. "The Co-evolution of the Internet and Civil Society in China." *Asian Survey* 43 (3): 405–422.
Yang, G., and Calhoun, C. 2007. "Media, Civil Society, and the Rise of a Green Public Sphere in China." *China Information* 21 (2): 211–236.
Yu, K. 2011. "Civil Society in China: Concepts, Classification and Institutional Environment." In *State and Civil Society: The Chinese Perspective*, edited by Z. Deng, 97–120. Singapore: World Scientific.
Zhai, B., and M. K. Ng. 2013. "Urban Regeneration and Social Capital in China: A Case Study of the Drum Tower Muslim District in Xi'an." *Cities* 35: 14–25.
Zhang, L. 2006. "Contesting Spatial Modernity in Late-Socialist China." *Current Anthropology* 47 (3): 461–484.
Zhu, Y. 2015. "Cultural Effects of Authenticity: Contested Heritage Practices in China." *International Journal of Heritage Studies* 21 (6): 594–608.
———. 2016. "Heritage Making of Lijiang: Governance, Reconstruction and Local Naxi Life." In *World Heritage on the Ground: Ethnographic Perspectives*, edited by C. Brumann and D. Berliner, 78–96. New York: Berghahn Books.
———. 2018a. "Uses of the Past: Negotiating Heritage in Xi'an." *International Journal of Heritage Studies* 24 (2): 181–192.
———. 2018b. *Heritage and Romantic Consumption in China*. Amsterdam: Amsterdam University Press.
Zhu, Y., and Y. Yang. 2017. "Travelling to the Past: Xi'an and Its Revived Tang Imperial City." In *Commercial Nationalism: Selling the National Story in Tourism and Events*, edited by L. White, 64–74. Bristol: Channel View.

6

'CONNECTING EMOTIONS THROUGH WELLS'

Heritage instrumentalisation, civic activism, and urban sustainability in Quanzhou, China

Yunci Cai

Introduction

In 2013, the Chinese president Xi Jinping unveiled plans for an ambitious development strategy, the Belt and Road Initiative (BRI), aimed at enhancing the trade cooperation and infrastructural connectivity between China and the Eurasian countries, based on reinvigorating two ancient trading routes: the overland Silk Road Economic Belt (SREB) connecting China to Europe, and the 21st-century Maritime Silk Road (MSR) connecting China to the Middle East through South and Southeast Asia. The BRI seeks to revitalise the historical precedents of the Silk Road to facilitate the formation of a new world order and a re-organised world economy led by China, based on the principles of cooperation, co-existence, and shared prosperity (Zhao 2015; Xin 2017).

A major focus of the MSR is the coastal city of Quanzhou in the Fujian Province, once hub of the maritime aspect of the historical Silk Road facilitating exchanges between China and the world. In 2016, the provincial government of Fujian applied for 16 historic monuments and sites in Quanzhou to be added to United Nations Educational and Scientific and Cultural Organization's (UNESCO) list of World Heritage Sites, citing their "contribution to the exchange system of the maritime Silk Roads and interchange of the Chinese people and foreigners in China on religious beliefs from the 10th century to the 14th century" (UNESCO n.d.) during the Song and Yuan dynasties. Riding on the Fujian Provincial Government's push for Quanzhou to become a UNESCO World Heritage Site, there has been a renewed interest in Quanzhou's history and heritage, which has been widely mobilised by different stakeholders in the city to promote their own agendas. One such effort is the 'Connecting EMOTIONS through WELLS' (触井生情) project, a community-led initiative to preserve and revitalise the old wells located within the Tongzheng community district (通政社区) in Licheng District

(鲤城区), a neighbourhood abutting the busy West Street near the Kaiyuan Temple, a key attraction proposed to be on the UNESCO World Heritage List.

In this chapter, I examine the cultural politics of the 'Connecting Emotions through Wells' project to shed light on how a community-led urban heritage initiative is drawing on heritage as a way of promoting community engagement, urban sustainability, and heritage tourism. Based on an ethnographic study of the project, I examine how positive discourses of urban sustainability, heritage preservation, and community-based, participatory approaches to urban development have been mobilised by state-endorsed civil society organisations, such as the community action group of the 'Connecting Emotions through Wells' project, to diffuse local resistance to the urban gentrification and touristification of the Tongzheng community district. I suggest that these can be construed as part of the technologies of governing that work to consolidate a post-political condition in urban Quanzhou that replaces overt political resistance with a more managerial-technocratic approach to governance characterised by rationalisation, compromise, and consensus.

Primary data for this research is derived from two week-long research stays in Quanzhou in January and August 2018, where I lived in a homestay within the Tongzheng community district, visited some of the wells in the community district, and held discussions with the community action group. This is supplemented with extensive notes from a WeChat discussion forum set up by the community action group that chronicles the development of the project from its initiation in December 2017 to February 2019. In what follows, I first set out the theoretical underpinnings of this chapter by exploring the role of heritage in the age of post-politics. I then introduce the 'Connecting Emotions through Wells' project, before delving into the cultural politics of the project and its implications for local communities and their neighbourhood. I outline how the project embodies the emergence of the post-political condition, characterised by a managerial-technocratic approach of government backed by hybrid institutions with expert administration and other technologies of governing that combine ideas of rationalisation, consensus, and compromise (Swyngedouw 2005, 2009). I conclude by reiterating how the 'Connecting Emotions through Wells' project has been a manifestation of the post-political condition, which by way of its positive discourses of promoting civic pride, social cohesion, urban sustainability, and heritage tourism, serves to transform local heritages whilst diffusing local resistance to urban gentrification and touristification.

Heritage in the age of post-politics

Critical scholarship on heritage has gradually moved beyond the preservation of cultural heritage for its own sake, to conceive heritage as a useful resource that can be mobilised to achieve a myriad of agendas and objectives (Appadurai 1986; Holden 2004, 2006; Smith 2006; Basu and Modest 2015). Heritage is "culturally ascribed" (Harrison 2010, 26), rather than being inherent and intrinsic. It is a value laden, loaded, and ambiguous concept, broadly defined as a perception of the past in the present, shaped by power relations and embroiled in questions of who it belongs to, who has the right to represent it, and for whom it is represented (Lowenthal 1998; Hall 1999; Graham, Ashworth, and Tunbridge 2000; Harrison 2013).

An official representation of heritage is often promoted, privileged, and normalised by the state and other establishments of power, in the form of an authorised (or authorising) heritage discourse, that contests and marginalises alternative perspectives of heritage, leading to heritage dissonance (Tunbridge and Ashworth 1996; Smith 2006; Harrison 2010). Heritage can thus be viewed as a kind of persuasion or rhetoric that has been 'mobilised creatively within a wide array of social, political, economic, and moral contexts where it gives persuasive force to particular standpoints, perspectives, and claims' (Samuels 2015, 4), which can provide a catalyst for changes and actions. As Hafstein (quoted in Samuels 2015, 6–7) argues, 'The major use of heritage is to mobilise people and resources, to reform discourses, and to transform practices ... Don't be fooled by the talk of preservation: all heritage is change'.

In the age of post-politics, heritage is increasingly mobilised as a resource and constituted as a field of expertise focussing on heritage resource management (Coombe 2013). Through the work of international organisations such as UNESCO, the International Committee on Monuments and Sites (ICOMOS), and other international heritage agencies, as well as their programmes such as the 1972 UNESCO World Heritage Convention and the 2003 UNESCO Intangible Cultural Heritage Convention, heritage is being instituted as a new system of governance through the formation of new technologies of governing such as selection, inventorying, standardization, and accreditation (Coombe 2013), to create a universalised and institutionalised form of world heritage, or what Kirshenblatt-Gimblett (2004) considers as 'the heritage of humanity'. In the institutionalisation of heritage, international heritage agencies such as UNESCO and ICOMOS, as well as academics and heritage professionals, are empowered and legitimised as key actors who can offer specialised knowledge and expertise to develop the heritage field of practice (Mattli and Buthe 2003; Coombe 2013).

The institutionalisation of heritage mirrors broader developments that have been unfolding in what Swyngedouw (2005, 2009) argues as the formation of a post-political condition, where political debate and disagreement are increasingly replaced by a post-democratic arrangement built around consensus, compromise, agreement, and a managerial-technocratic approach to governance backed by a stakeholder-based hybrid network of experts, civil society, and state actors. In the age of the post-politics, heritage has emerged alongside the environment as a depoliticised regime, grounded in global discourses of threat, vulnerability, and sustainability (Swyngedouw 2011). Similar to how socio-environmental conflicts have been depoliticised and subsumed under the hegemonic discourse on environmental sustainability (Swyngedouw 2009), dissonances around the management of heritage have also been depoliticised and incorporated within populist discourses on heritage sustainability. For the heritage movement, the threat arises from the overpowering modernity and the demise of traditional practices brought about by the advert of globalisation. This salvage paradigm underpins the narrative of the 1972 UNESCO World Heritage Convention, which conceives of heritage being "increasingly threatened with destruction not only by the traditional causes of decay, but also by changing social and economic conditions which aggravate the situation with even more formidable phenomena of damage or destruction" (UNESCO 1972). Similar to the global rhetoric eschewing the protection of the environment on ethical grounds, there is a moral imperative to the global discourse on heritage aimed at preserving and protecting cultural heritage from destruction and disappearance.

The depoliticisation of heritage under the neoliberal post-political regime leads not only to the up-scaling of governance to international agencies such as UNESCO and ICOMOS, but also to the downscaling of governance through deregulation to civil society organisations or other local groups (Swyngedouw 2005). In this vein, the onset of the post-political condition has provided a lacuna for the emergence of civil society organisations to fill the roles vacated by the retreat of the state, leading to a redistribution of roles from the state to civil society groups or other hybrid organisations. However, as Swyngedouw (2005) puts it, depoliticisation under the neoliberal regime produces a Janus-faced condition that serves to subordinate real political struggles to the overarching market forces.

In the context of post-political China, this appears to foster a 'top-down' pathway for the development of civil organisations, in which government departments in China or their related offices set up and manage these so-called civil organisations, with the primary objectives of serving the government agendas at an arm's length or as a bridge between the government departments and members of the general public (Jia 2011). This arrangement leads to the blurring of community-building efforts and civil society, which Salmenkari (2011, 103) considers as 'a rhetorical act to advocate civil society under the state-promoted programmes of community building, constructing a harmonious society and constructing a new countryside'. Rather than serving as non-governmental organisations representing the interests of the general public, these 'civil society organisations' in China often serve to entrench existing government rhetoric and extend the power of the state over the people. The emergence of the post-political condition has opened up possibilities for the instrumentalisation of heritage in China by different stakeholders, including state actors, operating under the post-political, neoliberal regime to achieve different agendas and interests, which produce complex ramifications for the local people and their places. In the following sections, I examine how the 'Connecting Emotions through Wells' project in urban Quanzhou embodies these complex dynamics, and consider the implications of the neoliberal heritage regime on the place and position of the local communities.

'Connecting Emotions through Wells': heritage revitalisation and gentrification of the Tongzheng community district in Quanzhou

The 'Connecting Emotions through Wells' project is a community project aimed at drawing on the old wells in the Tongzheng community district of the Licheng

District in Quanzhou to promote community engagement, urban improvement, and heritage tourism. In 2017, the Quanzhou Municipal Government contracted a capacity-development consultancy comprising architects, urban planners, and other urban development experts to run a series of training workshops on developing community-building projects for the local communities living in Quanzhou. The intention of the training workshops was to equip the local communities in Quanzhou with the expertise and technical 'know-how' to respond to a government's call for proposals for seed funding to implement a number of community-led urban improvement projects in the local areas.

The efforts of the Quanzhou Municipal Government in promoting community-led urban improvement projects can be considered within the broader context of urban heritage gentrification that has been unfolding in urban cities. Gentrification is a process of urban rehabilitation or regeneration of decaying and dilapidating neighbourhoods in central cities by more affluent occupants, often leading to the displacement of its original residents (Sassen 1991). Under the scheme, government officials from the local district offices, along with the local residents, were strongly encouraged to participate in the training workshops, so that they would qualify to bid for the seed funding from the Quanzhou Municipal Government to carry out urban improvement works in their local areas. The scheme resonates with a predominant trend in the neoliberal regime, which involves the downscaling of governance to civil society organisations or other local groups, which will take on the roles and responsibilities of certain social functions that have traditionally been performed by the state. In the context of 'Connecting Emotions through Wells' project, a local official working at the Licheng District Office with direct oversight of the Tongzheng community district later took on the task of leading a community action group to initiate the project for the competition, winning a grant of RMB 50,000 (£5,625) in February 2018 to realise the project.

Nested within the Quanzhou Old City, the Tongzheng community district is a quiet neighbourhood with a rich history which dates back to the Song dynasty (906–1279 AD), when it was predominantly a housing district for high-ranking government officials. During the Yuan dynasty (1271–1368 AD) and the Ming dynasty (1368–1644 AD), many government officials continued to reside in the area. During the late Qing dynasty (1636–1932 AD), many overseas Chinese who returned to China after their sojourns abroad bought properties in the area due to the safety offered by its layout of narrow alleys and limited entry points, which discouraged burglars and robbers from operating in the area. Once a prestigious residential area reserved for the upper echelons of society, the Tongzheng community district is now in a state of dilapidation. Whilst the narrow alleys and limited entry points into the neighbourhoods were largely valued in the past for the safety they offered, these features are generally perceived as obstacles for the redevelopment of the neighbourhood today.

With over 5,000 residents in 1,400 households residing in the community district, and a fifth of them being elderly residents, the community district is an aging district facing an exodus of young people to newer residential areas. As a result of local practices of land division and inheritance, many large residential sites of the past are also being sub-divided into smaller plots over generations, leading to the haphazard layouts within many private properties in the community district. Due to its strategic location within the Quanzhou Old City abutting a popular shopping district and a proposed UNESCO World Heritage Site—the Kaiyuan Temple—the community district is also under significant pressures to open up to tourism interests. Several old houses within the community district have already given way to the development of homestays for tourists, a phenomenon that has gained momentum over the last five years.

The idea of revitalising the old wells in the community district was selected as the subject of the community improvement project, as the project leader found meaning in the historical and emotional significance of the old wells in Chinese culture. As Quanzhou is the ancestral home of 15.8 million overseas Chinese, the wells are especially meaningful since they signify the tracing of one's roots in Chinese symbolism. The wells within the Tongzheng community district and around Quanzhou are rich in history, and many are intricately bound with the ebbs and flows of the city's development over time. For example, the Clarity Well (青白源井) behind the Chengtian Temple (承天寺) in Quanzhou bears testimony to the flourishing silk industry during the Song and Yuan dynasties, whilst the Germinating Seed Well (豆生井) on Zhongshan South Road was previously used in the growing of bean sprouts. A prominent landmark within the Tongzheng community district is the Calming Pagoda (定心塔) and the Serenity Well (玉泉井) (Figure 6.1), both constructed during the Ming dynasty, and later renovated during the Qing dynasty. The main alley within the neighbourhood, 'Pavilion Well Alley'

FIGURE 6.1 The Calming Pagoda after refurbishment

Source: Photograph: Author.

(井亭巷), draws its name from this pagoda and well, and an accompanying pavilion which has since been demolished. In the recent years, the pagoda was renamed Calming Pagoda from Sincerity Pagoda (诚心塔) by the local government. Today, the Calming Pagoda and the Serenity Well are under private ownership, nested within the private residence of 80-year-old Mr. Wan—a retired naval officer and a descendent of prominent Qing dynasty officer Wan Ti Du (万提督)—and kept out of public view (Shu 2018).

Based on a site survey conducted by the community action group in April 2018, there are seven public wells within the Tongzheng community district, of which two public wells sited at communal areas are still being used for washing purposes, whilst another five public wells are not put to any usage. There are also other wells which exist in the private domains within the courtyards of the houses and private residences in the Tongzheng community district, and there is no means to ascertain the number without the cooperation of the residents. The water from these wells is no longer consumed due to pollution, although residents would have consumed the water from these wells in the past. Many of these wells have also not been drained for some time. and hence, they have dried up, and are at risk of being covered up and demolished to make way for new developments.

For the community action group of the 'Connecting Emotions through Wells' project, the restoration of the old wells would not only improve the urban liveability of the community district for the residents and open up opportunities for heritage tourism, but also allow them to serve as conduits for evoking shared memories of their place histories, and foster a greater sense of belonging and community ownership amongst the residents. By collecting personal and family stories relating to these wells, the community action group seeks to draw these wells as a form of material evidence to forge a sense of shared history, identity, and ownership amongst the residents, which can be harnessed to revitalise the community spirit and imbue a sense of pride and belonging amongst the residents. The key objectives for the 'Connecting Emotions through Wells' project are thus to convert the spaces near the old wells into communal areas for community gatherings to promote social cohesion; re-discover uses for the old wells, focussing on the Calming Pagoda and its accompanying Serenity Well, as well as the Three Holes Well (三孔井); and create awareness for all the old wells in the community district.

To achieve their key objectives, the community action group has worked out an action plan, which includes strengthening their communal expertise by recruiting more volunteers, organising seminars taught by academics locally and field trips to other cities in China to expand on their knowledge of the subject matter, and engaging in discussions both offline at monthly meetings and online via a WeChat forum, as well as organising group outings to conduct site surveys within the neighbourhood to identify old wells, drain the wells to make them functional again, and speak with residents to understand the local place histories. The use of social media as a means of organising members of the community action group resonates with the changing organisational mechanisms of social movements, in which social media technologies such as Facebook and Twitter are increasingly being used to mobilise resources in support of activism, significantly altering the landscape of activist networks (Murthy 2018).

The community action group has also worked with the local authorities to test the quality of the water from the wells, but it appears that they are not safe for consumption, so their longer-term plan is to make the water in these wells clean and safe for consumption through the project. They also devised a programme to encourage the local communities to document the old wells in the neighbourhood by taking photographs, identifying their locations using a Global Positioning System online, and collecting stories about these wells through a storytelling competition. Through these programmes, the community action group and its volunteers are actively engaging in the 'staging' of local place histories, especially the histories related to these old wells, for the promotion of civic pride, social cohesion, urban sustainability, and heritage tourism within the Tongzheng community district.

As one of the objectives set out for the project is to promote community engagement, the community action group also sought to understand the sentiments of the local communities towards these old wells by speaking to the local communities residing in Tongzheng community district. The responses were rich and multi-layered, alluding to the different valorisation of cultural heritage amongst the local communities. The owner of Rong Gallery, a homestay nested within the Tongzhong community district, who is also an active volunteer on the project, said that they have an old well within their premises, and that they would like to use the water from the well to make tea someday, when the water quality improves. One long-time resident, Mr. Wan, who owns a prominent landmark, the Calming Pagoda and the Serenity Well, within his private residence, commented that the government should not have renamed the Sincerity Pagoda to Calming Pagoda, as both the pagoda and the well have spiritual values. A ten-year-old student who lives and goes to school in the community district perceives the wells as sites of fear, due to the possible risk of falling into these wells, as many are merely uncovered holes along the streets. The local communities also have different ideas about what they wish to do with the old wells. Some residents suggested that they would like to rent their courtyards to the local government so that tourists could view the wells in their courtyards, thus offering an opportunity for tourists to get a glimpse of the vernacular lives of the local communities. They could also then set up a shopfront in their courtyards to sell local snacks or souvenirs to the tourists, with permission from the local government.

As a form of heritage intervention, the 'Connecting Emotions through Wells' project is actively transforming the local place histories through the 'staging' of the histories of the old wells for the gaze of the both tourists and local communities. This overt intervention appears to be endorsed or even encouraged by Quanzhou Municipal Government, who awarded the community action group an initial funding of RMB 50,000 (£5,625) to implement their action plans. Part of the funding was used to replace a section of the broken wall of the private residence of Mr. Wan with a Chinese lattice panel which would allow passers-by to look into his private courtyard and view the Calming Pagoda and the Serenity Well from the main alley. The funding was also used to organise a series of community days where volunteers and members from the Tongzheng community district work together to make the wells in the community district functional again by cleaning and removing blockages in the wells. The community action group also supported an outreach programme at a local primary school within the community district, where students were encouraged to collect information and talk about a well in the community district, preferably one within the private domains, to add to the database of old wells in the community district. The students also participated in a storytelling competition about the old wells, thus creating new narratives to be woven into the local place histories. These activities were intended to endear the younger members of the communities to local place histories, enhancing their sense of pride and belonging to the Tongzheng district.

In the medium term, the community action group intends to use the funding to refurbish the communal areas and improve the provision of communal toilet facilities at some of these public wells, so that residents can organise social activities around these wells. There are also plans to refurbish and improve the underground water system, to make the public and private wells within the community district functional again. In the longer term, there are plans to enhance the accessibility of the community district by opening up new access points into the district, and to widen the narrow alleyways. The community action group hopes that these efforts will encourage the establishment of more homestays and community enterprises within the community district. This in turn will enhance the urban liveability and sustainability of the community district, transforming the aging neighbourhood into a buzzing town with a rich history, attracting tourists and locals alike. This redevelopment will help fulfil the vision of the community action group to gentrify the Tongzheng community district for the promotion of civic pride, social cohesion, urban sustainability, and heritage tourism, as well as facilitating better integration of the community district with the wider redevelopment of the Quanzhou Old City. This is all done through the 'bottom-up' performance and 'staging' of local place histories and heritage discourses relating to the old wells within the Tongzheng community district, as I will discuss in the next section.

Heritage instrumentalisation, civic activism, and urban governance

In the context of post-political China, heritage discourses appear to be mobilised by the state through hybrid institutions or local civil society organisations to promote urban gentrification in aging neighbourhoods. For the Tongzheng community district in the Quanzhou Old City, heritage has become a conduit for negotiating their marginalised status as an aging neighbourhood and for re-establishing its new place and position within these complex urban dynamics in Quanzhou. The community action group 'Connecting Emotions through Wells'—arguably a civil society organisation with government oversight—is mobilising heritage discourses, to achieve the agendas of promoting urban revitalisation and sustainability in the community district. This includes the historical narratives and local place histories relating to the old wells in the community district, which seeks to prevent the aging neighbourhood from being left behind in the wider redevelopment of the Quanzhou Old City.

Nonetheless, by mobilising the local place histories of the Tongzheng community district, the community action group has sought to make a convincing case both to the local communities and to the Quanzhou Municipal Government to invest in the gentrification of these old wells. Heritage can thus be viewed as a kind of persuasion or rhetoric that has been mobilised to serve broader social, political, and economic agendas of the community action group, and perhaps those of the Quanzhou Municipal Government. By tapping into the global rhetoric of 'heritage under threat' (e.g., overpowering modernity and disappearing traditions), the community action group of the 'Connecting Emotions through Wells' project is appealing on moral grounds to save the local place histories of the old wells from disappearance.

For the Quanzhou Municipal Government, this community-led 'Connecting Emotions through Wells' project will take the pressures off the local government to gentrify the Tongzheng community district. Since some of the urban improvement works within the community district will involve works undertaken on private lands, a top-down approach initiated by the Quanzhou Municipal Government could attract resistance from local communities seeking compensation from the government.[1] Conversely, a bottom-up, community-initiated approach spearheaded by a 'civil society organisation', such as the community action group of the 'Connecting Emotions through Wells' project, serves to diffuse and divert the overt resistance against the government to a more managerial-technocratic, stakeholder-based network of experts, civic society, and state actors, which aims to resolve these urban contestations through collaboration, compromise, and consensus. The community action group has been playing a brokerage and mediator role to assuage local resistance to the project by organising community visits to speak with the residents and to persuade them to support the project. The functions of the community action group of the 'Connecting Emotions through Wells' project resonates with the roles assumed by the hybrid institutions of managerial-technocrats in a post-political condition. This mode of governance, as Swyngedouw (2005, 2009) argues, ultimately leads to the depoliticisation of heritage that subordinates real politics under technical and administrative fixes. Heritage preservation, in this sense, becomes a driver for gentrification. Like gentrification, the process of heritagisation is reinforced by the capital accumulation and cultural reproduction of place (Herzfeld 2015). In the neoliberal regime, gentrification comes to be relegated in managerial-technocratic terms, downplaying the complex political and economic agendas that underpin these urban redevelopment projects whilst subordinating them to capitalist interests.

Whilst familiarity with the government bureaucracy has eased the ability of the community action group to utilise the seed-funding from the government, their association with the local government has led to some mistrust from the local residents of the project. Whilst the project leader has repeatedly expressed a desire for the team to relinquish their roles to a new fully independent project team in order for the project to be a truly community-based project, these efforts are in vain. This complicates the Janus-faced condition transpiring from the post-political condition, in that the local communities are actively resisting this managerial-technocratic arrangement by refusing to cooperate with the community action group due to their perceived association with the government.

The 'Connecting Emotions through Wells' project is not without its share of challenges and community resistance. Whilst most of the seminars conducted for the project went quite well, one seminar which took place in January 2018 was met with sharp divisions amongst the residents. This disagreement centred upon the overarching objectives of the project and how the old wells ought to be preserved. Whilst one group preferred a light-touch approach which would allow the local heritage to evolve more organically, another favoured an interventionist approach to restore and refurbish the old wells to promote heritage tourism and improve the urban environment of the community district. The differences in opinions of the residents on how and to what extent the old wells should be actively restored and refurbished as part of the 'Connecting Emotions through Wells' project point to the contestation or lack of agreement and consistency in the meanings of heritage. This is what Tunbridge and Ashworth (1996) term as 'heritage dissonance', rendering it susceptible to mobilisation under the neoliberal regime. Indeed, as emphasised by Herzfeld (2016, 194), economic development "is often more divisive than unifying". In line with the institutional fix in the post-political climate, a consensus was only achieved after the community action group stated that a bottom-up approach emphasising the needs of the residents would be taken.

Within the local communities of Tongzheng community district, there are those who prefer a more interventionist approach to refurbish the old wells within the neighbourhood. One idea is to develop a walking heritage trail around the wells, which would also provide greater accessibility for the owners of the homestays to pass through the narrow alleyways, as well as residents who suggest that the government could offer to pay them a monthly rent to open up their private wells to tourists. Yet, there are others who prefer to keep the peace and quiet of the neighbourhood, away from the prying eyes of the tourists, and allow the local heritage to evolve in a more organic manner. This also points to the problems of conceptualising the residents as a collective community with a common purpose and a clear position on the management of their cultural heritage. What is deemed as a collective local community is not homogenous but is in fact made up of different groups of social networks cutting across different situations, categories, and allegiances, each existing in its own right, and operating in a distinctive manner (Amit and Rapport 2002).

This dissonance therefore complicates the working dynamics of the 'Connecting Emotions through Wells' project. Whilst the predominant rhetoric of the 'Connecting Emotions through Wells' project has been to protect and preserve the cultural heritage of the old wells in the Tongzheng community district, the project is ironically leading to the creative destruction of these wells through the 'staging' and commodification of them for tourists. For instance, some residents will be enticed to sell their private residences and properties to tourism players for the establishment of homestays and other commercial uses to tap into the emerging opportunities offered by heritage tourism in the Quanzhou Old City. In neoliberal contexts, local communities are often reinvented as heritage entrepreneurs in order to capitalise on economic opportunities for their own personal gains, hastening the gentrification of the aging neighbourhood (Meskell 2018). The perceived economic gains on the private properties due to proposed improvement works in the community district have already triggered some conflicts amongst the claimants, some of whom wish to sell the properties to realise the financial gains against others who wish to live in the properties. Faced with the pressures of market forces, the organic development of the Tongzheng community district as a residential district will likely give way to its gentrification and touristification, accelerated by the activities promoted through the 'Connecting Emotions through Wells' project.

Through these processes of touristification and creative destruction, the local communities living in the Tongzheng district are likely to be squeezed out of the area, leading to the breakdown of the community ties and social cohesion. Although such processes are already playing out in the neighbouring Quanzhou Old City, the community action group and its volunteers prefer to focus on the benefits of the 'Connecting Emotions through Wells' project in promoting civic pride, social cohesion, urban sustainability, and heritage tourism. The community action group seems to constitute a powerful interest group drawing on the rhetoric of a ground-up, participatory approach and leveraging the endangerment and loss of cultural heritage. This is particularly the case for local place histories and heritage relating to the old wells, in addition to mobilising positive discourses of urban liveability and sustainability to gentrify the community district in ways contradictory to the project's goals. However, the local communities at Tongzheng community district are not passive agents either. Whilst some residents are adamant on the interventionist approach to heritage preservation taken by the community action group, other residents actively participate in the group to instrumentalise the local place histories for their personal gains.

In the post-political climate of contemporary China, there seems to be a convergence built around the positive discourses of urban sustainability, heritage preservation, and community-based, participatory approaches to urban development. These are often brokered or mediated through state-endorsed civil society organisations, leading to the promotion of a certain form of urban gentrification dominated by capitalist interests. There is arguably a diffusion of political resistance, through the 'Connecting Emotions through Wells' project, which mobilises positive discourses of urban sustainability, heritage preservation, and community-based, participatory approaches to urban development. In line with post-political tendencies, this movement is backed by a managerial-technocratic approach to governance to serve the agendas of the Quanzhou Municipal Government. The redevelopment of the Tongzheng community district—particularly through the actions of the 'Connecting Emotions through Wells' project—reinforces Swyngedouw's (2005) view that the emergence of the post-political condition subordinates political resistance to the hegemony of capitalist forces.

Conclusion

Through the case study of the 'Connecting Emotions through Wells' project in Quanzhou, I have demonstrated how the community action group and its volunteers have sought to promote community engagement, urban improvement, and heritage tourism. This has been done through the community action group's use of heritage discourses relating to the old wells in the community district. Whilst the community action group claims that the 'Connecting Emotions through Wells' project seeks to promote civil pride, social cohesion, urban sustainability, and heritage tourism, the activities pursued only serve to accelerate the urban gentrification and touristification of the Tongzheng community district. This could result in the squeezing out of the local residents and shops in favour of more tourist-friendly infrastructure in the community district, thereby breaking down the community ties and social cohesion that the project claims to forge.

The workings of the 'Connecting Emotions through Wells' project resonate with broader developments in the post-political condition, in which political debates and discussions about society are giving way to a post-democratic arrangement emphasising collaboration, compromise, and consensus. This process is supported by a managerial-technocratic approach to governance administered by a stakeholder-based network of state actors, civil society, and experts. In drawing upon the positive rhetoric of urban sustainability, heritage preservation, and community-based, participatory approaches to urban development, the community action group seeks to engender support from the local communities whilst diffusing local resistance to the interventionist approach to heritage preservation. The 'Connecting Emotions through Wells' project—whilst portrayed as a community-led project—thus serves to transform local heritages through the 'staging' and commodification of these heritage resources for the promotion of tourism. This aligns the interests of the Tongzheng community district and the broader agendas of the Quanzhou Municipal Government to gentrify the neighbourhood and capitalise on the economic potential of tourism, whilst diffusing local resistance to this process.

In the post-political context of contemporary China, there seems to be a depoliticisation of heritage characterised by the downscaling of governance to government-endorsed civil society organisations or local groups. This involves certain technologies of governing based on a technocratic mode of management and the production of consensus, compromise, and collaboration, aimed at diffusing political debates and discussions around urban gentrification. This process often dovetails with the adoption of positive discourses of urban sustainability, heritage preservation, and community-based, participatory approaches to urban development, which are often brokered or mediated through state-endorsed civil society organisations. As a result, familiar forms of urban gentrification prevail, benefitting capitalist interests. Indeed, rather than representing the diverse civil voices and interests of the local communities, these state-endorsed civil society organisations seem to be dominated by certain powerful interest groups seeking to extend the state agenda. In the age of post-politics, heritage, being a fluid and nebulous concept embroiled in power relations, thus becomes a resource mobilised by these state-endorsed agencies to serve their agendas, producing complex ramifications on the local people and their places.

Acknowledgements

I would like to acknowledge the assistance and advice of my informants from the community action group of the 'Connecting Emotions through Wells' project for their generous sharing, and for allowing me to use the materials which they have prepared for the project. I would like to acknowledge the generous support offered by the UCL Centre for Critical Heritage Studies Small Grant for funding my fieldwork to Quanzhou, China, and to the Asia Research Institute, National University of Singapore, and the University of Leicester for funding my travel expenses to attend the conference in Singapore, where this chapter was being presented and discussed.

Note

1 Such works include the opening up of the privately owned Calming Pagoda and the Serenity Well for public view, and the future acquisition of private lands to widen the narrow alleys.

References

Amit, V., and N. Rapport. 2002. *The Trouble with Community: Anthropological Reflections on Movement, Identity and Collectivity.* London: Pluto Press.

Appadurai, A. 1986. *The Social Life of Things: Commodities in Cultural Perspective.* Cambridge: Cambridge University Press.

Basu, P., and W. Modest., eds. 2015. *Museums, Heritage and International Development.* New York and London: Routledge.

Coombe, R. 2013. "Managing Cultural Heritage as Neoliberal Govern Mentality." In *Heritage Regimes and the State*, edited by R. Bendix, A. Eggert, and A. Peselmann, 375–387. 2nd rev. ed. Göttingen: Universitätsverlag Göttingen.

Graham, B., G. J. Ashworth, and J. E. Tunbridge. 2000. *A Geography of Heritage: Power, Culture and Economy.* London: Arnold.

Hall, S. 1999. "Un-settling 'the Heritage', Re-imagining the Post-Nation: Whose Heritage?" *Third Text* 13 (49): 3–13.

Harrison, R., ed. 2010. *Understanding the Politics of Heritage.* Manchester: Manchester University Press.

———. 2013. *Heritage: Critical Approaches.* Abingdon and New York: Routledge.

Herzfeld, M. 2015. "Heritage and the Right to the City: When Securing the Past Creates Insecurity in the Present." *Heritage and Society* 8 (1): 3–23.

———. 2016. *Siege of the Spirits: Community and Polity in Bangkok.* Chicago: University of Chicago Press.

Holden, J. 2004. *Capturing Cultural Value: How Culture Has Become a Tool of Government Policy.* London: Demos. Accessed July 7, 2017. www.demos.co.uk/files/CapturingCulturalValue.pdf

———. 2006. *Cultural Value and the Crisis of Legitimacy: Why Culture Needs a Democratic Mandate*. London: Demos. Accessed July 7, 2017. www.demos.co.uk/files/Culturalvalueweb.pdf

Jia, X. 2011. Civil Organization-Government Relationships: Functional Cooperation and Power Dilemmas. In *Emerging Civil Society in China: 1978–2008*, edited by M. Wang, 209–237. Leiden: Brill.

Kirshenblatt-Gimblett, B. 2004. "Intangible Heritage as a Metacultural Production." *Museum International* 56: 52–65.

Lowenthal, D. 1998. *The Heritage Crusade and the Spoils of History*. Cambridge: Cambridge University Press.

Mattli, W., and Buthe, T. 2003. "Setting International Standards: Technological Rationality or Primacy of Power?" *World Politics* 56 (1): 1–42.

Meskell, L. 2018. "Heritage, Gentrification, Participation: Remaking Urban Landscapes in the Name of Culture and Historic Preservation." *International Journal of Heritage Studies*. Online First. doi:10.1080/13527258.2018.1542334.

Murthy, D. 2018. "Introduction to Social Media, Activism, and Organizations." *Social Media and Society* 1–4.

Salmenkari, T. 2011. "Community Building, Civil Society and Society Service Production in China." *Journal of Civil Society* 7 (1): 101–118.

Samuels, K. L. 2015. "Introduction: Heritage as Persuasion." In *Heritage Keywords: Rhetoric and Redescription in Cultural Heritage*, edited by K. F. Samuels and T. Rico, 3–28. Boulder: University Press of Colorado.

Sassen, S. 1991. *The Global City: New York, London and Tokyo*. Princeton, NJ: Princeton University Press.

Shu, Y. 2018. "The Pagoda Emerges into View: The Calming Pagoda Comes into Public View, A Fresh New Lease of Life for an Old Alley." *Quanzhou Travel Journal*, June 6. https://mp.weixin.qq.com/s/0nLArHxUGYCEYCyn3Yg5OA

Smith, L. 2006. *Uses of Heritage*. London and New York: Routledge.

Swyngedouw, E. 2005. "Governance Innovation and the Citizen: The Janus Face of Governance-Beyond-the-State" *Urban Studies* 42 (11): 1991–2006.

———. 2009. "The Antinomies of the Postpolitical City: In Search of a Democratic Politics of Environmental Protection." *International Journal of Urban and Regional Research* 33 (3): 601–620.

———. 2011. "Depoliticized Environments: The End of Nature, Climate Change and the Post-Political Condition." *Royal Institute of Philosophy Supplement* 69: 253–274.

Tunbridge, J. E., and G. J. Ashworth. 1996. *Dissonant Heritage: The Management of the Past as A Resource in Conflict*. Chichester: Wiley.

UNESCO. 1972. "Convention Concerning the Protection of the World Cultural and Natural Heritage." Accessed November 15, 2018. https://whc.unesco.org/en/conventiontext/

———. n.d. "Historic Monuments and Sites of Ancient Quanzhou (Zayton)." Accessed September 20, 2017. http://whc.unesco.org/en/tentativelists/6073/

Xin, Z. 2017. "Chinese Capitalism and the Maritime Silk Road: A World-Systems Perspective." *Geopolitics* 22 (2): 310–331.

Zhao, H. 2015. "China's New Maritime Silk Road: Implications and Opportunities for Southeast Asia." Institute of Southeast Asian Studies, Trends in Southeast Asia Series No. 2015/3. Accessed September 20, 2017. www.iseas.edu.sg/images/pdf/Trends_2015_3.pdf

PART III
Post-politics in environmental governance

7

CONSTRUCTING SPACE FOR PARTICIPATORY GOVERNANCE IN VIETNAM

Reflections from the Hanoi tree movement

Seohee Kwak

Introduction

Even though public participation in matters of governance is regarded as a universally accepted ideal and is enacted in most societies, the way such participation manifests varies from country to country, and is constantly (re-)shaped and (re-)negotiated depending on the form of state-society relations and other sociopolitical contexts. In Vietnam, where the government uses a one-party socialist democratic model, no clear boundary is drawn between the one-party state and its people. More Vietnamese citizens are becoming active in expressing their voices on policies, with many forming strategic activities or groups that strive to become involved with matters of governance. However, space for public participation remains ambiguous, as the Vietnamese state takes a dual approach of simultaneously accommodating and controlling citizen voices. By examining a recent public protest against a massive tree-felling project carried out by the Hanoi municipal government, this chapter thus offers a contextualised analysis of the characteristics of public participation in Vietnam, to assess the relationship between the state and civil society.

By exploring the nexus of social movements and the conditions for public participation afforded by the party-state in Vietnam, this chapter explores (1) how the Hanoi tree movement is reflective of the current space for participatory governance in Vietnam and the nature of state–civil society relations, and (2) how the movement has contested or (re-)shaped this relationship within the current context. Documentary research and individual interviews were conducted during fieldwork in Hanoi from October 2017 to February 2018. Semi-structured interviews were conducted with a total of 50 people categorised by their affiliations: (1) government ministries or affiliated organisations, (2) Vietnamese social organisations, (3) bi- and multi-lateral development agencies in Vietnam, and

(4) international non-governmental organisations (INGOs).[1] These interviews covered several agendas pertaining to the practices and challenges of public participation in Vietnam. Due to the sensitive nature of this research topic, most of the interviewees wished to remain off the record and anonymous. Interview transcripts underwent a thematic analysis using the ATLAS.ti software, which identified, analysed, and reported patterns (or themes) within interview data (see Braun and Clarke 2006). As such, this study aims to connect key patterns which elucidate the reality and institutional characteristics of public participation in Vietnam.

Post-politics and participatory governance in Vietnam

According to Arnstein (1969, 2), citizen participation is a strategy as well as a means for citizens to be included in decision-making processes, "by which they can induce significant social reform which enables them to share in the benefits of the affluent society". In another definition from Roberts (2004, 230), public participation is "the process by which members of a society (those not holding office or administrative positions in government) share power with public officials in making substantive decisions and in taking actions related to the community". Public participation is not confined to specific forms, but includes various types of action and relational dynamics with power holders, to attain a stake in shaping decisions by which the public are affected. As suggested by Gaventa (2006), participation space is about an opportunity of empowerment: this space is 'closed' to the public when decisions are made by power holders, the public is 'invited' into this space when there are pre-set rules of the game posited by the state, or this space becomes 'claimed/created' through people's movements or actions. Hence, an autonomous form of public participation has different characteristics from invited participation, in which people are no more than invitees seated at a pre-arranged meeting (Cornwall 2008). In this sense, public participation is inherently political, and is linked to a society's unique political dynamics (White 1996). Taking the nuances of public participation in politics into consideration, it is therefore worth exploring whether and how public participation spaces and citizen mobilisations contest or reconcile with the post-political critique, which has been levelled at current modes of governance across the world.

Wilson and Swyngedouw (2014, 6) define post-politics as a condition in which "the political—understood as a space of contestation and agonistic engagement—is increasingly colonised by politics—understood as technocratic mechanisms and consensual procedures" under the influence of worldwide dominant models of representative democracy and free market economics. In discussing the concept of public participation, discourses on post-politics exclude disagreement and confrontation in the name of governance with an emphasis on consensus-oriented and pragmatic policy processes. Despite some divergence in epistemological and ontological details, a wide range of the literature on the critique of post-politics has conceptualised how space for political debates and contestations has been restrained or even oppressed within post-political, techno-managerial, (neo)liberal arrangements

(Mouffe 2005; Swyngedouw 2009; Wilson and Swyngedouw 2014; Žižek 1999). This chapter raises the question of whether post-political ideas can be used as an analytical tool to elucidate the reality of state-society relations in Vietnam. To what extent can post-political ideas explain manifestations of public participation in a non-liberal democratic regime? Does post-political discourse coincide or contrast with rationales embedded in Vietnamese state-society relations?

Several scholars have analysed the manifestations of public engagement or political action in Vietnam (Bui 2016; Dao and Nguyen 2015; Fforde 2011; Hoa and Garcia-Zamor 2017; Kerkvliet 2010, 2015; Nguyen 2014; Nguyen et al. 2015; Thayer 2010; Tortosa 2012; Vu 2017; Wells-Dang 2010). An extensive body of literature has examined to what extent civil society—as a sphere where individuals can form groups to raise their voices and take action independently from the government—has been developed or challenged (Bui 2013; Kleinen 2015; Landau 2008; Nguyen 2014; Salemink 2006; Thayer 2009; Wells-Dang 2014; Wischermann et al. 2015). It is important to connect the conceptual expectation of public participation to the real-life occurrence of public action seeking to oppose governmental policy. The case of the 2015 large-scale Hanoi tree movement is used as an illustrative example to detail the unfolding of societal action, as well as the nature of state response, in the city. Whilst Geertman and Boudereau (2018), Gillespie and Nguyen (2018), and Vu (2017) have provided in-depth insights into this case, this chapter goes further to integrate reflections from the Hanoi tree movement by providing a thematic analysis that focusses on how the governing institution imposes conditions that enables and constrains public participation. In doing so, this research seeks to answer the following questions: (1) What does the Hanoi tree movement signify in Vietnam's expanding space for public participation? (2) What are the characteristics of public participation in Vietnam, and how are they contested and/or (re-)shaped through the state-society dynamics in Vietnams?

The Hanoi tree movement

In November 2013, the Hanoi Department of Construction submitted a proposal (titled 'Overhauling and Replacing Urban Trees in Hanoi during the Period 2014–2015') to cut down and replace 6,708 trees on 190 streets of Hanoi, 45 of which were approved by the Hanoi People's Committee. Several rationales were used to justify this project. The local government, the Hanoi Municipal People's Committee, stated that the trees were hazardous to the flow of vehicular and pedestrian traffic, and that space needed to be created to accommodate the planned massive urban railway construction project that is co-funded by several external development agencies. The tree removal project began at a small scale, but from March 2015 onwards, it became more visible across the main streets of the city (see Table 7.1 for timeline of key events).

Having received little information about the project, Hanoi residents became suspicious about why the large, decades-old trees had to be removed and what the government would do with the cut-down trees. On 16 March 2015, a former

TABLE 7.1 Timeline summary of the Hanoi tree movement[2]

November 2013	• The Hanoi People's Committee issued Decision No. 6816/QD-UBND which approved the proposal of overhauling and replacing urban trees in Hanoi during the period 2014–2015 submitted by the Hanoi Department of Construction.
November 2014 to January 2015	• Hundreds of trees were cut down in the main streets of Hanoi.
January 2015 to March 2015	• The Hanoi Department of Construction pushed forward the implementation of cutting down more trees. The project became more visible.
16 March	• An ex-journalist posted an open letter to the president of the Hanoi People's Committee. It was spread by newspapers and social media.
17–30 March	• Three major Facebook groups were created by citizens. • A petition was drafted and circulated online and drew 22,000 signatures.
19 March	• Some undergraduate students gathered, hung up slogans, and tied ribbons around the trees on Giảng Võ Street.
20 March	• The petition was submitted to the Hanoi Department of Construction and the Hanoi People's Committee. • The Hanoi People's Committee announced that the project would be temporarily suspended and the officials involved would be disciplined. • A press conference was held by the Hanoi People's Committee, but questions from reporters were left unanswered (there was no interaction but an official response was released on 25 March).
21 March	• The government announced its plan of replacing the trees, but some experts stated that the new trees were not *Manglietia dandyi* but *Manglietia conifera*, which are much cheaper.

senior-level journalist posted an open letter on his Facebook account addressed to the chairman of the Hanoi People's Committee. With his post receiving over 500 shares and having been re-published in the mainstream media, his letter stated that public concerns about widespread tree removal were growing, and thereby requested that the project be suspended so that the viability of felling trees can be examined, that the government share information about the project with the public, and that the government listen to opinions from experts and citizens (Le et al. 2015, 16).

The Hanoi authorities pushed forward with the tree-felling plan with no sign of willingness to interact with the public, which further fuelled public grievances. The deputy head of the Hanoi Municipal People's Committee's Propaganda Department stated in a media interview that the letter was just sent by an ordinary citizen, and questioned whether the government has to ask the opinion of the public in every single policy ("Chặt cây xanh Hà Nội" 2015). On 20 March 2015, the Hanoi Municipal People's Committee held a press conference, where the vice president announced justifications for the project, leaving immediately afterwards without answering any questions from journalists ("Chặt cây xanh: Lãnh đạo Hà Nội" 2015).

With the advent of social media, where it is more easily accessible for people to express and exchange opinions with each other, the entry barriers to raising voices and taking action—online and offline—have been greatly reduced. Social media has created new contexts and platforms for social movements which were not possible with the unidirectional communication of traditional media (DeLuca, Lawson, and Sun 2012; Harlow 2011; Khondker 2011; Shirky 2011). A number of Vietnamese citizens shared images and their thoughts online, primarily through three Facebook pages that became key platforms for collective action. One page, named '6,700 People for 6,700 Trees' (*6,700 người vì 6,700 cây xanh*), was created by a housewife who cared about the loss of the beautiful trees, which drew over 60,000 likes and followers within two weeks and evolved into the main driving force of the citizen-led tree movement (Vu 2017). Another page, '6,700 Green Trees' (*6,700 cây xanh*), was created on 18 March 2015 by architects who planned to film a documentary on this topic, attracting over 5,000 members (Le et al. 2015). The third page, 'For a Green Hanoi' (*Vì Một Hà Nội Xanh*), was created in late March 2015, differing from the other groups in that it was created by environmental and political activists, adding a stronger political layer to their action, and their vehement demands for more transparency and accountability from the Hanoi government (Geertman and Boudereau 2018).

Participants in this movement were diverse. They included male and female teenagers, college students, and elderly people. Architects, artists, singers, environmental experts, lawyers, and social organisations got involved, indirectly or directly claiming the lack of justifiable elements and evidence in the municipality's decision to remove the trees (Le et al. 2015). No specific public group constituted a majority, and concerned individuals expressed their opinions in various ways, ranging from putting a campaign sticker on their bags to joining a street demonstration. The first action on the street was led by undergraduate students in Hanoi who attached signs to trees saying 'Please do not kill me' or tied ribbons around tree trunks on 19 March. In the meantime, a petition was initiated on Facebook, attracting over 22,000 signatures within several days, and it was submitted to the Hanoi Municipal People's Committee on 20 March 2015.

A few days after the petition was submitted, on 22 March 2015, a highly visible and organised demonstration was held in Hanoi, with an estimated 500 people participating. The protest was peaceful and friendly, with the participants standing hand in hand around the trees, chanting in groups, and marching with paper signs saying 'Tree Hugs Hanoi', calling for a stop to the tree-felling project. Experts and activists were committed to sharing relevant information, as they held a seminar on 23 March 2015 to discuss the status and problems of the project. Experts found that the information released by the local government, about the type of new trees to be planted as a replacement for the felled trees, was incorrect. They argued that the new replacement trees were not *Manglietia dandyi* as announced by the government, but rather the *Manglietia conifera*, which are usually much cheaper. This information spread like wildfire through social media, and public anger increased as greater transparency was demanded from the Hanoi government.

A series of public rallies were held from March to April 2015, and public dissatisfaction gradually expanded, leading to public mobilisations that demanded for greater government transparency and accountability to its citizens. Some members of the public held a banner with the slogan of the Vietnam Communist Party, 'People know, people discuss, people do, and people supervise' (*Dân biết, dân bàn, dân làm, dân kiểm tra*). Some bloggers emphasised the value of grassroots democracy which they revealed has been legally stipulated in government legislation, notably Ordinance No. 34/2007/PL-UBTVQH11 on Democratic Implementation at Communes, Wards and Towns (*Pháp lệnh số 34/2007/PL-UBTVQH11 ngày 20 tháng 4 năm 2007 về thực hiện dân chủ ở xã, phường, thị trấnidhhhr*). By referencing the law, the Hanoi government could not avoid addressing the public's political denunciations, as ignoring such public concerns was perceived to damage the government's 'moral legitimacy' (*uy tín*) (Gillespie and Nguyen 2018). In the later phase of a walk-out demonstration in April 2015, some participants started to criticise the Hanoi leaders and political figures, even though it was not the original purpose of the demonstration which primarily sought to oppose the tree-felling project (Le et al. 2015). As collective actions increasingly adopted an anti-governmental stance and contested the way the Hanoi government makes decisions, the authorities tried to terminate the movement more tyrannically: domestic security forces warned, interrogated, or physically harassed some protest participants, and mainstream media was forced to cease coverage of the movement (Vu 2017; Gillespie and Nguyen 2018).

When the government did respond to public concerns, their response was temporary, and more oriented to mitigating public denunciation, without preventing the trees from being removed or replaced. The government did not organise a platform to listen to public opinion, nor was any direct dialogue made between the Hanoi government and the public during the tree movement (Le et al. 2015; Gillespie and Nguyen 2018). The Hanoi Municipal People's Committee halted the project for a while, conducted an investigation of the tree-felling movement, and suspended a few working-level officials in the Hanoi Department of Construction for disciplinary reasons, but policy decisions were still made by and within the government, leaving little to no space for public involvement. The Hanoi Municipal People's Committee promised to conduct an investigation when public dissatisfaction rose, but such investigations only involved a closed group of invited experts. The Hanoi government implemented the project with no public consultations, and deliberately delayed its responses to the public as a 'cosmetic tactic' to soothe and thus minimise interactions with them (Vu 2017).

Initially, the central government of Vietnam did not take any specific measures, but rather stood on the sidelines because public complaints targeted the Hanoi Municipal People's Government. The central government eventually paid attention to and responded to public allegations of misconduct from the Hanoi government, and the Government Inspectorate, a ministry-level agency which handles public denunciations and state mismanagement such as corruption, asked the Hanoi government to submit a report on its management of this case (Le et al. 2015). The

Government Inspectorate noted some inappropriate actions of the Hanoi government, stating that the decision makers did not consult with experts or the public and that the local authorities made mistakes, such as providing incorrect information about the new replacement trees ("Review of Officials' Responsibility" 2015). However, as a larger number of people joined the movement and the arguments of the public became more politicised, both the central and Hanoi authorities became intolerant towards such citizen collective actions. With the state's forcible imposition of 'public order', public actions, which had blossomed within a short period, withered. All in all, the case did not make any transformative change in any institutional mechanism whereby citizens are able to engage in policy decision-making processes or hold the government to account.

Participation under the current institutions

Selective responses of the state

I argue that the severity of the Vietnamese state's responses to local social movements is selective, and differs according to the topic of the movement. In the case of the tree-felling project in Hanoi, public participation was tolerated when public demonstrations focussed on the tree-felling project itself, but the level of state suppression increased as the movement adopted an explicit political, anti-governmental bent by criticising the government's lack of transparency and accountability. If is the state perceives that an instance of public action challenges the firm objective of maintaining the status quo, state authorities will then seek to control and silence the dissenting public voices and actions. During fieldwork, many interviewees from social organisations and external development agencies in Hanoi stated that the scope of their work, which includes engaging in public awareness-raising programmes or in policy advocacy, is also topic dependent. As long as social organisations address a topic that is regarded by the relevant state agency or party as not posing a threat to the political structures and dynamics of the nation (e.g., poverty reduction or climate change adaptation), the authorities tend to be more receptive to input from the public and social organisations. In other words, state authorities are more open to hearing criticism and suggestions on what they consider as apolitical, which echoes research on post-democratic and post-political dynamics in Western contexts (e.g., Cochrane 2010; Swyngedouw 2011; Ward 2007).

Denunciations about leaders of the government or the party are rarely tolerated, and the Vietnamese are already aware of the negative consequences of such actions. An interviewee shared his experience of a nationwide survey exploring Vietnamese citizens' sentiments on governance, saying that the survey found how people are critical about policies or projects of the government, but often hesitate and do not really criticise the ruling Communist Party of Vietnam itself (interview no. 2, vice director, social organisation). Other topics citizens known to be out of bounds include human rights, multi-party democracy, transparency, and accountability. The view of the state is that these topics can be detrimental to maintaining the current institutions, so they are tied to a legally defined condition of 'disturbing public order'.

Another variable in the selective responses of the state is what approach people take. It is not just about whether protests occur individually or in a larger movement, but more about how aggressive they are towards the state. According to interviewees, the government is not very concerned about public demonstrations or pickets depending on the topic of contestation, whilst they would arrest an individual blogger who forcefully criticises the government or the Communist Party. A peaceful public rally may be tolerated or simply observed by plainclothes police officers, whereas participants—usually the leaders of a protest—are taken to the police if such mobilisations get too confrontational, or if people excessively criticise government policies online or in public space. The movement against the tree-felling project was not oppressed in its early phase, since participants were careful in their approach and made non-political arguments instead of fighting for political reconfiguration (Gillespie and Nguyen 2018).

From the government perspective, authorities prefer public participation in urban governance to take place within the officially established conventional mechanism within the current political system. One of the most representative examples of such a conventional channel is for citizens to use socio-political organisations established across the national, provincial, district, and communal levels across the country, to act as mediators with the governing bodies. However, the role of these socio-political organisations (also known as mass organisations) remains debatable, complicated by their organisational identity and their nature of independence and representativeness. Explaining the function of these mass organisations, some interviewees argue that mass organisations closely interact with local people through their local units, delivering local opinions and providing policy consultation to the government or Communist Party. One of the interviewees affiliated with a local socio-political organisation remarked that its main task is to process complaints and letters, to receive citizens' opinions and transfer them to responsible agencies to resolve, and to build a dialogic space between the leaders of the People's Committee or People's Council and local people, so that the latter can vocalise urgent matters of discontent (interview no. 40, deputy-manager level, socio-political organisation). Another interviewee who is involved with a socio-political organisation also commented about their role in bridging the gap between the government/Communist Party and people, saying that in the headquarters of their organisation there is a citizen reception room where any citizen can come to consult with them, which the organisation will then convey through the monthly meeting organised by the government or through the Vietnam Fatherland Front, an umbrella organisation of socio-political organisations (interview no. 41, deputy-manager level, socio-political organisation).

However, a more pessimistic perspective on the role of socio-political organisations emphasises their identity as the expanded arms of the Communist Party. Many other interviewees on the non-government side argued that these organisations do not serve as an intermediary of mutual interaction between the public and the state, but that their role is closer to disseminating propaganda than genuinely representing the voices of local people. What is inferred from the thematic analysis (see Figure 7.1) is that socio-political organisations play a dual role: they not only enable local people to make their voices heard by state agencies, but also act as a platform for the government or Communist Party to unilaterally announce policy decisions and mobilise support for them. Hence, the form of public participation through socio-political organisations can contain many contradictions: it may be self-driven (active) or mobilised (passive) depending on the case. Their different mixed identities and roles merit further research and classification.

Even though people are cautious not to provoke the government/Communist Party, the way the state applies its dual approach of accommodation and control of citizen voices is not always consistent. Instead, it depends on who makes the case, and what case is being made, and this can be arbitrary. Several interviewees claimed that the state response to public participation usually fluctuates depending on other factors, such as where citizen mobilisations occur (e.g., in urban and rural provinces) and how conservative the local leaders are (e.g., their political attitudes being restrictive or open to public voices). Moreover, there is no clear link between public participation and state responsiveness, which means that public efforts to voice discontent or engage with policy decision-making may lead to no response from state authorities. An interviewee argued that state responsiveness in Vietnam is still immature, as the state authorities barely respond to public inquiries or requests (interview no. 24, founder, unregistered group on human rights). Interviewees in all categories but the government sector remarked that the government takes the action of opening its ears, but its main aim is to keep society under its grip and prevent any unexpected confrontations against the party-state, arguing that formalistically there are channels to raise voices but the process is long. Another interviewee also stated that upon receipt of citizens' complaints, the government cares more about being publicly shamed than the nature of the problems expressed, so the police will visit a citizen's house to either calm them down or threaten them to keep them silent (interview no. 8, policy analyst, multi-lateral development agency).

Some interviewees in social organisations insisted that there are some interactions between the state and society which are meaningful, but that they represent no more than the state's superficial receptiveness. For example, it is common that the government invites a select number of citizens or social organisations to policy consultations, or for government officials to attend seminars organised by social organisations. However, such occasions tend to produce little real impact. As such, the Vietnamese state occasionally allows space for public engagement in policy decision-making when it seems acceptable from its point of view or when it is necessary to collect public opinion. As for the Hanoi tree-felling movement case, urban governance was perceived as "the exclusive preserve of the party-state", in which officials listened to public opinions only "when necessary" instead of accepting public participation as a basic right for the citizenry (Gillespie and Nguyen 2018, 12).

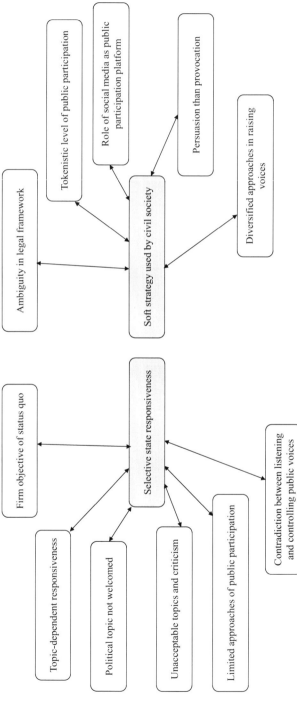

FIGURE 7.1 Thematic network of public participation contexts in Vietnam

Softer strategy within the reality

May interviewees argued that there is a wide gap between legal regulations and with the on-the-ground practices. Rhetoric about citizen participation in decision-making on paper merely serves as a way of constraining social disorder and maintaining the long-standing dominance of top-down state institutions (Dao and Nguyen 2015; Thayer 2010; Tortosa 2012; Wells-Dang 2010). An interviewee illustrated this claim by pointing out that the state tends to listen and respond to public opinion—instead of suppressing these opinions through the use of physical force—not to incorporate them into the decision-making process, but to merely placate public discontent and protect the legitimacy of the state (interview no. 25, chief researcher, development consulting firm in Vietnam).

At the same time, interviewees also repeatedly mentioned changes in state responsiveness towards public opinions. Plenty of interviewees in the non-governmental categories observed that the state is becoming more open and amicable towards citizens and social organisations. Regardless of the state's repressive measures, they have also shown greater tolerance to certain forms of individual and collective action as compared to the past, when the state was much more cautious towards practices of public action addressing state management. An interviewee remarked that in the past, local government leaders did not believe in the necessity of public participation in governance, but in recent years, the top-down form of governance has changed such that contemporary local governments care more about how they interact with their residents (no. 29, director general, central ministry). Despite these changes, ultimately, the party-state has not reformed spaces for public participation sufficiently to allow citizens to freely and actively engage with the policy decision-making processes.

Theoretically, a substantive social movement goes one step further than addressing a certain issue-specific social problem, but more broadly enhances "the role of civil society as a critical dialogue partner with the state" (Chambers and Kopstein 2008, 370). Considering that, public participation should ideally go further than facilitate people's 'participation in a given space', but should also realise their right to 'shape the space' (Gaventa 2006). In Vietnam, public participation has manifested in a limited space which is shaped not by the public themselves, but by the state's arbitrary discretion. Even though there exists legally recognised rights for the public to express their opinion and participate in decision-making processes, the Vietnamese state still prioritises their own political legitimacy over citizens' rights.

Whilst space for public participation is quite limited, at the same time, a move to promote public participation has emerged. Some interviewees mentioned the Hanoi tree-felling movement as a good example in which social media played a significant role in enabling more citizen voices to be asserted and heard. In contrast to the argument made by Kurfurst (2015, 142–143) that most online social movements are limited to cyberspace, 'hybrid spaces' have been formed by Vietnamese citizens through taking collective action in cyberspace which then permeated into the physical space of the city. For instance, the aforementioned Facebook pages enabled those who were concerned about the felling of trees to express their voices and mobilise a series of demonstrations in public spaces. Social media is a promising means of increasing public participation in matters of governance in Vietnam, providing an alternative platform for the public to exchange information and have a say on policy issues. Although cyberspace is subject to censorship by the authorities, social media has paved the way for collective action and allowed public voices to resonate to the extent that the government is now forced to pay attention to them. Since the voices of the Vietnamese public are not often heard by the government through official conventional channels (such as through the mediation of socio-political organisations), cyberspace, particularly social media, has come to function as a 'new public space' for the public to express opinions and share information (Duong 2017; Vu 2017). Many interviewees also noted the increasing presence of social media as being a solid ground for public action, with one individual commenting that using social media can be a time- and energy-efficient platform for citizens to lodge their complaints or make suggestions. Popular and widely disseminated messages on social media platforms are often covered by the mainstream media, which then grab the attention of the authorities, prompting these authorities to eventually respond (interview no. 14, researcher, university-affiliated research institute).

Furthermore, civil society has continued to mobilise in cyber space. For example, the '6,700 People for 6,700 Trees' Facebook page remains active. Some people share information and encourage others to sign the petition against the Law on Cybersecurity, passed in June 2018, which is interpreted as a means for the state to impose tighter control over online space and to access the personal information of Internet users. Setting aside the debate as to whether such online petitions made any measurable impact, the fact that citizens are putting their names and basic personal information out in the open by signing online petitions on various policy issues has substance in of itself, representing a willingness amongst the people to raise their voices on matters of governance, even though they run the risk of suppression by the state (Morris-Jung 2015). However, the impact of social media on current institutions needs to be considered with caution, as the state authorities still exercise power and influence by controlling the degree of public participation in governance (Bui 2016). Nonetheless, the Vietnamese public continue to use the Internet to enhance the possibility of claiming and creating space for public participation more widely.

Yet, public participation in Vietnam is developing in a way that conforms to whatever agenda the state pursues. Interviewees from both sides—government agencies and social organisations—remarked that it is more pragmatic to take a dialogical approach to making policy inputs through soliciting agreement and sustaining non-oppositional relationships. Due to heavy surveillance by the party-state, many Vietnamese social organisations avoid taking risks by standing against the government, but instead tend to place themselves under the auspices of the Communist Party (Landau 2008). An interviewee spoke of having to strike a balance between what they want to do, and what they can do under the current system (interview no. 34, vice-director, social organisation), a view shared by another interviewee, who also said that his organisation tries not to provoke the government by demanding policy changes, but that his organisation, as well as the government, tend to try to "work together in a team" (interview no. 45, coordinator, network of activists and organisations on governance). In addition, one interviewee stated that her organisation takes a "two-track approach", where they collect information about people's needs and provide the government with these research findings as evidence, and also confront the government when its policy decisions harm a particular community or social group (interview no. 46, vice-director, social organisation). In the Hanoi tree movement, individual activists and social organisations made it evident to the public that the use of a demonstrations was not their initial preference, but that they were prompted to launch such protest because their "non-violent and collaborative spirit" and demonstration was preceded by other forms of action, such as having previously attempted at initiating dialogue with the authorities or by submitting petitions (Vu 2017, 1194).

The party-state is concerned that greater public participation may become uncontrollable and develop into political resistance not just against specific issue-specific matters, but against the governing bodies. Whilst some citizens and organisations face strong oppression for actively criticising the government or the Communist Party, much civic action works to gradually stretch out the boundary of participation space through a strategic combination of advocacy and persuasion, rather than by engaging in radical revolt. The approaches used by techniques of advocacy and persuasion range from providing evidence-based policy consultancy, such as disseminating research or survey findings in which the needs of local people are reflected, to organising policy workshops with invited government officials. This tendency of seeking cooperation rather than confrontation is attributed to an inevitable political compromise arising from the clearly demarcated boundaries of the space for public participation in Vietnam.

Conclusion

The case of the Hanoi tree movement offers mixed findings regarding the extent to which public participation is substantive in present-day Vietnam. The movement began with environmental concerns over large-scale tree felling across Hanoi, but calls for government transparency and accountability soon came to the fore. As Vu (2017) argues, local environmental activism acted both as a medium to integrate the political demands of citizens and organisations for increased government accountability, and as a catalyst to the development of further collective action. In this sense, the movement has been successful in carving a path towards enhancing state-society relations. The widespread collective actions taken by ordinary Vietnamese citizens are significant, in that they are not merely limited to one-time, single-issue events, but represent a series of sustained public engagements involving a range of petitions to public rallies on the streets, the latter of which are still rare in Vietnam. Moreover, social media use has risen in Vietnam as an alternative platform for public participation in policy affairs. On the other hand, actions taken by individual citizens or organisations are oppressed as soon as the state authorities start to feel threatened by them. For instance, the state authorities shut down public demonstrations if the demands of protest participants became overtly politicised, even if the participants held rallies in a non-violent manner.

From the thematic analysis summarised in Figure 7.1, two trends in political participation in Vietnam can be highlighted. Firstly, public participation in governance is topic dependent, as the government forecloses politically sensitive topics such as human rights and democratic pluralism. Whilst the public can have a say about certain policy issues, public action remains subject to suppression in the name of protecting public order, with notions of public order defined at the government's discretion. Secondly, public participation space in Vietnam is approach dependent: interviewees widely believe that a cooperative approach, and not a confrontational approach, between the state and society better allows space for citizen participation to be stretched out and to expand. For citizens, engaging in dialogue and evidence-based discussions with policy makers may take longer for substantial change to be actualised, but such approaches are adopted as a form of compromise due to Vietnam's inconsistent and uncertain participation space.

The notion of public participation is recognised and practised by Vietnamese citizens: people talk to local officials, sign petitions, criticise policies, and form groups and some organise individual or small-scale demonstrations in public spaces. One of the main reasons for people taking such action is to express disagreement with, or to denunciate, state authorities or institutions. The Vietnamese state does not always repress public participation. However, public participation has a weak relationship with government responsiveness. The state's politicised 'accommodate-and-control' approach leaves public participation tokenistic, and further, the state authorities are not willing to share decision-making power with the public despite the legal documents enshrining grassroots democracy and public consultations in the policy-making process. Vietnamese individuals and social organisations are aware of such restrictive conditions, and have responded by adopting 'softer' strategies of initiating dialogues and attempting to persuade the state through evidence-based approaches, which are deemed as safer ways of making their voices heard by the state authorities.

These characteristics of state-society relations in Vietnam may look similar to what the post-politics literature describes as governance based on consensual, pragmatic, and expertise-oriented politics. However, the non-liberal democratic structure of Vietnam results in a model of public participation that is far removed from the form of techno-managerial decision-making described in much of the post-politics literature. For instance, the Vietnamese state exercises control over social mobilisation to sustain the socio-political status quo, which is vital to maintaining the current democratic socialist regime. The power of state control and regulation and the prevailing state ideology on participation work to constrain public participation. Public action and contestation must therefore be depoliticised, which is premised on a very limited view of public participation adovated by the party-state.

Acknowledgements

I would like to thank my interviewees and Linh Khanh Luu, who was my local research assistant during the fieldwork. I also extend my gratitude to my promotors, Prof Wil Hout and Dr Joop de Wit, for their support and valuable advice. Last but not least, I appreciate the Asia Research Institute of the National University of Singapore for its invitation to present this chapter in draft form at a conference organised in August 2018.

Notes

1 Organisations that are established and operated by citizens are called 'social organisations' (*tổ chức xã hội*) or 'associations' (*hội*) in official policy documents and discourses. According to the Decree No. 45/2010/ND-CP on the Organisation, Operation and Management (*Nghị định số 45/2010/NĐ-CP ngày 21 tháng 4 năm 2010 của Chính phủ: Quy định về tổ chức, hoạt động và quản lý hội o vul*), an association is defined as "a voluntary organisation of Vietnamese citizens or institutions with the same business or interest or in the same circle that unite for a common goal and operate regularly and disinterestedly" (np). In practice, social organisations are often regarded interchangeable with 'civil society organisations' or 'non-governmental organisations' which are grounded on the liberal democratic model, but it needs to be noted that they are not completely synonymous in the Vietnamese context, conceptually or operationally.
2 For further details, refer to Le et al. (2015) and "Timeline of the Tree-felling Project" (2015).

References

Arnstein, S. R. 1969. "A Ladder of Citizen Participation." *Journal of the American Institute of Planners* 35 (4): 216–224.

Braun, V., and V. Clarke. 2006. "Using Thematic Analysis in Psychology." *Qualitative Research in Psychology* 3 (2): 77–101.

Bui, T. H. 2013. "The Development of Civil Society and Dynamics of Governance in Vietnam's One Party Rule." *Global Change, Peace & Security* 25 (1): 77–93.

———. 2016. "The Influence of Social Media in Vietnam's Elite Politics." *Journal of Current Southeast Asian Affairs* 35 (2): 89–112.

Chambers, S., and J. Kopstein. 2008. "Civil Society and the State." In *The Oxford Handbook of Political Theory*, edited by J. S. Dryzek, B. Honig, and A. Phillips, 363–381. Oxford: Oxford University Press.

Chặt cây xanh Hà Nội không phải hỏi dân [Cutting Trees in Hanoi does not have to be asked to People]. 2015. *Vietnamnet*, March 17. http://vietnamnet.vn/vn/thoi-su/chat-cay-xanh-ha-noi-khong-phai-hoi-dan-226164.html

Chặt cây xanh: Lãnh đạo Hà Nội nhận lỗi và "nợ" 21 câu trả lời [Cutting Green Trees: Hanoi Leader Talks and 'Owes' 21 Answers]. 2015. *Nguoi Lao Dong*, March 20. https://nld.com.vn/thoi-su-trong-nuoc/chat-cay-xanh-lanh-dao-ha-noi-nhan-loi-va-no-21-cau-tra-loi-20150320161623631.html

Cochrane, A. 2010. "Exploring the Regional Politics of 'Sustainability': Making up Sustainable Communities in the South-East of England." *Environmental Policy and Governance* 20: 370–381.

Cornwall, A. 2008. "Unpacking 'Participation': Models, Meanings and Practices." *Community Development Journal* 43 (3): 269–283.

Dao, T. H. M., and T. A. T. Nguyen. 2015. "Citizen-Centered Local Governance in Vietnam: The Participation at Local Level." In *Citizen Participation in Selected Local Governance of Asia Pacific Countries*, edited by A. Nurmandi, S. Roengtam, E. P. Purnomo, and A. W. Tamronglak, 111–128. Indonesia: Asia Pacific Society for Public Affairs and Jusuf Kalla School of Government.

DeLuca, K. M., S. Lawson, and Y. Sun. 2012. "Occupy Wall Street on the Public Screens of Social Media: The Many Framings of the Birth of a Protest Movement." *Communication, Culture and Critique* 5 (4): 483–509.

Duong, M. 2017. "The Beginning of Online Social Movements in Vietnam." Paper presented at the 2017 ANZCA Conference: Communication Worlds: Access, Voice, Diversity, Engagement, Sydney, July 4–7.

Fforde, A. 2011. "Contemporary Vietnam: Political Opportunities, Conservative Formal Politics, and Patterns of Radical Change." *Asian Politics & Policy* 3 (2): 165–184.

Gaventa, J. 2006. "Finding the Spaces for Change: A Power Analysis." *IDS Bulletin* 37 (6): 23–33.

Geertman, S., and J. Boudereau. 2018. "'Life as Art': Emerging Youth Networks in Hanoi and the Tree Hug Movement." *City & Society* 30 (1): 1–27.

Gillespie, J., and Q. H. Nguyen. 2018. "Between Authoritarian Governance and Urban Citizenship: Tree-Felling Protests in Hanoi." *Urban Studies* 56 (5): 1–15.

Harlow, S. 2011. "Social Media and Social Movements: Facebook and an Online Guatemalan Justice Movement that Moved Offline." *New Media & Society* 14 (2): 225–243.

Hoa, T. T. T., and J. Garcia-Zamor. 2017. "Citizen Participation in Vietnam's Local Government: Impact on Transparency and Accountability." *Journal of Public Administration and Governance* 7 (4): 38–57.

Kerkvliet, B. J. T. 2010. "Governance, Development, and the Responsive-Repressive State in Vietnam." *Forum for Development Studies* 37 (1): 33–59.

———. 2015. "Regime Critics: Democratization Advocates in Vietnam, 1990s—2014." *Critical Asian Studies* 47 (3): 359–387.

Khondker, H. H. 2011. "Role of the New Media in the Arab Spring." *Globalization* 8 (5): 675–679.

Kleinen, J. 2015. *Vietnam: One-party State and the Mimicry of Civil Society*. Bangkok: Research Institute on Contemporary Southeast Asia (IRASEC).

Kurfurst, S. 2015. "Networking Alone? Digital Communications and Collective Action in Vietnam." *Journal of Current Southeast Asian Affairs* 34 (3): 123–150.

Landau, I. 2008. "Law and Civil Society in Cambodia and Vietnam: A Gramsci an perspective." *Journal of Contemporary Asia* 38 (2): 244–258.

Le, Q. B., T. H. Doan, T. T. N. Nguyen, and T. T. Mai. 2015. *Report on Movements to Protect 6700 Trees in Hanoi*. Hanoi: Hong Duc Publisher.

Morris-Jung, J. 2015. "Online Petitions: Promoting a Public Voice in Vietnamese Politics." *ISEAS Perspective* 38. www.iseas.edu.sg/images/pdf/ISEAS_Perspective_2015_38.pdf

Mouffe, C. 2005. *On the Political*. Oxford: Routledge.

Nghị định số 45/2010/NĐ-CP ngày 21 tháng 4 năm 2010 của Chính phủ quy định về tổ chức, hoạt động và quản lý hội [Decree No. 45/2010/ND-CP of April 21, 2010, on the Organization, Operation and Management]. https://thuvienphapluat.vn/archive/Nghi-dinh/Decree-No-45-2010-ND-CP-on-the-organization-operation-and-management-vb108162t11.aspx

Nguyen, H. H. 2014. "Political Parties, Civil Society and Citizen Movements in Vietnam." In *Political Parties and Citizen Movements in Asia and Europe*, edited by R. Cordenillo and S. van der Staak, 141–159. Sweden: Asia-Europe Foundation, Haans Seidel Foundation, and International Institute for Democracy and Electoral Assistance.

Nguyen, T. V., C. Q. Le, B. T. Tran, and S. E. Bryant. 2015. "Citizen Participation in City Governance: Experiences from Vietnam." *Public Administration and Development* 35 (1): 34–45.
Pháp lệnh số 34/2007/PL-UBTVQH11 ngày 20 tháng 4 năm 2007 về thực hiện dân chủ ở xã, phường, thị trấn [Ordinance No. 34/2007/PL-UBTVQH11 of April 20, 2007, on Exercise of Democracy in Communes, Wards and Townships]. https://vanbanphapluat.co/phap-lenh-thuc-hien-dan-chu-o-xa-phuong-thi-tran-2007-34–2007-pl-ubtvqh11#luoc-do
Review of Officials' Responsibility in 'Tree Massacre' Must Finish in June: Hanoi Authorities. 2015. *Tuổi Trẻ*, March 20. https://tuoitrenews.vn/society/28171/window.print
Roberts, N. 2004. "Public Deliberation in an Age of Direct Citizen Participation." *The American Review of Public Administration* 34 (4): 315–353.
Salemink, O. 2006. "Translating, Interpreting and Practicing Civil Society in Vietnam: A Tale of Calculated Misunderstandings." In *Development Brokers and Translators: The Ethnography of Aid and Agencies*, edited by D. Lewis and D. Mosse, 101–126. Bloomfield, CT: Kumarian Press.
Shirky, C. 2011. "Political Power of Social Media Technology, the Public Sphere, and Political Change." *Foreign Affairs* 90 (1): 28–41.
Swyngedouw, E. 2009. "The Antinomies of the Postpolitical City: In Search of a Democratic Politics of Environmental Production." *International Journal of Urban and Regional Research* 33 (3): 601–620.
———. 2011. "Interrogating Post-Democratization: Reclaiming Egalitarian Political Spaces." *Political Geography* 30 (7): 370–380.
Thayer, C. A. 2009. "Vietnam and the Challenge of Political Civil Society." *Contemporary Southeast Asia: A Journal of International and Strategic Affairs* 31 (1): 1–27.
———. 2010. "Political Legitimacy in Vietnam: Challenge and Response." *Politics and Policy* 38 (3): 423–444.
Tortosa, A. J. P. 2012. "Grassroots Democracy in Rural Vietnam: A Gramscian Analysis." *Socialism and Democracy* 26 (1): 103–126.
Vu, N. A. 2017. "Grassroots Environmental Activism in an Authoritarian Context: The Trees Movement in Vietnam." *VOLUNTAS: International Journal of Voluntary and Nonprofit Organizations* 28 (3): 1180–1208.
Ward, K. 2007. "'Creating a Personality for Downtown': Business Improvement Districts in Milwaukee." *Urban Geography* 28 (8): 781–808.
Wells-Dang, A. 2010. "Political Space in Vietnam: A View from the 'Rice-Roots'." *The Pacific Review* 23 (1): 93–112.
———. 2014. "The Political Influence of Civil Society in Vietnam." In *Politics in Contemporary Vietnam: Party, State, and Authority Relations*, edited by J. London, 162–183. London: Palgrave Macmillan.
White, S. C. 1996. "Depoliticising Development: The Uses and Abuses of Participation." *Development in Practice* 6 (1): 6–15.
Wilson, J., and E. Swyngedouw. 2014. "Seeds of Dystopia: Post-Politics and the Return of the Political." In *Post-Political and Its Discontents: Spaces of Depoliticisation, Spectres of Radical Politics*, edited by J. Wilson and E. Swyngedouw, 1–22. Edinburgh: Edinburgh University Press.
Wischermann, J., T. C. Bui, Q. V. Nguyen, T. V. P. Dang, and T. M. C. Nguyen. 2015. "Under the State's Thumb: Results from an Empirical Survey of Civic Organizations in Vietnam." GIGA German Institute of Global and Area Studies No. 276. Germany: German Institute of Global and Area Studies.
Žižek, S. 1999. *The Absent Centre of Political Ontology*. London: Verso.

8

ENVIRONMENTAL CIVIL ACTIVISM IN CENTRAL ASIA

Emerging civil society governance and fragile relations with the state

Reina Artur Kyzy

Introduction

Central Asian republics have existed as *de jure* independent nations since the collapse of the Soviet Union in 1991, and they have evolved out of communist systems where ideas of civil society had been intrinsically attached to the state agenda. Kyrgyzstan, Kazakhstan, Uzbekistan, Tajikistan, and Turkmenistan are five *stan*-countries which have very common cultural and social characteristics, but simultaneously differ significantly in their current political regimes. At the moment, Kazakhstan, Tajikistan, and Turkmenistan have a more authoritarian leadership, whereas Kyrgyzstan has gone through two coup d'états and is the only country with renewed presidents, and Uzbekistan elected their second president, Shavkat Mirziyoyev (2016–present), just one year after the death of the first president, Islam Karimov, who ruled for 27 years (1991–2016). However, according to variety of independent international organisations such as Transparency International, Human Rights Watch, Amnesty International, and others, all five countries are considered amongst the countries with the lowest rates of democracy and with weak or even an absent fundamental democratic freedoms (Transparency International 2018). Obviously, in addition to poor economic prosperity and complicated social and cultural norms, civic freedoms are the least developed in the region.

Nevertheless, each country has a long history of thorny relations between civil society dynamics and the state, which makes the region a fascinating one to study. Although the relationship between governments and civil society has never been a simple affair in any society, the diverse historical and geographic conditions of the region itself (being located at the crossroads of Europe and Asia and possessing scarce resources in its landlocked geography, as well as having inherited ideologies and practices derived from Islamic rule and Soviet communism) present interesting potentials for the reconfiguration of state-society relations. This chapter will provide an overview of civil society in modern Central Asia with an emphasis on environmental groups. In particular, it will elaborate on the third sector's relationships with governments in Central Asia, focusing on the case study of Kyrgyzstan, and finally, assess the potentials of civil society in the region.

Environmental NGOs in Central Asia

After the fall of the Soviet Union, and with increasing support from Western organisations and governments, the number of non-governmental organisations (NGOs) and civic unions has significantly increased in Central Asia. Despite the wide range of NGOs engaged in diverse activities, environmental NGOs have played an especially significant role in the development of civil society in Central Asia. Environmental groups are considered the strongest and most experienced amongst the civic sector. This is evidenced not just through their numbers, but also their strong solidarity network of civic activists and vigorous campaigns. Whilst democratic freedoms have yet to reach Central Asia, civic activists have been building liberal democratic mechanisms to address important urban and environmental problems in support of the state's activities, or more frequently, in opposing state's decisions, connivances, or ignorance. Despite the wide range of challenges, environmental NGOs and activists have shown a high level of development in building trustworthy relationships with most of the different actors by offering strategic decisions to important environmental problems, thus resulting in attractive investments and international grants.

Despite this variety of hardships, the environmental NGOs have affected a broad development of civil society in four areas: developing community support, networking and coalition building, working with and affecting change in government, and establishing international contacts (Watters 1995). Hundreds of small NGOs continue to develop small communities and transform local society, whereas larger organisations work on broader issues, and have a substantial influence over countrywide and national decisions.

In light of the growing urbanisation over the last 15 years, administrations of capital cities in Central Asia such as Bishkek, Almaty/Astana, Dushanbe, and Tashkent have been taking unpopular and highly contested decisions over the cities' landscapes and infrastructure or ignoring very urgent environmental issues. In addition to massive tree cutting in order to widen the roads for cars, there is also the expansion of garbage dumps around cities, ignorance of drastic air pollution increases, and privatisation of public parklands and forests. Most of these activities have been actively confronted by local environmental activists in the form of public dialogues, policy proposals, roundtable discussions, and riots and protests. However, ubiquitous corruption, authoritarian regimes, fragile democracies, and other socio-economic problems at both national and local levels have hampered local civil society's activity. Nevertheless, environmental activists and NGOs have played a significant role in the development of civil society in Central Asia. Environmental civil groups are amongst the strongest organisations; they have the longest history and have made significant contributions in the development of urban landscapes through collaboration with governments and international organisations.

Conceptualising civil society relations in Central Asia

The actions of civil society groups are always highly dependent on a given state's regime. In simple terms, governance is an important process which regulates a broad range of problems and issues, where actors arrive to mutually agreed decisions through cooperation and discussions. Schmitter defines governance-beyond-the-state systems as horizontal, networked, and "based on interactive relations between independent and interdependent actors" who share a common objectives, ideas and problems with a "high degree of trust", even though there might be internal disputes and problems (Schmitter 2002; Swyngedouw, Page, and Kaika 2002, 112). As Lemke would add, this results in a transformation of politics that changes the power structures in society. What we have today is not a diminishment of state sovereignty and managerial capacities, but a restructure of both formal and informal approaches of government and the appearance of new participants on the scene of government (e.g., NGOs), that indicates a fundamental difference in the statehood and relationship between the state and civil society actors (Lemke 2002). This includes a threefold re-organisation (Swyngedouw 2009). The first one considers the externalisation of state functions through privatisation and decentralisation. Both mechanisms inevitably imply that civil society or market-based groups become increasingly involved in regulating, governing, and organising a series of social, economic, and cultural activities. Second is the up-scaling of governance where the national state increasingly delegates tasks to higher scales or levels of governance, and third is the downscaling of governance to 'local' quasi-autonomous and multi-stakeholder-based practices in the arena of governing. This includes processes of vertical decentralisation towards sub-national forms of governance (Swyngedouw 2009).

Traditionally, the notion of 'community' has been understood as a group of people with close relations between one another, sharing a sense of inclusiveness and solidarity. Before modern urban and civil society discourses, the prevailing idea was also on territorial residence. Community members were supposed to share a territory of residence. Durant (2011, 11) defined community as "a territorial group of people with a common mode of living striving for common objectives". However, with the urbanisation process on the rise, it is clear that sharing close ties and a sense of belonging are not crucial to modern society and civic incentives. Moreover, with constant technological development, physical and territorial attachment has become a less salient and even downgrading feature, thus locality becomes a less important characteristic of communities (Knox and Pinch 2010). The use of computer-mediated communication serves as an additional platform for solidarity without replacing in-person relationships entirely (Knox and Pinch 2010). In countries where freedom of speech and civil rights are fragile and civic activism can be persecuted, raising one's voice via the Internet can be safer and a channel for spreading progressive ideas amongst previously indifferent residents.

Nevertheless, it does not undermine the grassroots nature of civil activism, because such manifestations still emerge as a response to various threats and urgent needs in local areas (Swyngedouw 1997). Nowadays, examples of such grassroots groups are numerous: from groups exposing unsafe buildings and structures caused by corruption to larger movements of saving green spaces. Usually, these sorts of movements are bounded within a certain territory and have a specific agenda. What sets urban social movements apart from grassroots efforts is that they aim to bring about 'a structural change' in social institutions and policy direction (Knox and Pinch 2010).

More recent studies of grassroots and civil activities with a modern technological blueprint indicate an importance of the network amongst them. In simple terms, most accomplishments that any civil society organisation can achieve are done through uniting its efforts. In this case, what becomes more important is uniting efforts of institutionally organised civil society and grassroots communities, where both formal and informal relations can play a significant role, in particular in the developing world, where local residents can usually be ignored by the state or be subject to discrimination. This relates to Diani's (2015) notion of civil society as a web of interdependence, where networks serve as the cement of civil society. Network studies thus point to the importance of collective action mobilisation, which enables local urban residents to ask authorities for responsibility and accountability.

Emerging civil society and state-society relations

The constitution of each country in the Central Asian region states that the political system is democratic. The collapse of the Soviet Union introduced two interrelated logics into Central Asia: democracy and capitalism. Thus, contemporary democratic language employs and reinforces the rhetoric of capitalism: freedom, liberty, satisfaction, communication, connection, and diversity. Like any media-savvy corporation, democratic activists would like to ensure that their voices are heard and their opinions are registered. But in the case of Central Asia, nothing is that simple because in the fight for a democratic and capitalistic state, civil society's relationship with the state is continually challenged.

It is clear that civil society will not achieve progressive results without governmental support, especially in such a fragile democratic and authoritarian setting like Central Asia. When one considers to what extent the work of civil society with the government is effective, the reality of Central Asia shows a bleak picture of this dynamic, especially when compared with more successful post-Soviet Eastern European countries (Georgia, Estonia, Russia, etc.).[1] Today, NGOs maintain limited partnership with government and are primarily more active at the local levels. The government realises that due to its limited financial and human capabilities and the development of Internet (as a modern means of communication and coordination), it can be helpful to cooperate with NGOs as these organisations have some resources and enjoy support from the government's constituents. NGOs would also like to maximise their effectiveness, which can be achieved only in cooperation with the government, including the regulatory agencies. In an ideal democratic setting, this would truly be a win-win relationship, but in reality this has assumed a very different picture.

In Central Asia, the experience of NGO-government cooperation tends to be very diverse and varies from community to community. In Uzbekistan and Turkmenistan, where the government is more repressive towards liberal basic freedoms and does not really tolerate NGO activities, environmental groups and organisations work primarily on issues which do not openly challenge the government's position and activities.

Despite many internal discussions regarding the collapse of urban planning in both countries, deforestation, and significant water pollution, local NGOs have long struggled to bring these problems to the fore of the government's actions. Cotton production (a major agricultural activity in the region) has caused wide-scale problems, mainly the scarcity of drinking water, for ordinary citizens both in urban and rural areas. However, NGOs and activist groups remain afraid to openly address this problem and try instead to seek small-scale solutions at the local levels or solicit the involvement of international donors. However, due to the complicated bureaucratic system controlling international donors' support for local organisations, which usually passes through governmental agencies, it can take years to implement even small projects in Uzbekistan and Turkmenistan. Due to this, the local community tends to lose confidence in NGOs and their associated credibility. Moreover, corrupt systems of government result in systematic barriers that slow down and limit NGO's activity. Thus, major developments are clearer at the local level where small-scale projects have the ability to generate results.

One interesting case is NGO-government cooperation in Tajikistan. Despite weak democratic freedoms, the presence of an authoritarian regime, and persistent socio-economic problems, several major NGOs have developed a strong position within society. The civil war and wide-scale economic problems have weakened the position of the state, which did not have the time and energy for dealing with the rising number of NGOs, and therefore allowed for some issues to be addressed by civil society (ICNL 2019). This situation therefore helped Tajikistan's NGOs to build a strong network of solidarity for further development.

Another example from Tajikistan is very illustrative, as it shows the level of interaction which occurs both at a local and at a national level. A coalition of more than 20 environmental NGOs united under the name 'Citizen's Council on the Environment' has been providing consultancy services to the Ministry of the Environment, with a focus on advising the national environmental policy (CEPGRT 2010). With the support of international donors, such as the International Center for Not-for-Profit Law and United States Agency for International Development (USAID), the council lobbied for the ratification of several important international laws and conventions on the environment. Furthermore, they have lobbied at the Parliament International Convention on the Desertification and Convention on International Trade in Endangered Species. Finally, a new alternative law on social organisations has been a result of such a productive cooperation. This law has played a crucial role in developing civil society in Tajikistan, working as a legal basis for opening and developing new organisations and initiative groups. However, the currently existing environmental NGO sector is very much dependent on international donors and foreign funds. The government sporadically implements barriers to civil society if its actions somehow contradict lucrative businesses or questions (corrupt) government schemes. It should be noted that a very high rate of labour migration of educated males to Russia has significantly challenged the potential of Tajikistan's civil society, leaving a very small number of talented NGOs and professionals to develop the third sector.

Examples from Kazakhstan and Kyrgyzstan have been more successful, because so far their governments do not perceive civil activists as a real threat to their legitimacy. Environmental NGOs have contributed significantly to the development of civil society culture after the 1990s, even whilst battling an array of obstacles and barriers. For the last 28 years of independence, a variety of examples of NGO-government cooperation can be seen. The following example of the Green Salvation–government partnership demonstrates that the openness and readiness of the government can positively contribute solutions by working with civil society partners

The Almaty-based group Green Salvation is one of the oldest environmental groups in the region. It has developed three new nature protection laws for the country and cooperated in the discussion of dozens of ecological regulations. In early 1990, the organisation was invited to participate in working groups with other NGOs and state agencies to develop the country's legislation, which has resulted in an entirely new text on the environmental impact assessment. Later, in 1998, Green Salvation co-authored a law on radiation safety. Whilst participating in the working groups, Green Salvation has provided comprehensive recommendations for other environmental draft laws which were later passed on to parliament. This high level of cooperation built credibility and trust in NGOs in the country from local and nationwide authorities, and international donors have continued to actively invest and support their projects.

Whilst earlier civil society in the region tended to be more of a charismatic nature, NGOs have now started to recognise the importance of grassroots schemes, thus involving more communities in their work. Green Salvation has also understood that without community support, they cannot achieve their mission and gain credibility and public legitimacy, as it is incredibly important to have influence in the community and in relationships with the government. However, this relationship is still limited and remains in a nascent state. For instance, it is unclear whether Kazakhstan's government has treated Green Salvation as a partner, or whether the Ministry of the Environment is led by strong managers and experts in the area of environmental science. This is unlikely, since the state still continues to be very interested in the lucrative oil extraction business and constructions, though it has been proven to be very harmful to the environment (Mondiaal Nieuws 2014). In other words, Kazakhstan's third sector remains constrained by what is permitted by the government and oligarchs.

Existing barriers to civil society–state partnerships

Amongst the most prominent problems are corruption, bureaucracy, incompetence, and the unprofessionalism of governmental officials in important issues. Most of the remaining legal regulations follow those of Soviet times, which bring complications to modern strategies of addressing urban planning and related environmental issues. For example, despite a large protest by environmental activists against the sporadic building of multi-story houses around the capital city Bishkek and the destruction of green parks, the mayor's office has been distributing lands in city parks for wide-scale construction of private houses and business properties. Legal regulations are hardly followed, and permissions for construction are distributed through highly corrupt channels. Thus, even when government institutions support the activities of NGOs in a variety of fields, money-driven and corrupt activities pose significant complications to successful cooperation. Moreover, in a state of weak rule of law, there are often unjust persecutions of civil activists, thus putting even more barriers in the way of civil society (Transparency International 2018).

Environmental organisations in Central Asia also complain about a lack of accountability and transparency on the part of government. Obviously, due to a lack of sufficient information about urban planning and environmental issues, it is becoming more complicated to plan the work and write project proposals. With the development of the Internet, more and more information is becoming available for wider publicity, but still the government decides what sort of information can be accessible to a wider audience. Moreover, the Ministry of the Environment and other related agencies usually lack financial and human resources to address urban environmental problems, but when NGOs try to do it instead of state agencies, access to important information and bureaucratic permissions are difficult to get (Timofeeva 2018). This situation of state-controlled data and corruption significantly challenges and reduces the work of NGOs and governmental authorities itself.

Moving forward: the promising development of urban civic activism in Bishkek

Civil society in the Kyrgyz Republic has developed more rapidly compared to other countries in Central Asia, which is considered a central component of the country's willingness to change and adapt in the process of democratisation. Kyrgyzstan has the highest level of external support for civil society, which exists largely without governmental controls. The country thus has a substantial NGO sector with more than 4,000 NGOs officially registered at the time of writing (National Statistical Committee of Kyrgyzstan 2018). The registration process is one of the easiest in the region—a low fee of KGS$ 40 (£0.46) that the majority can afford, and a simple set of documentation. The law that regulates NGOs was adopted after the collapse of the Soviet Union in 1991, and little has changed from previous laws on public associations. Though most NGOs in registration documents indicate one goal in particular (women's rights, youth rights, environmental protection, human rights, etc.), all have diverse fields of work that include more than one mission. NGOs with an environmental mission comprise around nine percent, but have always played a significant role in the development of civil society in the country. They have the longest history, greatest funding possibilities, and comparatively less problems with the government in most cases. Environmental NGOs tend to be grassroots in nature, especially when organisations are formed around local civil activists. Recent trends show a drastic change in relationships between environmental civil activists and government.

For the last five years, the relationship between Bishkek's civil activists and the municipality has been contentious, but in 2017 it reached its most dangerous point. In the spring of 2017, the municipality commenced one of the largest street reconstructions in Bishkek, which resulted in more than 7,000 trees being cut down. The Dushanbinka neighbourhood was most severely affected by the tree cutting, and its local residents joined environmental civic activists in a month-long resistance against authorities. Protesters received extensive support from the online community, and even brought the case before city court, claiming that authorities had violated the master plan of the capital. But the case was lost quickly despite clear and strong evidence.

However, their protesting activities mobilised a variety of human rights organisations, urban activists, journalists, and even residents of other neighbourhoods who were also frustrated with the authorities. Resistance against the municipality became so fierce that local police detained protesters, including senior citizens and mothers with children. The protesters blamed authorities for their poor knowledge about the environmental consequences of the municipality's actions, and corrupt relationships with lucrative construction businesses. The authorities refused to acknowledge the grassroots nature of the protests and resistance, but instead labelled the protesters as conspiring foreign agents who wanted to destabilise the politics of the country. With officials dismissing protesters' demands, the municipality continued developing and acting on its comprehensive plan for the city centre. Civil activists continued their resistance, but began to actively call for public discussions and moved their protests in front of the offices of authorities.

Later in 2018, environmental problems became the most hotly disputed topic in the capital city, and the government of Kyrgyzstan even admitted that a serious air pollution problem had arisen in Bishkek which posed serious risks to public health. The main reasons for the poor air quality have been associated with errors made in previous urban environment planning decisions, when infill construction had a negative impact on the capital's air quality. Another cause for the deterioration of air quality is the heating of private houses by coal and automobile emissions. Civil activists have added that the tree cutting further amplified this problem by eliminating their ecosystem services (e.g., carbon sequestration). The situation has also been aggravated by a lack of national standards for measuring air pollution. Despite assurances by the government that the situation would be taken under control, and that the state would promote the development of green areas, including switching towards environmentally friendly technologies, and even ban the use of plastic products, civil activists are not convinced. Instead, they claim that Bishkek is gradually turning from one of the greenest cities of the former Soviet Union into a polluted, smoggy, and dirty one (Sarkeyeva 2018).

In early 2019, environmental civic activists have announced that the city municipality is planning to cut down another 4,000 trees to widen the roads for more cars. The Internet community of the country was stunned, because at the same time, the country's prime minister, Mukhammedkalyi Abylgaziev, was actively delivering populist speeches about the importance of the environment and green spaces. An online petition was initiated and has already received thousands of supporters. Supporters of the petition are varied, ranging from prominent environmental NGOs to individual civil activists, and although they have forwarded the petition to the municipality's office, no response has been received yet. This is the dominant form of grassroots activism in the modern world, as captured by Castells's 'network society', which is characterised by "a relational network system that connects territories through information and communication flows" (Castells 1996, 471). As such, communications and movements within cyberspace have direct implications on physical places. As Gunnell and Marolt (2014, 381–85) have argued, if "a subject is not part of the pattern of power that configures the network, it loses control of the capacity to alter the network according to its needs, desires, and projects".

Despite the uneven path and questionable outcomes of these recent civil society movements, they indicate that grassroots communities have really started to engage in contentious politics in Bishkek. For instance, 2018 and 2019 have seen discussions of a new master plan for the city centre and renewed protests. The issues of clean air and environmental protection have provided an overarching agenda for demonstrations and discussions. More and more media and urban activists augmented interest in the environmental agenda by publishing stories about corruption in the municipality and the rationale behind new urban developments. Yet, how this civic activism shapes the local urban population and civic participation more generally remains to be determined. Are we witnessing the rise of new civic communities and networks in the city, or are the current problems just mobilising a thin layer of politically active residents?

If we take Castells's position and argue for a politics which stems from a base made up of local grassroots movements made up of shared social identities and common understanding—then it is definitely an indicator of a new civic realm, or a 'network society' (Castells 1983). Indeed, movements and grassroots mobilisations are communities in action (Roberts and Sykes 2000); they challenge the current state of affairs and typically employ bottom-up mobilisation (Day 2006, 242). A majority of studies on civil society and grassroots activism conclude that the success of their demonstrations depends on their networking potential and ability to engage with local systems. In the case of Kyrgyzstan, where civil society is seen more as a threat to the state than a partner, network studies might shed more light on the condition and promises of civil society development. However, local scholars have concluded that there is a relative fragmentation of Bishkek's civil society groups and communities and different patterns of cooperation between them. This fragmentation of different civil society groups and communities is a result of very different missions, funding issues, members, and relationships with the government (Sarkeyeva 2018). Finally, structural gaps in Bishkek's civic networks usually collude with the extant social divides in the city: spatial, economic, and linguistic. Thus, these structural gaps will need to be bridged in order to raise the potential of the third sector.

Concluding remarks

Civic activism has had a difficult and thorny trajectory in Central Asia. For it to make some headway, links between civil society and the state have to be considered. The very relationship between the state and the third sector has not yet been fundamentally established. Moreover, the sectors do not share equal rights, and have a high level of mistrust towards each other. Central Asian governments are either interested in promoting and supporting lucrative businesses, or preserving their power and authority—this is the classical reality of developing countries, and is the reason for their place at the top of the list of the world's most corrupt countries. Meanwhile, civil society is not yet able to sustain itself without international funding, and remains too scattered to interfere significantly into major domestic issues. Nonetheless, as the Central Asian governments are unlikely to undergo radical political changes anytime soon, the importance of civil society and its accomplishments become even more significant.

To be successful, civil society organisations must continue implementing their programmes, searching for any sustainable funds, working collaboratively inside communities, and most importantly, stop local governments from blocking foreign grant support of the third sector. As mentioned earlier, there needs to be a framework of representative democracy, free market economies, and cosmopolitan liberalism for civil society development. The NGO sector should also continue engaging citizens in decision-making over community issues, in order to preserve their grassroots nature and to get more support from citizens' and foreign donors' trust. The importance of building up a network society in Castells's conception is crucial for making the third sector sustainable, with less dependence on foreign aid and government interference. This network society perspective should confront the system through diverse approaches—both online and on the ground. Emerging networks should be horizontal, leaderless solidarities amongst civic organisations and ordinary citizens.

Moreover, structural changes within the government are needed. High-level positions in ministries of the environment and related agencies should be filled with professionals and managers with a background in environmental sciences or sustainability, civil society and grassroots activists should play a decisive role in approving any municipal strategic urban plans, and outcomes of most political decisions should be in line with existing regulations. This is a long way from happening in Central Asia, but that does not mean it will not happen in the future. In the meantime, there is a need for sustaining the work of the third sector and building a strong network society of Central Asian green organisations.

At the present level of political development, the countries of Central Asia demonstrate, in varying degrees, the power of the state in constraining the development of a stronger participating civil society. These conditions require us to describe the limited contentious politics and also forms of participation which stem from an emerging civil society trying to assert itself whilst at the same time trying to work with the state. In Central Asia, the state is very much in control. The more direct regulatory and coercive powers of the state make unnecessary more subtle post-political strategies described in the other chapters. Seen in this light, a post-political situation may possibly be a more desired state of development, for it requires a more enlightened civil society before the deceptive post-political strategies of the state become deployed.

Note

1 Eastern and Central Europe was also a part of the Soviet Union, and achieved independence almost at the same time as Central Asia did.

References

Castells, M. 1983. *The City and the Grassroots: A Cross-Cultural Theory of Urban Social Movements*. Berkeley, CA and Los Angeles: University of California Press.
———. 1996. *The Rise of the Network Society*. Oxford: Blackwell.
Committee on Environmental Protection under the Government of the Republic of Tajikistan (CEPGRT). 2010. "National Report on the Implementation of the AARHUS Convention in Tajikistan for 2008–2010." https://wedocs.unep.org/bitstream/handle/20.500.11822/9637/-National_Report_on_the_Implementation_of_the_Aarhus_Convention_in_Tajikistan_for_2008_to_.pdf?sequence=2&isAllowed=y
Day, D. 2006. *Community and Everyday Life*. New York: Routledge.
Diani, M. 2015. *The Cement of Civil Society: Studying Networks in Localities*. Cambridge: Cambridge University Press.
Durant, T. J., Jr. 2011. "The Utility of Vulnerability and Social Capital Theories in Studying the Impact of Hurricane Katrina on the Elderly." *Journal of Family Issues*, 11.
"Giant oil field in Kazakhstan is a ticking time bomb." 2014. *Mondiaal Nieuws*. www.mo.be/en/article/giant-oil-field-kazakhstan-ticking-time-bomb
Gunnell, T., and P. Marolt. 2014. "Cities and Their Grassroutes." *Environment and Planning D: Society and Space*, 32 (3): 381–385.
ICNL (The International Cenyer for Not-for-Profit Law). 2019. *Civic Freedom Monitor: Tajikistan*. www.icnl.org/research/monitor/tajikistan.html
Knox, P., and S. Pinch. 2010. *Urban Social Geography: An Introduction*. 6th ed. London: Pearson.
Lemke, T. 2002. "Foucault, Governmentality, and Critique." *Rethinking Marxism, In Journal of Economics, Society and Culture*, 14 (3): 49–64, Taylor and Francis.
National Statistical Committee of Kyrgyzstan. 2018. "Data of 2018." www.stat.kg/ru/bazy-dannyh/
Roberts, P., and H. Sykes, eds. 2000. *Urban Regeneration: A Handbook*. London: Sage.

Sarkeyeva, R. 2018. "Rethinking Urban Activism and Civil Society: Insights from Analysis of Bishkek Civic Networks." CAP Paper #208 (CAAP Fellows Paper). http://centralasiaprogram.org/wp-content/uploads/2018/06/Sarkeyeva-CAP-Fellows-Paper-June-2018-1.pdf
Schmitter, P. 2002. "Participation in Governance Arrangements: Is There any Reason to Expect It Will Achieve 'Sustainable and Innovative Policies in a Multi-Level Context'?" In *Participatory Governance: Political and Societal Implications*, edited by J. Grote and B. Gbipki, 51–69. Opladen: Leske and Budrich.
Swyngedouw, E. 1997. "Neither Global nor Local: 'Glocalization' and the Politics of Scale." In *Spaces of Globalization: Reasserting the Power of the Local*, edited by K. Cox, 137–166. New York: Guilford.
———. 2009. "The Antinomies of Post-Political City: In Search of a Democratic Politics of Environmental Production." *International Journal of Urban and Regional Research*, 601–620.
Swyngedouw, E., Page, B., and M. Kaika. 2002. "Sustainability and Policy Innovation in a Multi-Level Context: Crosscutting Issues in the Water Sector." In *Participatory Governance in Multi-Level Context: Concepts and Experience*, edited by H. Heinelt, P. Getimis, G. Kafkalas, R. Smith, and E. Swyngedouw, 107–132. Opladen: Springer Fachmedien Wiesbaden.
Timofeeva, D. 2018. "Jiteli Bishkeka hotyat suditsya s Vlastyami iz-za Smoga nad Gorodom. [Bishkek Residents Want to Sue the Authorities Because of Smog over the City]." *Current Times*, November 18. www.currenttime.tv/a/smog-air-pollution-bishkek/29608764.html
Transparency International. 2018. "Corruption Perception Index in Kyrgyzstan, Kazakhstan, Uzbekistan, Tajikistan." Corruption Trends in Asia. www.transparency.org/country/KGZ
Watters, K. 1995. "Environmental NGOs and the Development of Civil Society in Cental Asia." In *Civil Society in Central Asia*, edited by M. H. Ruffin and D. Waugh, 85–108. Seattle: University of Washington Press.

9
POST-POLITICAL PLANNING AND INSURGENT MOBILISATION IN THE POST-DISASTER CITY

The experience of Tacloban City, Philippines, after Typhoon Haiyan

Dakila Kim P. Yee

Introduction

Contemporary urban environments have become increasingly vulnerable and exposed to problems caused by natural disasters such as typhoons and monsoon flooding, along with issues associated with rising sea levels (Dasgupta et al. 2009). This has led to a proliferation of research on disaster mitigation in cities, addressing topics ranging from urban regeneration (MacLeod 2011; Ruming 2018), urban planning (Allmendinger and Haughton 2012), the creation of 'green cities' (Rosol, Beál, and Mössner 2017), to the threat of climate change (Swyngedouw 2010; Kenis and Mathijs 2014). But much of this work notes that a 'post-political' bent—where political disagreements between the state and civil society has been subsumed by the prioritisation of consensus building and cooperation—has emerged within discourses about disaster management.

Through an ethnographic study focussing on the post-disaster recovery process of Tacloban City, in the aftermath of Typhoon Haiyan in 2013, this chapter reviews the mitigation and negotiation of risks within the urban contexts of the Philippines (Curato 2018; Yee 2018a Balgos 2015). This chapter seeks to examine the implication urbanisation has on the production of discourses on risks and disaster management in the Philippines (Saguin 2017; Yee 2018a; Loh and Pante 2015), and explore state–civil society interactions by focusing specifically on the housing contestations of the urban poor (Porio 2002; Shatkin 2005; Karaos 1993, 1998). By looking at these themes together, this chapter is able to articulate how post-politics is deployed in the urban planning of Tacloban City after Typhoon Haiyan. I argue that Tacloban City's post-disaster reconstruction is influenced by factors that simultaneously facilitate the emergence of, and conversely challenge, the post-political condition.

On the one hand, post-disaster urban planning in Tacloban is driven by a post-political discourse. The Filipino state has historically implemented disaster risk mitigation within the framework of 'high modernism' (Shatkin 2005) which places a strong emphasis on centralised planning and technocratic knowledge and expertise. Thus, risk mitigation in the Philippines, a process inclusive of post-disaster reconstruction, has largely been constructed along the lines of improving infrastructural designs that will enable cities to absorb the risks associated with hydrological disasters such as flooding (Saguin 2017; Loh and Pante 2015) and by removing urban poor slum dwellers from risk-prone areas (Balgos 2015; Warren 2013). Under the direction of policy makers and state actors, post-disaster reconstruction efforts after Haiyan have similarly been approached in a centralised and technocratic manner (Hilhorst 2003), and claim to strive towards fostering urban competitiveness and urban sustainability (Davidson and Iveson 2014), seemingly positive ideals which are difficult to dispute and disagree with. Furthermore, the event of a disaster lends itself to the creation of post-political conditions by inducing consensus throughout society. The shared difficulties and sufferings experienced by populations affected by the disasters create a sense of solidarity amongst them. During and immediately after disasters, divergent interests derived from everyday class, race, and gender distinctions become obfuscated (Fassin and Vasquez 2005), and political disagreements between individuals and groups are suspended as they are deemed inappropriate (Curato 2017a). As such, this chapter finds that reconstruction efforts in Tacloban City limit the possibility for debate and antagonistic politics, in regard to how the post-disaster city takes shape, to arise from civil society. At the same time, this chapter also recognises that post-politicisation is never complete. Although Tacloban City's reconstruction efforts seek to impose and enforce consensus throughout society, such consensus is not always actualised. As this chapter shows, one reason for this is the long history of distrust between the military establishment that plays a large role in the Philippine's disaster management, and the radical leftist civil society organisations that are the purveyors of antagonistic politics (Bankoff and Hilhorst 2009). Another reason is that the marginalised urban poor of Tacloban City are excluded from the city's post-disaster urban plans, prompting such communities to mobilise and contest such conditions (Cretney 2018).

This chapter begins by tracing the development of the post-political framework in the discipline of urban studies, and then assesses how such a framework can be useful in the context of disaster studies, especially in the Philippines. The third section discusses the process of post-politicisation in Tacloban City in the wake of the devastation caused by Typhoon Haiyan. The 'resilient' city modelled by planners in the wake of the typhoon echoes some basic characteristics of the 'post-political' city, particularly the emphasis on economic competitiveness and urban 'sustainability'. The fourth section explores the insurgent mobilisations of People Surge, a grassroots organisation that challenges the technocratic approach to disaster reconstruction in Tacloban City. The chapter concludes by exploring the prospects of the post-political framework in understanding post-disaster reconstruction.

Understanding the post-political condition

The characterisation of the post-political condition draws mainly from Rancière's formulation of the 'police', 'political', and 'politics'. For Rancière, the concept of 'police' consists of the creation of socio-political order through the 'distribution of the sensible'. To elaborate, this order is instituted through the distribution of names, places, and functions to select subjects and objects, thus rendering them 'sensible'—able to acquire recognition and acknowledgement within the 'police' order. As a system of administration, the 'police' are based on the social organisation of space, and this distribution of what is recognised and what is ignored is the basis of governance (Dikéc 2017; Swyngedouw 2009); in other words, the process of ascribing this sensibility is determined by the parameters of the state's needs and interests. However, this police order is not necessarily completely closed, as those excluded from the distribution of the sensible exist outside of police order and therefore outside the control of the state, potentially challenging and destabilising the police order (Swyngedouw 2009). The political emerges when the police order is challenged by "those who have no part" of this order, subsequently exposing the 'politics'—defined here as "the production of spaces, the making of environments and the recognition of the principle of dissensus" and antagonisms (Swyngedouw 2009, 607)—that are normally suppressed under the police. Because this political antagonism emerges outside of the police order, Swyngedouw (2014) argues that proper political acts operate at a distance from the state, and instead occur within public spaces such as streets and squares. Examples of such actions include the Occupy Movement, the Arab Spring, and the Indignados movement in Spain. Such encounters between the political and the police results in the reordering of the distribution of the sensible, and ultimately, of the police order itself (Swyngedouw 2014, 130).

As mentioned, under conditions of the post-political, cities aim to achieve economic growth, attain 'global city' status, secure the city from threats, and ensure environmental sustainability (Davidson and Iveson 2014; MacLeod 2011; Swyngedouw 2009). There is an emphasis that these ideals are acquired through the propagation of a 'participatory' approach to urban governance. However, these forms of participation are 'managed' by the state and experts in a way wherein the parameters for what can be debated are already defined at the onset (Haughton and Allmendinger 2011). Any dissent and disruption that may arise within this post-political condition are "over the institutional modalities of governing, the accountancy calculus of risk and the technologies of expert administration or management" (Swyngedouw 2009, 609), rather than ideological divisions. In other words, when disagreement does emerge in the post-political city, they pertain to how these ideals of urban sustainability and security are to be actualised, as opposed to questioning the premise behind these ideals in the first place. This evacuation of genuine debate and dissent within processes of urban governance allows policy makers to concentrate on imposing a policy agenda that is predominantly centred on neoliberal and growth-driven principles (Swyngedouw 2009; Haughton and Allmendinger 2011).

Whilst the post-political framework provides a strong case for the description and analysis of how democratic politics operate in Western liberal societies, the literature has identified several critiques of this framework. Firstly, there is an essentialising tendency to frame the post-political as an affixed condition that characterises all contemporary societies. This tendency assumes that conditions of the post-political have manifested as a coherent set of urban policies (Ruming 2018), which have now taken hold (Davidson and Iveson 2014) across late-capitalistic societies in the same manner (Swyngedouw 2009), and cannot be challenged nor dispelled. Such an approach ignores the differences in the geographical and societal contexts wherein the practice of post-politics is observed, and how these varying contexts influences the actual exercise of the post-politics. Also, treating post-politics as a consistent and static condition ignores empirical evidence showing how post-politics is contested across varying spaces and scales (Ruming 2018; Swyngedouw 2014). Towards this end, I follow the suggestion of Ruming (2018) in analysing the post-political as a process. Such an approach analyses the complexities of the labour and politics involved in deploying a post-political approach to urban planning (Ruming 2018), and that what is understood as the post-political is prone to develop and change over space and time, rather than assuming this as a given condition in late capitalist societies.

The second critique of the post-political framework is its emphasis on what has been termed a 'proper political moment', referring to the re-emergence of a dissent and debate that is not mediated by the state or experts, as exemplified by street protests and occupations (Indignados and Occupy Wall Street) that are driven by an evolutionary bent (Beveridge and Koch 2017; Millington 2016). This critique is levied against the simplistic juxtaposition of a 'strong' state within the post-political framework (Millington 2016; Thomas 2017) against such 'insurgent' forms of political activity (Swyngedouw 2014) that seek to directly challenge state power. Emphasis on an insurgent form of political activity downplays a multitude of other less visible and long-term political activities in the realm of urban studies as falling outside of the 'proper political moment', which may include volunteerism, community building, and engaging in debates in colloquial conversations, to name a few. With only revolutionary activities being considered as the 'proper political moment', this remains problematic as it excludes and denigrates other reformist actions that strive for incremental gains (Beveridge and Koch 2017).

Political development in the Philippines

One key theoretical concern arises from the application of the post-political framework, derived from analyses of contemporary liberal democracies in the West (see Swyngedouw 2009), to the context of developing countries in Asia. I consider the viability of the post-political framework in the Philippines, one of the oldest democracies in Asia.

In the early 20th century, American colonisers introduced electoral democracy in the Philippines in an attempt to integrate and absorb indigenous elites into the formal structures of state governance. This electoral system was largely biased towards the elites, with property ownership and literacy deemed as prerequisites for participating in the voting process (Quimpo 2009). After World War II, the electoral system shifted towards patronage politics wherein Filipino elites offered jobs and money to their constituents in exchange for votes (Quimpo 2009, 340). These elections were also dominated by two parties, the Nacionalista and the Liberal Party which espoused similar ideologies to each other, making them almost indistinguishable (Quimpo 2009, 340). This electoral system would later be interrupted by 20 years of years of dictatorial rule under Ferdinand Marcos (1965–1986) (Abinales and Amoroso 2005), where Marcos centralised power, destroyed oppositional voices, and plundered state resources. The creeping authoritarianism of Marcos's first term as president also generated the growth of leftist social movements in the Philippines during the late 1960s and early 1970s (McCoy 2009a). Tracing their lineage to the old Soviet-aligned Partido Komunista ng Pilipinas, new youth organisations organised by English lecturer Jose Ma. Sison, the Kabataang Makabayan emerged at the forefront of student activist protests in the late 1960s to early 1970s. The increasing militancy of the Sison-organised groups eventually resulted in a split in the old communist party, resulting in the establishment of the Maoist-inspired Communist Party of the Philippines on 26 December 1968 (Abinales and Amoroso 2005, 199). The student activists aligned with Kabataang Makabyan, and other left-leaning organisations such as the Samahang Demokratikong Kabataan launched massive protests in the early 1970s which eventually became known in local Filipino as the First Quarter Storm (Lacaba 1982; Pimentel 2006). Leftist protest groups were able to attract intellectuals from the student sector through the penetration of student councils and other student organisations in the major universities of Metro Manila (Abinales and Amoroso 2005, 200). The clampdown on activism brought about by the declaration of martial law forced many activists to go underground and eventually join the clandestine organisation of the Communist Party of the Philippines. Some activists were forced to go incognito, joining the New People's Army, the armed wing of the Communist Party of the Philippines. The armed rebellion waged by the communists during the heyday of the Marcos dictatorship, in addition to the revival of street protests in the early 1980s, brought about by the assassination of opposition senator Benigno "Ninoy" Aquino Jr. would eventually contribute to the erosion of Marcos control of the Philippine state. However, it was not until the aborted coup d'état by young military officers of the Reform the Armed Forces of the Philippines Movement that a massive street protest evicted Ferdinand Marcos from power in February of 1986[1] (Abinales and Amoroso 2005, 224).

With the downfall of Marcos in 1986, a process of 'redemocratisation' was initiated wherein electoral democracy was restored (Brillantes 1998), but this did not necessarily lead to radical socio-political reform and change in the Philippines. The redemocraticsation process, involved the simple reintroduction and reinstatement of past electoral practices, which meant that the traditional elite politicians from the pre-Marcos years were voted back into power (Quimpo 2009). Post-authoritarian transition has been difficult, marred by slow economic growth, democratic institutions being dominated by the elites, and contentious politics from leftist social movements (Rivera 2002).

Whilst the post-Marcos transitions were marred by conservative and traditional forces, some innovations for democratic reforms were eventually introduced as a means of broadening the scope of the redemocratisation efforts. This was to be actualised by granting greater political autonomy to local government units (LGUs), and widening the access of the populace to local state structures (Brillantes 1998). One of the key reforms introduced into legislation was the Local Government Code of 1991, which initiated the decentralisation of power from the national (federal) government, and towards LGUs. In practice, decentralisation involves the transferring of services and functions traditionally performed by the national government agencies to LGUs, and also involves increasing LGU's taxation powers, thereby granting them financial autonomy from the national coffers (Legaspi 2001). Whilst a comprehensive review of how decentralisation in the Philippines was enacted and manifested is beyond the scope of this chapter, what should be noted here is that decentralisation is now the primary governance framework used throughout the country. LGUs now assume many of the responsibilities previously ascribed to the national government, as seen in service delivery (see Atienza 2004 for the health sector; Go 2016 for the education sector) and in natural resource management (see Holden and Jacobson 2006 for mining; Dressler, Kull, and Meredith for natural parks management 2006).

Paralleling the political institution, civil society in the Philippines has similarly evolved markedly through the years, especially within the urban areas (Karaos 1998). Civil society mobilisation in cities during the Marcos dictatorship in the late 1960s and early 1970s took the form of 'squatter movements' (homeless people's movements) that resisted evictions caused by urban renewal projects in Manila that were designed to enhance the capital's image to the emergent middle-class within the nation and to an international audience (Shatkin 2005, 585–87). The restoration of the electoral democracy under President Corazon Aquino (1986–1992) prompted a shift in the political ideologies and mobilisation practices of civil society organisations campaigning for the rights of the urban poor, moving away from leftist-inspired organising and mass mobilisation, and becoming a reformist and policy-oriented movement (Karaos 1998, 145–46). The introduction of decentralisation through the Local Government Code of 1991 also provides a greater role for civil society organisations such as non-governmental organisations (NGOs) to fulfil governance functions that were previously provided for by the national government (Brillantes 1994, 581). This shift has increased the capacity of several urban poor civil society organisations to achieve policy outcomes, especially in regard to securing housing tenure (Porio 2002), and the ability to engage with state agencies such as the Presidential Commission of the Urban Poor (Karaos 1998). Today, these civil society organisations initiating reform-oriented movements exist side by side with other urban poor movements such as Kalipunan ng Damayang Mahihirap, which advocates for direct confrontation with the state and conducting militant activities by occupying housing units built by state agencies (Arcilla 2018).

It is in this context that we can understand the existing governance structures of Tacloban City. Tacloban City was also subject to the national government's policy of redistributing political power to LGUs as part of the redemocratisation efforts across the Philippines. But what has yet to be addressed is that such redemocratisation ideals are not reflected at the LGU level, wherein political power remains retained amongst a select few. For example, at the time Haiyan struck, the mayor of Tacloban City was Alfred Romualdez, a nephew of Imelda Romualdez Marcos, the wife of Ferdinand Marcos. The Romualdez clan has held a stranglehold on the mayorship of the city over the past two decades, as the previous mayor was Alfred's father, Alfredo "Bejo" Romualdez. At the writing of this chapter, the mayor of the city is Alfred's wife, Cristina Gonzales Romualdez. The succession of Romualdezes' controlling the mayorship of Tacloban City is a classic case of Alfred McCoy's 'anarchy of families'—the domination of the Philippine political system by powerful political families whose successive control of electoral positions evoke dynastic characteristics. The basis for the formation and persistence of political families is an aggressive practice of rent-seeking behaviour—that is, "the active pursuit of political influence to gain market advantage" (McCoy 2009a, xii). The Romualdez family benefited from expansive rent-seeking behaviour during the Marcos dictatorship. McCoy (2009b, 401–402) pointed out that Bejo Romualdez was awarded several licences to operate gambling facilities in Metro Manila during the dictatorship. Rent-seeking behaviour feeds into local political dominance, as these funds are then used to cultivate local patron-client relationships with the votes (primarily through the practice of buying votes). At the same time, there are minimal efforts to initiate local development because of the short electoral terms (three years), which means that once the local officials win, they are already gearing up for the next electoral cycle.

This problematic combination manifested in Tacloban City during the lead-up to Typhoon Haiyan. The local electoral dominance of the Romualdezes meant that there was no public accountability on inaction in disaster preparedness prior to Typhoon Haiyan.[2,3] Mangada (2016, 105) notes how the local City Disaster Risk Reduction Management Office was ill-equipped with resources and manpower, which affected the city's ability to respond effectively immediately after of the typhoon. In an earlier paper, Mangada (2015) documents how local governance dynamics contributed to a non-functioning City Disaster Risk Reduction Management Office. These include that (1) the local city ordinance (city-level law) that created the office was not supported by Mayor Alfred Romualdez, as this was sponsored by a councillor from the opposition; (2) there was a of permanent administrative staff because most of the personnel were transferred from other city departments and were on short-term contracts, thus the lack of motivation; (3) and the lack of institutional formalisation meant that there was no secure funding for the office, as all of the funds were released during emergency situations only.[4]

Aside from problematic governance, the local government is also characterised by a constricted space for civil society actors. Holden (2009, 2011) has documented the harassments and killings of activists in the city, and within the wider Eastern Visayas region of which Tacloban City is located. The next section shows how processes of post-politicisation unfolded in Tacloban City during the post-disaster reconstruction phase.

Post-politics and post-disaster reconstruction in Tacloban City, Philippines

Conducting my fieldwork in Tacloban a year after Typhoon Haiyan devastated the city, from November 2014 to November 2015, I observed the post-disaster reconstruction and its impact on coastal communities that were slated for eviction due to their exposure to the risks associated with storm surge. I interviewed 40 informants considered stakeholders in the reconstruction process, including individuals residing in areas designated as a 'no-build zone' after the disaster; local government officials, city planners, and administrators that designed and implemented the reconstruction plan; and community activists that resisted the urban reconstruction and rehabilitation plan of the government. Interviews were supplemented by participant observation of local consultation activities implemented by the government, dialogues launched by community residents with government officials, and protest actions launched by residents against local and national government agencies. I also analysed planning documents published by the local government, as well as public statements and critiques released by the activists.

Tacloban City, located at the island of Leyte, is the administrative and economic capital of the Eastern Visayas Region of the Philippines. The city hosts a population of at least 240,000 people (Philippine Statistics Authority 2016), and is vulnerable to natural disasters induced by typhoons, earthquakes, storm surges, and tsunamis. When Typhoon Haiyan made landfall on 8 November 2013, it unleashed towering storm surges that pummelled the coastal barangays and villages of the city, and inundated the city's entire business district. Typhoon Haiyan left at least 6,300 people dead and around 1,000 people missing in the affected areas in the Philippines; in Tacloban City, at least 2,000 people died to the impact of the typhoon (National Disaster Risk Reduction Management Council, n.d).

After the typhoon, the national government created the Office of the Presidential Assistant for Reconstruction and Recovery to oversee reconstruction and recovery efforts across regions affected by Typhoon Haiyan. In Tacloban, the LGU, with support from the United Nations Human Settlements Programme team, created the Tacloban Recovery and Sustainable Development Group (TacDev). TacDev initiated the formulation of a post-disaster reconstruction and recovery plan that would guide the reconstruction process in the city. Through a series of planning charrettes, the United Nationals Development Program and the LGU invited select representatives from national government agencies, local government officials, barangay unit heads, and international non-government organisations (INGOs) to help draft the Tacloban Recovery and Rehabilitation Plan (TRRP), which became the basis for the reconstruction visions and efforts of the LGU after Typhoon Haiyan. TacDev claimed that the drafting of the TRRP would be conducted through a holistic and inclusive approach. Whilst the planning process did incorporate the voices of select NGOs and members of professional communities (such as architects and engineers), members of the public who would be affected by the plan were excluded from the planning and decision-making processes surrounding the making of the TRRP. Rather, public participation was limited to information dissemination, whereby they were simply told the plans were after the plans were already made by the government and experts (Curato 2018).

The TRRP is composed of five components, with the main report accompanied by four sector-specific plans: economic development, infrastructure, social services, and environmental protection. One objective of the TRRP is to create potential development districts that will provide a "useful reference in defining the site of future public investments for investors and locators concerned with making sound business decisions for projects" (Tacloban Recovery and Sustainable Development Group 2014a, 16). The plan proposes to reorder the current land-use plan of Tacloban, and proposes four development districts to be located in the North, Mid-Coast, Upland, and South Coast of the city. The TRRP uses post-disaster urban planning and reconstruction to maximise the investment potential of the city. The cornerstone of this plan is the massive redevelopment of the northern sections of the city, specifically a former agricultural area known as Tacloban North that has been considered a proposed relocation site for at least 14,000 families residing along sections of the Tacloban coastline now been labelled as a 'no-build zone'. There are three objectives for the development of Tacloban North: (1) development of mixed-use areas, (2) the creation of a new settlement site (township), and (3) the development of coastal production as well as the conversion of land use for recreational (tourism) purposes.

The goal of achieving economic development in the aftermath of the disaster also hinged on a strategy of "ecological modernization" which aims to synergise growth objectives with environmental conservation and sustainability (Bäckstrand and Lövbrand 2006, 52). The technocratic roots of this strategy are also emphasised in this goal to reach ecological modernisation as stated in planning documents:

> The reconstruction . . . provided an opportunity for urban planners, policy makers, scientists and politicians to formulate an urban reconstruction plan that attempts to harmonize economic growth and the protection of the environment. One of the guiding principles of the recovery and rehabilitation process outlined in the TRRP is an "inclusive and holistic" process that aims to promote "socially, environmentally, economically and culturally balanced redevelopment" by utilizing the recovery and reconstruction process as an "opportunity" for improving the system in the city.
>
> *(Tacloban Recovery and Sustainable Development Group 2014, 5)*

These plans are implemented alongside a disaster risk-reduction plan that is heavily driven by infrastructural development. The notion of disaster recovery and 'resilience' in Tacloban is based on the territorialisation of risks (Rebotier 2012). During this territorialisation of risk, representations and discourses of risks are simplistically understood as being exposed to geophysical hazards, which then transforms the material spaces of the city where the urban poor reside. The manifestations of this plan include the demarcation of a 40-metre 'no-build zone' in the city, along with the creation of tide embankments and other coastal defence measures along 27 kilometres of the coastline, enhancing the urban ecological security (Hodson and Marvin 2009) of Tacloban against the threat of a potential 'Haiyan-like' typhoon in the future. I argue in another article (Yee 2018a) that these notions of resilience after typhoon Haiyan is premised on a form of 'bourgeoisie environmentalism' (Baviskar 2003) that seeks to erase the poor from the shorelines of the city. Many officials proclaim that they have long intended to remove the urban poor from coastal areas, and Typhoon Haiyan gave them the justification to do so.

The visions for the post-disaster city is hinged on achieving economic growth and environmental sustainability, two key values that are venerated and supposedly shared by all within the post-political city (Davidson and Iveson 2014). Whilst Curato (2018) notes that post-political consensus was enforced because the local government in Tacloban City provides limited avenues for public participation and deliberation over its post-disaster policies, the creation of an external 'other' in the form of climate change and disasters (see Swyngedouw 2010) helped create consensus to support the implementation of the plan, as seen from civil society attitudes towards the proposed relocation of the urban poor living along the coastline. Even amongst a number of urban poor communities that I met during my fieldwork in Tacloban City, there was a general sense of agreement from these individuals that their areas are vulnerable to hazards and that their eventual relocation to the northern areas of the city was beneficial, as this would render them safe from calamities. Meanwhile, most civil society organisations involved in the city's post-disaster response also conceded with the objectives of the TRRP. In several planning workshops that I observed, there was no disagreement over the overall design of the TRRP, but only on the modalities of its implementation. For example, the relocation plan of at least 14,000 families was never questioned by civil society organisations involved in the process. The only debates generated were centred on the schedule of the implementation of the relocation project. For example, the Urban Poor Homeless Group (pseudonym), an NGO that lobbies for urban poor land rights in the city, organised a rally attended by at least 1,000 people outside the city hall, calling not for the abolition of the relocation plan, but to ask for the postponement of the relocation as the resettlement housing sites were not yet completed. The organisation also mobilises for 'inclusivity' and transparency in the planning process, demands that do not radically challenge the institutional framework for civil society organisation participation, as pointed out by other scholars who have analysed the concept of the post-politics (Allmendinger and Haughton 2012).

The institutional framework in the Philippines that provides the necessary support to state–civil society collaboration in disaster management is Republic Act (RA) 10121, also known as the Philippine Disaster Risk Reduction Management (DRRM) Act of 2010. RA 10121 has been lauded for marking a shift in the state's perspective regarding disasters, from one that was reactive and treating disasters as 'external threats', to an approach that recognises vulnerability reduction in communities that are exposed to hazards. The DRRM also represents a marked shift in disaster governance, from one that is based on centralised state responses, to a networked form of governance whereby decision-making power is distributed throughout the country, enhancing the participation of communities and civil society organisations at the local level. However, under the DRRM, the participation of civil society organisations is ensured as long as they comply with the coordination mechanisms set forth by the national and local disaster risk-reduction management councils. The selection of civil society organisations' representatives to the National Disaster Risk Reduction Management Council (NDRRMC) is done based on how these civil society organisations are ranked against one another within the criteria set forth by the NDRRMC.[5] In sum, civic involvement in participatory urban governance is premised on civil society organisations meeting the selection criteria established by those in power, and is also contingent on the civil society organisations abiding by the government's rules of engagement in the deliberation process. By selecting which sectors of civil society are able to partake in post-disaster governance, the government is able to control the type of discourse that emerges during the planning process.

In Tacloban, only a select range of civil society organisations are included in post-disaster planning. For example, a former city councillor expressed frustration that the reconstruction process was dominated by INGOs whose personnel were not from the city. In contrast, a number of local civil society organisations encountered difficulties in getting official accreditation from LGUs to become official members of the NDRRMC. Jose, a local officer of a leftist grassroots environmental NGO in the city, recalls how their application to the local housing office was not acted upon. He also narrated how they were ignored when they wanted to set up meetings with the local officials. The key implication from barring leftist civil society organisations from the official coordinating structures was that those who were proposing alternative perspectives and plans on the post-disaster reconstruction were sidelined. Firstly, competing visions and interests on certain disaster reconstruction plans were muted. Jose narrated how his NGO attempted to gain an audience with the regional economic body to report on the negative ramifications that the government's proposed tide embankment project will have on the locality. The NGO also tried contacting partner organisations who had access to governing boards, but they were never given the opportunity to talk to government officials. Secondly, alternative development programmes were not recognised by government officials nor able to be implemented widely, as they did not fit the state's reconstruction framework. For example, Jose's organisation received a grant from an international funding agency to provide shelter kits to those affected by the typhoon. However, officials refused to give permission to Jose's NGO to distribute these shelter kits within the no-build zone,[6] with a city social welfare officer explaining that these shelter kits allow residents to rebuild inside the no-build zone, which will encourages residents to stay in this zone rather than relocate to the housing resettlement sites. City officials claim that relocating households residing within the no-build zone is to ensure their safety in case another typhoon arrives. Although some residents and NGOs have raised concerns pertaining to how relocated households can continue pursuing their existing livelihoods, and also question the available services and the structural integrity of houses found within permanent and non-permanent resettlement sites. Overall, the basic premise of relocation to another area is not challenged in its entirety (Shelter Cluster Philippines 2014).

Even as problems and controversies mar Tacloban's City's rehabilitation process, civil society organisations barely criticise the state. Furthermore, despite the integration of civil society organisations and private-sector representatives inside the NDRRMC, the influence of the Philippine military remains strong, with the NDRRMC being headed by the secretary of the Department of National Defense (Brower and Magno 2011). This has important implications regarding the exercise of antagonistic politics, as those that become overtly critical of state management of disaster response and reconstruction become labelled as anti-state actors (Bankoff and Hilhorst 2009), and those who harbour alternative conceptions of post-disaster reconstruction are marginalised in the reconstruction process.

Insurgent politics and the emergence of the political after Typhoon Haiyan

Whilst a consensus in post-disaster recovery and reconstruction was taking hold over Tacloban City, there emerged several pockets of resistance and community opposition towards these plans. Observing a meeting of Tacloban City activists composed of individuals living in the coastal areas one month after the disaster, I heard these activists state their opposition to the proposed evictions of coastal communities and to the imposition of the 40-meter "No-Build Zone" in their area, as they would be uprooted from the sources of their livelihood and community support networks.[7] Some also criticised the plan as "benefiting only those with capital and real estate interests".[8] Several households openly defied the imposition of the no-build zone by rebuilding their shacks within the demarcated danger zone. While they recognise that their areas are prone to risks, moving into resettlement sites in the north constitute a "disaster after the disaster", as these areas are far from their sources of livelihood and at the same time, they will be forced to pay rent since these social housing are provided for by the state.[9]

Community opposition to the government's reconstruction plan started to take shape with the formation of People Surge—a social movement organisation of disaster survivors formed in the wake of Typhoon Haiyan. The seeds of this social movement were planted as early as December 2013, one month after the typhoon, when community leaders and activists had already discussed opposing plans regarding the 'no-build zone', as well as generating public outcry towards the government response to the disaster which was characterised by their slow response time and factional politics[10] (Yee 2016). The first mobilisation launched by the organisation was on 24 January 2014, when an estimated 8,000 disaster survivors staged a protest in a city that was still practically in rubbles. People Surge was supported by other national activist organisations such as Bagong Alyansang Makabayan, Anakbayan (a youth activist organisation), and leftist parliamentary group BAYAN MUNA.

The emergence of contentious politics in the aftermath of a disaster is influenced by the confluence of political networks that operate in a given locality (Yee 2016). Many organisers of People Surge belong to the network of activist groups mentioned previously, and these networks play an important role into the creation of an insurgent politics (Swyngedouw 2014) that questions the distribution of the sensible in the post-disaster plans in Tacloban City.

After the massive mobilisation in January 2014, the organisation embarked on an array of activities that seek to contest the recovery plan presented by the government. Some of the activities include small discussions held within communities, public meetings, dialogues and negotiations with government officials, painting street graffiti, and protesting at local and national government offices. These activities challenge the consensus of state planners and their networks of technocrats and advisers, and paint a picture of the disaster that emphasises the suffering of the poor. The activities of the organisation also challenge the notion of "performative resilience" (Ong 2015, 614) exhibited by the middle-class of the city, wherein representations of the poor's post-disaster suffering are elided by emotions of hope, gratefulness, and a call for national unity and solidarity that echoes post-political ideals of consensus building (Ong 2015). By challenging the premise of unity and solidarity in the aftermath of the typhoon, and by problematising the government's recovery plan, the People Surge social movement re-introduces the political in post-disaster reconstruction of the city.

The mobilisation of People Surge renders the issues of post-disaster reconstruction political by emphasising the antagonistic politics of the survivors, many whom were not included in the recovery planning process. The movement frames post-disaster reconstruction plans in terms of class conflict, analysing these plans not as the collective aspirations of Tacloban City residents affected by the typhoon, but as a vehicle for advancing business interests at the expense of the poor. This is reflected in the statement by Rita, an organiser of the group, who mentioned that the "farmers, fishermen, workers and urban poor who have been systematically excluded from the pro-business rehabilitation plan of the Philippine government, are now making themselves heard in the streets to oppose the plan of the government".[11] This statement highlights how the poor were rendered unintelligible in the planning process, as their aspirations and perspectives were barely taken into account by the government and by other institutional bodies. The former president of People Surge, Efleda Bautista, highlights the discrepancy in the government's priorities in the post-disaster plans:

> Rehabilitation, for whom? The Aquino government's Reconstruction Assistance for Yolanda (RAY) is focused on heavy privatized infrastructure distributed among Pres. Noynoy Aquino's big business allies, debt-driven micro-financing for agriculture and the anti-poor, pro-big business No-Build Zone policy in coastal communities. Meanwhile, only 1% of survivors that require shelter aid, which number at around 1.2 million homes have actually received permanent shelter.[12]

The organisation goes on to criticise government plans, such as the construction of tide embankments and other infrastructural improvements that they deem as being built as "money-making ventures". They also attack the consultation process of the government as "non-democratic" and not genuine. Jack, a community activist, says that

> we know that most of their projects, even if there are consultations, most of them do not really have consultation . . . they will call you, the attendance will be taken, after the meeting people will go home, and now, all of a sudden, they will claim there is consultation even if they just took attendance. We are always duped by the government, that's why we oppose their projects.[13]

To counter the plan initiated by the government, community organisations affiliated with People Surge pushed for a counter proposal of "on-site" development that will give the urban poor concrete resettlement sites within their barangays of origin. Jojo, one of the community activists, explains that

> a better solution would be . . . if they build [houses] near the city because most of the people's livelihood are in the city . . . that's why we are demanding an "on-site" development. They should be here, so that they will not experience hardships, anyway there's money [from donations], there's funding, why don't they build it?[14]

These proposals received lukewarm reactions from the city government. A LGU official claimed that the proposal for tenement housing in urban poor areas have been approved at the council meeting, but has not been acted upon by the office of the mayor.[15] A department officer insisted that they will not entertain a proposal for an on-site development, because these areas are deemed by experts as dangerous and unsuited for occupation. A planner involved in the reconstruction process stated that the city government has already made up its mind, and was determined to move people to the resettlement sites in the north:

> The power of the mayor to declare that everyone will be transferred to the north even though there were many warnings from humanitarians, . . . if ever the need arises to decide that they will be transferred to the North, the decision . . . should be nuanced, should not create more risk, should be sustainable . . . and most of all should be deeply democratic. It should not be a hasty decision . . . that process is dangerous . . . if you look at the last version of the [land use plan] shown by the LGU [local government unit], there is an implicit bias against the urban poor. I am afraid because if you look at the maps, they are really intent on removing the poor from the coastal areas.[16]

People Surge displayed the characteristics of insurgent mobilisations that bring about the political to urban governance. The protests and activities of the organisation, whilst primarily aiming to gain short-term concessions in the form of aid and relief,[17] represented a "demand by those 'that do not count' to be counted, named, and recognized" (Swyngedouw 2014, 129). The poor in Tacloban City, having been marginalised by the exercise of 'performative resilience' (Ong 2015, 614) amongst the middle-class and by technocratic urban planning processes in the aftermath of the typhoon, took to protesting on the streets to make themselves and their demands visible, and subjected the state's efforts at consensus to questioning and critique. The mobilisations also operated within various public spaces—ranging from the city streets, public squares, and even at a local state university—which are distanced from the state, thereby affording these civil society actors an opportunity to exercise their expressions of the political (Swyngedouw 2014, 130). The movement can be classified as an insurgent form of mobilisation, seeking to disrupt and create rupture in the city's post-disaster reconstruction, defying Tacloban City's post-disaster realities that does not afford a space for the expression of the political (Curato 2017b). These grassroots mobilisations, and their assertion for the right to occupy risk prone areas, are expressions of the people's ability to "self-manage and organize their affairs" (Swyngedouw 2014, 131).

However, such an insurgent mobilisation is often subjected to the "violence inscribed in the everyday . . . functioning of the police" (Swyngedouw 2014, 133). The post-disaster reconstruction process in areas affected by Typhoon Haiyan are inscribed in the social and spatial contexts of violence, where activists associated with People Surge have been attacked by state actors (Yee 2018b). This context is rooted in the civil war between the Philippine government and the Communist Party of the Philippines (CPP) which occurred throughout the latter half of the 20th century. Groups such a People Surge, because of their leftist associations, are tagged as front organisations of the CPP. This distrust between the Philippine government and seemingly leftist civil society organisations have resulted in parallel forms of disaster response in areas where these civil society organisations are active, wherein they organise disaster response activity independent of the mechanisms put in place by the government (Bankoff and Hilhorst 2009). It was during one instance of such parallel disaster response activities when the first casualty of People Surge, Jefferson Custodio, was shot down by suspected military elements. The military allege that Custodio is a member of the New People's Army, the armed wing of the CPP, whilst the members of Custodio's organisation assert that Custodio is a development worker engaged in humanitarian relief efforts. Data from a Philippine-based human rights organisations reveal that 13 community organisers and volunteers were killed under similar circumstances in the aftermath of Typhoon Haiyan.

The use of physical force against leftist dissidents have been practised in the Philippines since the 1980s with the rise of paramilitary groups in different regions in the country as part of counter-insurgency efforts against communist rebels in the Philippines (Bello 1987, 82–84). The patterns of assassination and intimidation against leftist activists in the Philippines bears resemblance to 'Operation Phoenix', a large-scale counter-insurgency plan launched by the United States in Vietnam during the late 1960s (Holden 2011). These counter-insurgency practices typically target suspected sympathisers of the underground communist rebels with the goal of intimidating suspected rebel sympathisers (Holden 2011). Whilst communist rebels in the Philippines are nowhere near capturing state power, thereby posing no tangible threat to the local and national governments. The killing and harassment of civil society organisation actors with supposed leftist ties are a means of restricting leftist participation in the electoral process and wider structures of governance (Holden 2009), and act as a means of limiting political activities and mobilisations that can muster critical mass to challenge the government (Quimpo 2009).

Conclusion

This chapter explores the applicability of the post-political framework in analysing post-disaster reconstruction in Tacloban City after the city was devastated by Typhoon Haiyan. Despite survivors still reeling from the impact of the natural disaster, the government have worked together with a select number of international and local civil society organisations, to institute a post-disaster reconstruction plan that espoused ideals of urban growth and sustainability that have come to characterise the post-political city devoid of contestation and dissent (Davidson and Iveson 2014). These plans revolved around the notion of ecological modernisation to tap into the city's potential as an investment site, whilst constructing environmental sustainability as a foundation for such growth. The grounding of this vision of the post-political city was founded in the exclusion of the voices and visions of Tacloban City's urban poor from post-disaster reconstruction plan. As a result, the urban poor in the city have become 'part of those who have no part' constituting the outside of the 'distribution of the sensible' (Ranciere 2010 in Derickson 2017). I also show how the institutional framework of state-civil society engagement during post-disaster response and reconstruction efforts in the Philippines lends itself to the articulation of post-political engagements of consensus-building between these two domains.

At the same time, the chapter shows that the post-political condition in the Philippine context is not absolute. The emergence of People Surge as a social movement representing disaster survivors, whose voices have been excluded from the reconstruction process, was a moment of insurgent mobilisation that re-introduced notions of the political in the post-disaster reconstruction in the city. This movement relied on articulating an 'anti-capitalist' critique, whilst also mobilising to render the urban poor visible on Tacloban City's social and political landscape. Yet this movement has been marred by state-induced violence that impedes and suppresses the emergence of politics proper and the redistribution of the sensible. Nonetheless, the chapter has highlighted how the political emerges even from conditions of despair and crisis, providing disaster survivors opportunities to register their dissent and to demand to be treated as equals.

Notes

1 The Communist Party of the Philippines–New People's Army continues to exist today, 50 years after their inception, still pursuing a Maoist-inspired protracted people's war with the goal of establishing a socialist state (Guerrero 1970). Prospects for peace talks were revived when self-proclaimed socialist President Rodrigo Duterte released key

communist officials, including alleged CPP Chair Benito Tiamzon and his wife and alleged CPP Secretary General Wilma Austria-Tiamzon in 2016, to participate in the peace talks with the Philippine government (Marcelo 2016). However, in 2019, Duterte formally terminated the peace talks with the CPP-NPA leadership (ABS-CBN News 2019). The administration has opted for a 'localized' approach to peace negotiations which has been criticised by rebels as nothing more than a surrender package to communist combatants (Colina IV 2018).
2 In the 2013 local elections, reports of vote buying where the name of Alfred Romualdez appeared in sample ballots together with other local politicians circulated online (Rappler 2013). Vote buying is a rampant electoral violation in Tacloban City (Center for People Empowerment in Governance 2010), yet the Commission on Elections, the office that regulates elections in the Philippines, has not filed a case. These cases are generally not filed in court as it is difficult to ascertain who committed the violations.
3 Former mayor Alfred Romualdez has been tagged by the Commission on Audit (COA) for "misspending" almost Php900 million (GBP£13.3 million) for post-disaster rehabilitation (Rappler 2016a). The camp of the former mayor has since responded, saying that they gave the money to those who deserved help, adding that the stringent government rules on procurement made it difficult to spend the money. No further cases have been filed stemming from this COA report (Rappler 2016b).
4 After typhoon Haiyan, the City Disaster Risk Reduction Management Office has become a permanent department of the Tacloban City LGU. As of my last visit to their office, they have more adequate facilities and an emergency response van.
5 While the formal rules stipulate these criteria, according to my NGO informants on the ground, this varies depending on whether the local government implements these criteria or not. One informant noted that being able to apply for accreditation depends on the strength of civil society organisation lobbying in the area (Interview with Rachel, officer for a national NGO).
6 Interview with Ron, community organiser.
7 Interview with Jojo, community resident.
8 Interview with Frank, urban poor organisation officer.
9 Interview with Mark, community organiser.
10 While secretaries from different national government agencies were present before the typhoon made landfall (Mangada 2015), the immediate response was characterised by 'missing' officials, as no one seemed to be in charge of the situation (Mangada 2015). The former interior local government secretary was also caught on video telling former Mayor Romualdez that he had to comply with certain procedures because Romualdez belonged to a rival political family as the former president, Benigno Aquino III. No government response was felt in the immediate days after the typhoon, prompting some typhoon survivors to loot some shops and abandoned homes (Yap 2013).
11 Interview with Rita, community organiser, 2015.
12 Interview with Bautista, former president of People Surge, 2014.
13 Interview with Jack, community activist, 2015.
14 Interview with Jojo, community resident.
15 Interview with Pedro, city politician.
16 Interview with Mario, urban planner, 2015.
17 Interview with Ron, community organiser, 2015.

References

Abinales, P. N., and D. J. Amoroso. 2005. *State and Society in the Philippines*. Boulder: Rowman & Littlefield.
ABS-CBN News. 2019. "Duterte announces 'permanent termination' of peace talks with Reds." *ABS-CBN*, March 21. https://news.abs-cbn.com/news/03/21/19/duterte-announces-permanent-termination-of-peace-talks-with-reds

Allmendinger, P., and G. Haughton. 2012. "Post-Political Spatial Planning in England: A Crisis of Consensus?" *Transactions of the Institute of British Geographers* 37 (1): 89–103.

Arcilla, C. A. C. 2018. "Producing Empty Socialized Housing: Privatizing Gains, Socializing Costs, and Dispossessing the Filipino Poor." *Social Transformations: Journal of the Global South* 6 (1): 77–105.

Atienza, M. E. L. 2004. "The Politics of Health Devolution in the Philippines: Experiences of Municipalities in a Devolved Set-up." *Philippine Political Science Journal* 25 (48): 25–54.

Bäckstrand, K., and E. Lövbrand. 2006. "Planting Trees to Mitigate Climate Change: Contested Discourses of Ecological Modernization, Green Governmentality and Civic Environmentalism." *Global Environmental Politics* 6 (1): 50–75.

Balgos, Benigno C. 2015. "Securing the Safety of Informal Settler Families Along Waterways in Metro Manila, Philippines: Government-Civil Society Organisation Partnership." In *Disaster Governance in Urbanising Asia*, edited by M. A. Miller and M. Douglass, 177–193. Singapore: Springer Singapore.

Baviskar, A. 2003. "Between Violence and Desire: Space, Power and Identity in the Making of Metropolitan Delhi." *International Social Science Journal* 55 (175): 89–98.

Bankoff, G., and D. Hilhorst. 2009. "The Politics of Risk in the Philippines: Comparing State and NGO Perceptions of Disaster Management." *Disasters* 33 (4): 686–704.

Bello, W. 1987. "U.S.-Sponsored Low-Intensity Conflict in the Philippines." Food First Development Report No. 2. San Francisco: The Institute for Food and Development Policy.

Beveridge, R., and P. Koch. 2017. "The Post-Political Trap? Reflections on Politics, Agency and the City." *Urban Studies* 54 (1): 31–43. doi:10.1177/0042098016671477.

Brillantes, A. B., Jr. 1994. "Redemocratization and Decentralization in the Philippines: The Increasing Leadership Role of NGOs." *International Review of Administrative Sciences* 60 (4): 575–586.

———. 1998. "Decentralized Democratic Governance under the Local Government Code: A Governmental Perspective." *Philippine Journal of Public Administration* 42 (1–2): 38–57.

Brower, R. S., and F. A. Magno. 2011. "A 'Third Way' in the Philippines: Voluntary Organizing for a New Disaster Management Paradigm." *International Review of Public Administration* 16 (1): 31–50.

Center for People Empowerment in Governance. 2010. "The CENPEG Report on the May 2010 Automated Elections in the Philippines." Accessed March 22, 2019. www.cenpeg.org/publications/The_CenPEG_Report.html

Colina, A. L., IV. 2018. "NDFP-Southern Mindanao Calls Localized Peace Talks a 'Surrender Package'." *Mindanews*, July 26. www.mindanews.com/peace-process/2018/07/ndfp-southern-mindanao-calls-localized-peace-talks-a-surrender-package/

Cretney, R. 2018. "An Opportunity to Hope and Dream: Disaster Politics and the Emergence of Possibility through Community-Led Recovery." *Antipode* 51 (2): 497–516. doi:10.1111/anti.12431.

Curato, N. 2017a. "'We Haven't Even Buried the Dead Yet': Ethics of Discursive Contestation in a Crisis Situation." *Current Sociology* 65 (7): 1010–1030.

———. 2017b. "Flirting with Authoritarian Fantasies: Rodrigo Duterte and the New Terms of Philippine Populism." *Journal of Contemporary Asia* 47 (1): 142–153.

———. 2018. "From Authoritarian Enclave to Deliberative Space: Governance Logics in Post-Disaster Reconstruction." *Disasters* 42 (4): 635–654. doi:10.1111/disa.12280.

Dasgupta, S., B. Laplante, S. Murray, and D. Wheeler. 2009. "Climate Change and the Future Impacts of Storm-Surge Disasters in Developing Countries." Working Paper 182. Washington, DC: Center for Global Development. Accessed October 30, 2018. http://citeseerx.ist.psu.edu/viewdoc/download?doi=10.1.1.625.424&rep=rep1&type=pdf

Davidson, M., and K. Iveson. 2014. "Recovering the Politics of the City: From the 'Post-Political City' to a 'Method of Equality' for Critical Urban Geography." *Progress in Human Geography* 39 (5): 543–559.

Derickson, K. D. 2017. "Taking Account of the 'Part of Those That Have No Part'." *Urban Studies* 54 (1): 44–48.

Dikéc, M. 2017. "Disruptive Politics." *Urban Studies* 54 (1): 49–54.

Dressler, W., C. A. Kull., and T. C. Meredith. 2006. "The Politics of Decentralizing National Parks Management in the Philippines." *Political Geography* 25 (7): 789–816.

Fassin, D., and P. Vasquez. 2005. "Humanitarian Exception as the Rule: The Political Theology of the 1999 *Tragedia* in Venezuela." *American Ethnologist* 32 (3): 389–405.

Go, J. R. R. 2016. "Political Leadership and Education Politics: The Mayor and Education Services in Nasugbu, Batangas." *Philippine Political Science Journal* 37 (2): 111–134.

Guerrero, A. 1970. *Philippine Society and Revolution*. Accessed August 13, 2019. http://bannedthought.net/Philippines/CPP/1970s/PhilippineSocietyAndRevolution-4ed.pdf

Haughton, G. and P. Allmendinger. 2011. "Moving On - From Spatial Planning to Localism and Beyond." *Town and Country Planning* 80 (4): 184–187.

Hilhorst, D. 2003. "Responding to Disasters: Diversity of Bureaucrats, Technocrats and Local People." *International Journal of Mass Emergencies and Disasters* 21 (1): 37–55.

Hodson, M., and S. Marvin. 2009. "'Urban Ecological Security': A New Urban Paradigm?" *International Journal of Urban and Regional Research* 33 (1): 193–215.

Holden, W. 2009. "Ashes from the Phoenix: State Terrorism and the Party-List Groups in the Philippines." *Contemporary Politics* 15 (4): 377–393.

———. 2011. "Neoliberalism and State Terrorism in the Philippines: The Fingerprints of Phoenix." *Critical Studies on Terrorism* 4 (3): 331–350.

Holden, W. N., and R.D. Jacobson. 2006. "Mining amid Decentralization. Local Governments and Mining in the Philippines." *Natural Resource Forum* 30 (3): 188–198.

Karaos, A. M. 1993. "Manila's Squatter Movement: A Struggle for Place and Identity." *Philippine Sociological Review* 41 (1–4): 71–91.

———. 1998. "Fragmentations in the Urban Movement: Shift from Resistance to Policy Advocacy." *Philippine Sociological Review* 46 (3–4): 143–157.

Kenis, A., and E. Mathijs. 2014. "Climate Change and Post-Politics: Repoliticizing the Present by Imagining the Future?" *Geoforum* 52: 148–156.

Lacaba, J. F. 1982. *Days of Disquiet, Nights of Rage: The First Quarter Storm & Related Events*. Manila: Salinlahi Publishing House.

Legaspi, P. E. 2001. "The Changing Role of Local Government under a Decentralized State: The Case of the Philippines." *Public Management Review* 3 (1): 131–139.

Loh, K. S., and M. D. Pante. 2015. "Controlling Nature, Disciplining Human Nature: Floods in Singapore and Metro Manila, 1945–1980s." *Nature and Culture* 10 (1): 36–56.

MacLeod, G. 2011. "Urban Politics Reconsidered: Growth Machine to Post-Democratic City?" *Urban Studies* 48 (12): 2629–2660.

Mangada, L. L. 2015. *Missing: Who Is in Charge?* A case study published by the William Davidson Institute at the University of Michigan. Madison, WI: WDI Publishing.

McCoy, A. W. 2009a. *An Anarchy of Families: State and Family in the Philippines*. Madison, WI: The University of Wisconsin Press.

———. 2016. "Post-Haiyan Adaptation and Institutional Barriers to Women Survivors in Tacloban." *Philippine Political Science Journal* 37 (2): 94–110.

———. 2009b. *Policing America's Empire: The United States, the Philippines and the Rise of the Surveillance State*. Madison, WI: The University of Wisconsin Press.

Millington, G. 2016. "'I Found the Truth in Foot Locker': London 2011, Urban Culture and the Post-Political City." *Antipode* 48 (3): 705–723.

National Disaster Risk Reduction and Management Council. n.d. "NDRRMC Update: Final Report re Effects of Typhoon Yolanda 'Haiyan'." Final Report in a Series of Government Report from November 2013—April 2014. Quezon City: National Disaster Risk Reduction and Management Centre. Accessed May 1, 2015. http://ndrrmc.gov.ph/attachments/article/1329/FINAL_REPORT_re_Effects_of_Typhoon_YOLANDA_(HAIYAN)_06-09NOV2013.pdf

Ong, J. C. 2015. "Witnessing Distant and Proximal Suffering within a Zone of Danger: Lay Moralities of Media Audiences in the Philippines." *International Communication Gazette* 77 (7): 607–621.

Philippine Statistics Authority. 2016. "Population of Region VIII—Eastern Visayas (Based on the 2015 Census of Population)." www.psa.gov.ph/population-and-housing/title/Population%20of%20Region%20VIII%20-%20Eastern%20Visayas%20%28Based%20on%20the%202015%20Census%20of%20Population%29

Pimentel, B. 2006. *U.G.: An Underground Tale: The Journey of Edgar Jopson and the First Quarter Generation*. Manila: Anvil Publishing.

Porio, E. 2002. "Urban Poor Communities in State-Civil Society Dynamics: Constraints and Possibilities for Housing and Security of Tenure in Metro Manila." *Asian Journal of Social Science* 30 (1): 73–96.

Quimpo, N. G. 2009. "The Philippines: Predatory Regime, Growing Authoritarian Features." *Pacific Review* 22 (3): 335–353.

Rancière, J. 2010. *Dissensus: On Politics and Aesthetics*. New York: Bloomsbury Publishing.

Rappler. 2013. "Offline and Online Reports of Vote Buying." *Rappler*, May 13. www.rappler.com/nation/politics/elections-2013/28941-offline-online-reports-vote-buying

———. 2016a. "Tacloban Misspent Nearly P1B in Yolanda Funds—COA." *Rappler*, July 31. www.rappler.com/nation/141258-coa-tacloban-misspent-yolanda-funds

———. 2016b. "Ex-Tacloban Mayor: Yolanda Funds Not Misspent." *Rappler*, July 31. www.rappler.com/nation/141486-ex-tacloban-mayor-yolanda-funds-not-misspent

Rebotier, J. 2012. "Vulnerability Conditions and Risk Representations in Latin America: Framing the Territorializing Urban Risk." *Global Environmental Change* 22 (2): 391–398.

Rivera, T. C. 2002. "Transition Pathways and Democratic Consolidation in Post-Marcos Philippines." *Contemporary Southeast Asia* 24 (3): 466–483.

Rosol, M., V. Beál, and S. Mössner. 2017. "Greenest Cities? The (Post-)politics of New Urban Environmental Regimes." *Environment and Planning A* 49 (8): 1710–1718.

Ruming, K. 2018. "Post-Political Planning and Community Opposition: Asserting and Challenging Consensus in Planning Urban Regeneration in Newcastle, NSW." *Geographical Research* 56 (2): 181–195. doi:10.1111/1745-5871.12269.

Saguin, K. 2017. "Producing an Urban Hazardscape Beyond the City." *Environment and Planning A* 49 (9): 1968–1985.

Shatkin, G. 2005. "Colonial Capital, Modernist Capital, Global Capital: The Changing Political Symbolism of Urban Space in Metro Manila, Philippines." *Pacific Affairs* 78 (4): 577–600.

Shelter Cluster Philippines. 2014. "Shelter Cluster Meeting." http://sheltercluster.org/sites/default/files/docs/140603%20Tacloban%20City%20Shelter%20Cluster%20Minutes.pdf.

Swyngedouw, E. 2009. "The Antinomies of the Postpolitical City: In Search of a Democratic Politics of Environmental Production." *International Journal of Urban and Regional Research* 33 (3): 601–620.

———. 2010. "Apocalypse Forever? Post-Political Populism and the Spectre of Climate Change." *Theory, Culture & Society* 27 (2–3): 213–232.

———. 2014. "Where Is the Political? Insurgent Mobilisations and the Incipient 'Return of the Political'." *Space and Polity* 18 (2): 122–136.

Tacloban Recovery and Sustainable Development Group. 2014. *The Tacloban Recovery and Rehabilitation Plan: Main Report*. Tacloban City, Philippines: City Government of Tacloban.

Thomas, A. 2017. "Everyday Experiences of Post-Politicising Processes in Rural Freshwater Management." *Environment and Planning A* 49 (6): 1413–1431.

Warren, J. F. 2013. "A Tale of Two Decades: Typhoons and Floods, Manila and the Provinces, and the Marcos Years." *The Asia-Pacific Journal* 11 (43): 1–22.

Yap, D. J. 2013. "Days after Yolanda's Wrath, Looting Erupts in Tacloban City." *Philippine Daily Inquirer*, November 10. https://newsinfo.inquirer.net/524731/days-after-yolandas-wrath-looting-erupts-in-tacloban-city

Yee, D. K. P. 2016. "Staking the Claim to the Post-Disaster City: An Ethnographic Account of a Post-Disaster Social Movement in Tacloban City, Philippines." Paper presented at the Disaster Justice in Anthropocene Asia and the Pacific Conference held at the Asia Research Institute, November 17–18.

———. 2018a. "Constructing Reconstruction, Territorializing Risk: Imposing 'No-Build Zones' in Post-Disaster Reconstruction in Tacloban City, Philippines." *Critical Asian Studies* 50 (1): 103–121.

———. 2018b. "Violence and Disaster Capitalism in Post-Haiyan Philippines." *Peace Review* 30 (2): 160–167.

INDEX

Note: Page numbers in *italics* indicate figures and in **bold** indicate tables on the corresponding pages.

Abylgaziev, M. 148
Agonism and Antagonism: Past and Future Possibilities of Radical Democracy 28
Aquino, B., Jr. 156
Aquino, C. 157
Arab Spring 27, 33, 154
Arnstein, S. R. 124
Asian urbanism 5–6
Aung San Suu Kyi 37

back-to-the-land movement: atomised desire for breaking away in 77; decentring environmental post-politics 75–79; farming as heritage and 78–79; introduction to 72–75; organic as part of an every (market) utopia in 77; organic utopias and 83–85; politics of 85–86; in Tiruvannamalai, India 72, 79–83; village frontier and 81–83
Bautista, E. 164
Baviskar, A. 75
Belt and Road Initiative (BRI) 106
Berlin Wall, fall of the 38
Beveridge, R. 3
Bishkek, Kyrgyzstan 146–149
Boudereau, J. 125
Brown, W. 24, 26–27

Castells, M. 148–149
Central Asian republics: conceptualising civil society relations in 142–143; emerging civil society and state-society relations in 143–145; environmental NGOs in 141–142; existing barriers to civil society-state partnerships in 146; introduction to 140–141; promising development of urban civic activism in Bishkek in 146–149; structural governmental changes needed in 149–150
Cheng U Wen Lena 29
Chennai, India *see* India
Cheonggyecheon project 59–62, **60**
Chinese heritage practices 103–104; in the age of post-politics 107–109; in contemporary cities 93–95; contested landscape and 99–102; cultural salon and social media in 101–102; for governance and urban renewal in Xi'an 97–99; in heritage instrumentalisation, civic activism, and urban governance 114–118; introduction to 93; rethinking civil society in China and 95–97; in revitalisation and gentrification of Tongzheng community district in Quanzhou 109–119, *111*; Silk Road and 106–107
citizen-state relations, reconfiguration of 40–41, 47–50
civil society 6, 21–23; in China 95–97; conceptualised in Central Asia 142–143; existing barriers to

partnerships in 146; mobilised in cyber space in Vietnam 134; promising development of urban civic activism in Bishkek and 146–149; in Singapore 30; in Thailand 31–32
collective action, the political as 25
Community Driven Operation Grievance Mechanism (CDOGM) 44, 50
'Connecting Emotions through Wells' program *see* Quanzhou, China
consensus democracy 40; reconfiguration of citizen-state relations in 40–41
contested landscape in Xi'an, China 99–102
Cooper, D. 77
creative cities 2
cultural salon 101–102
Custodio, J. 166

Diani, M. 143
Disagreement 26, 33
dissent, suppression of 5, 28, 40, 129
Durant, T.J., Jr. 142

English Romantic movement 73, 82
Eurocentrism 4; ideas of post-politics based on liberal democracies 22–23, 33, 38, 124, 154–155

farming *see* back-to-the-land movement

Gandhi, M. 78, 82
Gaventa, J. 124
Geertman, S. 125
George, C. 30, 34
Gillespie, J. 125
global cities 2, 154
Goh Chok Tong 29
government-organised non-government organisations (GONGOs), Chinese 97
green cities 2
Guha, R. 75, 82
Gunnell, T. 148

Hankow: Commerce and Society in a Chinese City 96
Hanoi tree movement, Vietnam: history and development of 125–129, **126**; introduction to 123–124; participation under current institutions 129–135, *132*; post-politics and participatory governance in 124–125
Han River Renaissance Project, South Korea 63–64, 135–136

heritage: in the age of post-politics 107–109; civic activism, urban governance, and instrumentalisation of 114–118; in contemporary Chinese cities (*see* Chinese heritage practices); farming 78–79; in Vietnam (*see* Hanoi tree movement, Vietnam)
Holden, W. 158
Hong Lim Park 30

ICOMOS 108–109
incomplete depoliticisation 41
incompleteness of post-politicisation 41–42, 50–51
India: breaking away in Tiruvannamalai 79–83; decentring environmental post-politics in 75–79; farming as heritage in 78–79; introduction to back-to-the-land movement in 72–75
Indignados movement in Spain 154, 155
International Center for Not-for-Profit Law 144

Japan International Cooperation Agency (JICA) 43–44, 46; reconfiguration of citizen-state relations and 47–50
Japan Thilawa Development Ltd. (MJTD) 43–44, 46; reconfiguration of citizen-state relations and 47–50

Kamat, S. 23–24, 25, 26, 38; on integration of democracy in post-politics 39–40; on suppression of dissent 40
Kim Jong-un 56
Kirshenblatt-Gimblett, B. 108
Koch, P. 3
Korea *see* Seoul, South Korea
Kyrgyzstan *see* Bishkek, Kyrgyzstan

Larner, W. 24
Lee Myung-bak 59, 61, 62, 63
Lin, W.-I. 3
local *versus* national politics in South Korea 55–56

Ma, J. 156
Mangada 158
Marcos, F. 156–158
Marcos, I. R. 158
Maritime Silk Road (MSR) 106
Marolt, P. 148
Mirziyoyev, S. 140
Moong over Microchips: Adventures of a Techie-Turned-Farmer 81–82

Mouffe, C. 2, 22, 27
Multi-Stakeholder Advisory Group (MSAG) 44, 46, 49
Mya Hlaing 43
Myanmar 51–52; complaints management procedure in 42–45; inevitable incompleteness of post-politicisation in 41–42, 50–51; integration of democratic principles into 39–40; project-affected persons (PAPs) in 46–47; reconfiguration of citizen-state relations in 41, 47–50; TCMP and age of post-politics in 45–51; transition away from military governance in 37–38

Nammālvār, G. 82, 84
National Council for Peace and Order (NCPO) 31
neoliberalism 24, 26, 39; as planning strategy and practice 5, 25, 45, 61, 109, 117, 154, 160–161; political antagonism against, in South Korea 59–64, **60**
New Town Programme (NTP), South Korea 62–64
Nguyen, Q. H. 125
nongovernmental organisations (NGOs): in Central Asia 141–142; in the Philippines 157; state-society relations and 143–145
North Korea 57

Occupy Movement 6, 27, 33, 41, 154, 155
Oh Se-hoon 59, 62, 63, 64–65
Oosterlynck, S. 76
organic farming *see* back-to-the-land movement

Park Geun-hye 57, 65–67
Philippines, the *see* Tacloban City, Philippines
Phongphisoot B. 32
post-disaster planning *see* Tacloban City, Philippines
The Post-political and Its Discontents 54
post-politics: decentring environmental 75–79; disagreement in 25; with 'good governance,' in Seoul 64–68, *66*, **68**; heritage in the age of 107–109; history and definition of 23–25; incompleteness of 41–42, 50–51; integration of democratic principles into Myanmar's governance and 45–46; interaction between state and society in (*see* Chinese heritage practices); in Korea (*see* Seoul); in Myanmar (*see* Myanmar); opposed in non-democratic regimes 32–35; and participatory governance in Vietnam 124–125; in the Philippines (*see* Tacloban City, Philippines); in post-disaster cities (*see* Tacloban City, Philippines); puzzles and pathways in Asian 8–13; returning to the political in 25–28; rise of 1–4; state-society relations and 4–7; TCMP and 42, 45–51

Quanzhou, China 118–119; heritage revitalization and gentrification of the Tongzheng community district in 109–114, *111*; introduction to 106–107

Raco, M. 3, 25
radical democracy 27; opposing post-politics in non-democratic regimes and 32–35; in Singapore 29–31; in Thailand 31–32; theory and practice in 28–29
Rancière, J. 2, 22, 26, 27, 38, 52, 153–154; on consensus democracy 40; on partition of sensible 51, 154
Reynolds, L. 41
Roberts, N. 124
Romualdez, A. 158
Romualdez, A. B. 158
Romualdez, C. G. 158
Rowe, W. 96
Ruming, K. 1, 5, 155

Salmenkari, T. 109
Saramago, J. 54
Scott, J. C. 75
Seeing 54
Seoul, South Korea 68–69; current divisions between local and national politics in 55–56; explosion of political antagonism against New Town Programme and Yongsan disaster in 62–64; historical background for underdevelopment of urban politics in 56–59; introduction to post-politics in 54–56; as post-political city with 'good governance' 64–68, *66*, **68**; rise of political antagonism through Cheonggyecheon project in 59–62, **60**
Silk Road Economic Belt (SREB) 106–107
Singam, C. 29–30, 31
Singapore 29–31
smart cities 2
social capacity 28
social media 101–102; Hanoi tree movement and 126–127, 134; Quanzhou

Municipal Government and 112–113; computer-mediated communication facilitating civil society actions and networks, Kyrgyzstan 142, 148
South Korea *see* Seoul, South Korea
state-society relations: in Asian urban context 4–7; in Central Asian republics 143–145; existing barriers to partnerships in 146
Sunflower Movement 6, 34
Sustainable Development Goals, United Nations 7
Swyngedouw, E. 2–3, 21, 33, 42, 45, 49, 52, 54, 76; on depoliticisation under neoliberalism 109; on disagreement in post-politics 25; on grievance management in post-politics 37–38; on incomplete depoliticisation 41, 50; on political acts in public spaces 154; on post-political formation 24, 103, 108, 117–118; on return to the political 21–23, 27–28, 124
Szerszynski, B. 41

Tacloban City, Philippines: insurgent politics and emergence of the political after Typhoon Haiyan in 163–167; introduction to 152–153; Local Government Code (LGU) and 157–158; Philippine Disaster Risk Reduction Management (DRRM) Act of 2010 and 161–163; political development in 155–158; post-politics and post-disaster reconstruction in 159–163; Tacloban Recovery and Rehabilitation Plan (TRRP) in 159–160; understanding post-political condition in 153–155
Tamilnadu *see* India
Thailand 31–32
Than Shwe 37, 42, 45, 46

Thein Sein 37
Thilawa SEZ Complaints Management Procedure (TCMP) 42, 45–52
Thilawa Social Development Group (TSDG) 43
Thilawa Special Economic Zone (SEZ), Myanmar *see* Myanmar
Tin Hsan 43
Tiruvannamalai, India 72, 79–83; *see also* India
Trump, D. 56
Typhoon Haiyan *see* Tacloban City, Philippines

Umbrella Movement 6
UNESCO 108–109
United States Agency for International Development (USAID) 144
utopias, organic 83–85

Vietnam *see* Hanoi tree movement, Vietnam
Vu, N. A. 125

Weber, M. 57
WeChat 101, 107
Wilson, J. 21, 54, 124

Xi'an, China: contemporary urban development in 102–103; contested landscape in 99–102; cultural salon and social media in 101–102; heritage governance and urban renewal in 97–99, 103–104; Muslim quarter of 99–101
Xi Jingping 106

Yongsan Redevelopment Project, South Korea 63–64
Yu Keping 96

Žižek, S. 2, 22, 40